Studies in the History of Law and Justice

Volume 19

The purpose of this book series is to publish high quality volumes on the history of law and justice. Legal history can be a deeply provocative and influential field, as illustrated by the growth of the European universities and the *Ius Commune*, the French Revolution, the American Revolution, and indeed all the great movements for national liberation through law. The study of history gives scholars and reformers the models and courage to question entrenched injustices, by demonstrating the contingency of law and other social arrangements. Yet legal history today finds itself diminished in the universities and legal academy. Too often scholarship betrays no knowledge of what went before, or why legal institutions took the shape that they did. This series seeks to remedy that deficiency.

Studies in the History of Law and Justice will be theoretical and reflective. Volumes will address the history of law and justice from a critical and comparative viewpoint. The studies in this series will be strong bold narratives of the development of law and justice. Some will be suitable for a very broad readership.

Contributions to this series will come from scholars on every continent and in every legal system. Volumes will promote international comparisons and dialogue. The purpose will be to provide the next generation of lawyers with the models and narratives needed to understand and improve the law and justice of their own era. The series includes monographs focusing on a specific topic, as well as collections of articles covering a theme or collections of article by one author.

More information about this series at http://www.springer.com/series/11794

Mélanie Bost · Antoon Vrints
Editors

Doing Justice In Wartime

Multiple Interplays between Justice and Populations during the Two World Wars

Springer

Editors
Mélanie Bost
CegeSoma/Royal Military Academy
Brussels, Belgium

Antoon Vrints
Ghent University
Ghent, Belgium

ISSN 2198-9842 ISSN 2198-9850 (electronic)
Studies in the History of Law and Justice
ISBN 978-3-030-72049-0 ISBN 978-3-030-72050-6 (eBook)
https://doi.org/10.1007/978-3-030-72050-6

This Springer imprint is published by the registered company Springer Nature Switzerland AG
The registered company address is: Gewerbestrasse 11, 6330 Cham, Switzerland

Acknowledgements

This book has been published with the support of

- The Interuniversitary Attraction Poles, Programme initiated by the Belgian Science Policy Office (Interuniversitary Attraction Pole 'Justice and Populations: The Belgian Experience in International Perspective [1795–2015]')
- FNRS—Fund for Scientific Research Wallonia-Brussels Federation

.arch CEGESOMA

GHENT UNIVERSITY

centre d'histoire du droit et de la justice

UCLouvain

HUMBOLDT-UNIVERSITÄT ZU BERLIN

belspo

be just 2.0

fnrs
FREEDOM TO RESEARCH

Introduction

The impact of war on justice and crime has been discussed in criminology for more than a century now. The question even seems to have had a decisive impact on the development of criminology as a discipline. At the beginning of the twentieth century, European criminologists were intensely divided over the precise weight that should be given to psychological, biological and social factors in the origins of crime (Muncie 1999, 86). Some scholars focused on biological and psychological factors, situating the causes of crime predominantly within the individual. Others analysed the impact of the social context. According to criminologist Hermann Mannheim, European counterparts were more inclined to an 'individual, endogeneous theory of criminality' than were the overall socially oriented American and Russian criminologists. In his view, this difference was obliterated by the experience of the First World War and the post-war period, which, as he wrote in 1955, 'brought home to European criminologists the importance of social factors' (Mannheim 1955, 82). The rise in crime figures during and after the First World War all over Europe could not be credited plausibly to biological or psychological factors or to changes in legislation. According to Mannheim, this recognition led to a re-evaluation of social factors among European criminologists during and after the First World War. The First World War and the rapid societal changes it provoked were analysed by criminologists as a giant social experiment to measure the impact of (changing) environmental factors.

Indeed, during the First World War, already all over Europe, even in non-belligerent countries, criminological interest in the impact of war on crime popped up. In the 1920s this interest resulted in an impressive corpus of criminological overviews and national case studies (for France, Germany, Austria, Hungary, Czechoslovakia, The Netherlands, Norway, Sweden, Britain …) on this topic. The two most elaborate studies (on the German and the Austrian cases) were published by the German criminologist Moritz Liepmann and the Austrian criminologist Franz Exner in a series of the *Carnegie Endowment for International Peace* (Exner 1927; Liepmann 1930). In the 1930s the interest in the relationship between war and crime apparently faded away. For obvious reasons, this interest was resurrected during the Second World War. Not only did scholars analyse the current situation but also some, such as Hermann Mannheim in his *War and Crime* (1941; written as a German exile in Britain) looked back to the previous war for a better understanding. For Edith Abbott, a Chicago-based economist and social worker who had already published on the relationship between war and crime during the First World War, the Second World War offered a convenient occasion to publish an unedited manuscript on juvenile delinquency in Britain during the First World War, written in spring 1919 (Abbott 1918, 1943; Leeson 1917). In the wake of both world wars, international criminological conferences were organised to exchange views on the impact of war on crime (Cornil 1951). This impressive corpus of scholarship may have contributed to an awareness of the importance of social factors in crimonology but does not offer a true social analysis of the impact of war on crime and justice. This body of research takes police and judicial statistics, its main source, at face value and therefore primarly reflects the moral preoccupations and perceptions of criminal-justice professionals. After the memory of both world wars faded away, scholarly interest in the issue decreased to a similar degree (see Tham 1990). The experience of the Vietnam War provoked only a temporary renewal of interest among criminologists.

It is only quite recently that the relationship between war and crime started to attract the interest of historians (for discussion of recent historiographical production, see Rousseaux 2013; Emsley 2017). The organisation of an international conference in Brussels in 2011 entitled *Justice in Wartime and Revolutions. Europe, 1795–1950* is significative in this regard (De Koster et al. 2012). Different fields of interest can be observed in the emerging historical production on this topic. Without any doubt the most firmly established field is that of transitional justice. Since the 1990s historians, like other social scientists, have been researching the question of how post-conflict societies dealt with the violent past by doing justice or not. It is therefore no coincidence that half of the contributors to the above-mentioned conference treated a transitional-justice subject. Another theme that is gaining interest is that of military justice, focusing on the judicial treatment of soldiers. What was considered a crime in armies, and how was it punished? (Emsley 2013; Rousseaux et al. 2013). Lastly, and somewhat hesitantly, some work has been done on civilian crime in wartime, one of the preoccupations of the post-war scholarly production (Eggens 2005). However, historical interest in the relationship between war and crime still needs to be broadened and deepened. The initiators of the IUAP (Interuniversity Attraction Poles) project 7/22, 'Justice and Populations: The Belgian Experience in International Perspective, 1795–2015', a multidisciplinary programme funded by the Belgian Science Policy Office, wanted to address this need by creating a special work package on justice in wartime. The IUAP organised with the same goal an international conference on this topic in Brussels on 3–4 December 2015.[1] The present volume consists of a selection of papers delivered at this conference.

Periods of wars and foreign domination are indeed of crucial importance in the history of justice. They have led to important shifts in the expectations, practices and actors involved in the field of justice. As a result of the often sudden change

[1] This conference was entitled 'Doing Justice in Wartime. Multiple Interplays between Justice and Populations during the Two World Wars' and was organised by five partners (CegeSoma, Ghent University, Université catholique de Louvain, the Royal Military Academy of Belgium and the Humboldt Universität zu Berlin).

provoked by war, existing routines in the broad field of justice came under serious pressure. The disruption of predictable patterns stimulated inventiveness. The way in which actors of justice dealt with those sweeping changes is an important research question. Although different aspects of the impact of armed conflict on justice have been studied, the dominant approach of most of this work is top-down and highly institutional. As a result of this bias, the actual actors of justice and their practices and expectations in war settings have been largely neglected so far. Drawing from current trends in criminology and the social history of justice, this edited volume starts from an interactionist perspective. It focuses on the impact of war on the complex interactions between different actors of justice: individuals and social groups on the one hand; 'the justice system' (police, judiciary and penitentiary professionals) on the other hand. The volume aims to highlight the emergence of new expectations of justice among these actors that resulted from the war. It also tackles justice practices, strategies to cope with the changing circumstances, new forms of negotiation, interaction, relationships between populations and the formal justice system in this particular context, and the impact of this renegotiation in the long run.

War led to the redefinition of the roles of the different actors involved in justice. New roles emerged, and room to operate shifted. The claim of the professionals from the formal justice system on the monopoly of justice was, of course, to a large extent fictional even in peacetime. 'Doing justice'—a notion we borrowed from historian Rebekka Habermas (2008)—is, even in a context of a consolidated state, always the outcome of a complex interplay between informal and formal actors of justice, as indicated, for instance, by the importance of the willingness to report crimes. In wartime, the balance in this interaction seems to have shifted at the expense of the formal justice system. Military courts experienced exceptional growth, and their authority gradually expanded at the expense of regular courts. In areas occupied by foreign armies, the impact on the judicial system was even more substantial. When they were not simply removed, the national courts had to coexist with those of the occupier; new bodies and players then competed with traditional judicial authorities. Moreover, people seemed to be more inclined to take justice into their own hands. Significantly, all major waves of informal justice in Europe during the last two centuries took place during wars and revolutions. The distinction between insiders and outsiders of the formal justice system tended to blur as a result of warfare. Informers to secret police and political factions (like collaborators and resistance fighters) acquired a share of the power of constraint that in peacetime was monopolised by state agents. Unusual collaborations, sometimes at the margins of legality, were established between judges and civil society (like charity organisations). The proliferation of judicial actors altered the balance of power within the system. However, justice officials did not undergo these changes passively. Even if their autonomy was reduced from above and rival forces gained power, judges retained discretion in the application and implementation of laws, and in a broader sense they tried to cope with the changing circumstances.

Wars also changed the margins of tolerance of all the actors of justice mentioned above. This was marked by a blurring of the distinction between normal and abnormal, tolerated and prohibited behaviour. New forms of 'crime' and new 'criminals' emerged. These shifts are particularly revealing in the frame of the expectations of justice held by all these actors. These expectations could converge, as shown by the generally shared ambition to see collaborators punished at the end of occupations, but could also diverge. The reconstruction of the expectations of justice among different actors not only allows access to the moral framework of these actors in the war context but also reveals possible conflicts caused or intensified by this experience.

As a result, of course, the concept of the transgressor was redefined. Specific categories of people facing sanctions emerged (i.e., the enemy, collaborators, foreigners, new citizens, Jews, minorities, black marketeers), while existing categories were extended due to the exceptional circumstances. Finally, certain categories of the population became subjects of increased surveillance, being considered dangerous in view of the continuing tension (e.g., juveniles, tramps etc.).

The diversification of the actors in the justice system and the shifting thresholds of tolerance of course had an impact on the practices of justice. Indeed, we can observe a blurring of the borders between popular, criminal, military, administrative and colonial law. Criminal punishment was supplemented by non-standard popular, military or administrative practices. Exceptional measures were taken and often became semi-permanent, as for example the administrative internment of different types of 'suspects'. Usual sanctions were equally transformed, as judges adapted penalties to the changing circumstances. In order to reconstruct the complex landscape of actors of justice in wartime, and their expectations and practices, a grassroots approach imposes itself for this book. For this approach to be feasible, it is essential to prioritise archives resulting from actual justice activities. Judicial archives not only form the main source but also constitute an ideal observatory for interactions between the different actors. Archives stemming from police operations, the prison system and administrative surveillance are equally suitable. The privileging of this kind of 'operational sources' of the criminal justice system in its broadest sense enables us to go beyond a top-down approach based predominately on policy sources.

Ten out of the 11 chapters of this book deal with Belgian issues, equitably distributed between the two world wars. Due to the diversity of its war experiences in the twentieth century, Belgium is a particularly interesting case for studying the impact of war on the dynamics of 'doing justice'. The Belgian Army fought in both world wars, for five years in the First World War and for 18 days in the Second World War. The vast majority of the Belgian population experienced both world wars as a period of occupation. The two long-lasting military occupations generated various forms of collaboration with the enemy. After both wars, these phenomena required from the barely reinstalled Belgian State the implementation of a large-scale judicial process of repression of these 'antipatriotic' behaviours, in order to restore both its authority and legitimacy and to re-establish the social peace among its citizens. Moreover, Belgium as a colonial power mobilised its African empire as part of the war effort during both world wars, a mobilisation that influenced populations and justice relationships. While most works on justice and war emphasise the study of penal justice, Aurore François and Mélanie Bost's chapters look into the juvenile and civil-justice systems. Based on the archives of the Brussels juvenile court, **Aurore François's** study is conducted according to a twofold perspective. On the one hand it looks at the survival strategies of juvenile delinquents during the First World War, a population particularly weakened by the subsistence crisis generated by the German occupation. On the other hand it deals with the question of how a relatively young institution responded to the youngsters' offenses. For the Belgian juvenile court, created in 1912, the war was to some extent a baptism of fire. The essay shows how judges perceived the survival strategies of the youth and their families and dealt with offenses deriving from it. It reveals the moral hierarchisation operated by the judicial actors between different delinquent behaviours, tolerating some (as theft) because of the wartime context and, in contrast, stigmatising others (such as mendicity). The essay also illustrates the shifts in tolerance thresholds among victims of juvenile crime, highlighting how wartime exacerbated social tensions over scarce resources.

Mélanie Bost's contribution explores the judicial dimension of another vivid social question during World War One: the rent issue. Beyond the social problem, also the legitimacy of the occupier's legislative power and, consequently, the applicability of its decrees by the judges were at stake for the Belgian magistrates. The question led to a major controversy in the judiciary, provoking a rift in the patriotic front. Very interestingly, this contribution shows us magistrates dealing for the first time with the very recent international occupation law. It also highlights the extent to which civil law cases, to which little attention has yet been paid in comparison with criminal ones, can be used to study military occupations.

The next three chapters address post-war issues, in particular how the legal and judicial systems managed the various categories of former collaborators with the enemy after the First World War. **Gertjan Leenders** focuses on denunciation to the enemy, a new offense introduced in the Belgian penal code in 1917 by the government-in-exile. In an original way, Leenders adopts the suspects' perspective. His careful analysis of their discourses and defence strategies shows how, far from being passive, these outsiders tried to instrumentalise the judicial system. The author also attempts to assess the impact of the defendants' strategies on court judgements, delivering quite surprising results. In addition, the essay looks at the origin of the complaints.

Martin Schoups's essay is innovative in several respects. Up to now, studies in the field of transitional justice regarding post-war Belgium concentrated on the repression of the crimes and offences against national security—a chapter of the Belgian Criminal Code that punishes the various collaborations with the enemy. Highlighting the close ties between an apparently more 'trivial' matters—post-war food legislation—and the prosecution of economic collaboration, his study urges us to consider a set of measures much more extensive. His results also confirm that, for Belgians, economic collaboration and war profiteering were a more serious concern than political collaboration. The criminalisation of numerous economic practices related to food immediately after the war attests to the moralisation of economy, a phenomenon that for a few years weakened the economic liberalism traditionally in force in the country. Complementing Schoups's examination of the legislation, his study of the judicial statistics and of local court records explores how the judiciary effectively applied the food legislation. He also investigates the nature of the prosecuted offenses and the socio-economic profile of the defendants.

To end this section devoted to the First World War, **Florent Verfaillie** analyses an aspect of punishment for collaboration with the enemy that has so far been neglected: its confinement component. He aims to provide a first overview on the role played by prisons in the restoration of the post-war political rule of Belgium. After a detailed review of the legal and statistical data, a more qualitative approach gives insight into the detention experiences of different categories of detainees. The penitentiary perspective also sheds new light on the notion of political crime in the post-war period. Again the exploitation of the judicial archives attests to the erosion of the liberal regime by the war.

The next six chapters focus on Second World War issues. Only two decades after the first German invasion and occupation, Belgium had to face the consequences of a second one, this time like large parts of continental Europe. As the ideological ambitions of the national-socialist occupier were far bigger than those of his imperial predecessor, the second occupation led to a far more outspoken political polarization in Belgian society. As a result, political violence on a previously unknown scale erupted. The number of murders committed by civilians, often in a context of struggle between collaboration and resistance movements, grew dramatically. Two of these six chapters are devoted to the very delicate position of central state agents—the police and justice—facing the loss of their monopoly over legitimate violence. The German occupation therefore strongly affected their professional practices.

Jonas Campion compares the impact of the 1940–1944 occupation on relations between gendarmes and populations in the Belgian province of Hainaut and the French administrative region of Nord-Pas-de-Calais. During the war, the numerous reforms of the institution, the intrusion of collaborationist elements in the staff and the transformations of security matters on both sides of the Franco-Belgian border forced the gendarmes to redesign their professional practices. Relations between gendarmes and local populations were also deeply affected. Increasingly, the gendarmes perceived the majority of the population as a source of risks that must be controlled instead of people needing protection. The people's subsequent lack of confidence in the gendarmes led, after the war, to questioning the very existence of the institution. Even though, as an independent body, the Belgian magistrates probably suffered less intrusion from the occupier and fewer bottom-up pressures than the gendarmes, they also faced difficult dilemmas. **Jan Julia Zurné** examines the issue of political attacks on collaborators carried out by resistance groups and, more particularly, how the Brussels public prosecutor's office dealt with this. Her clear and well-conducted case study invites us to a more general investigation of the options and choices of the magistracy at war. Amongst other interesting findings, Zurné reveals a very amazing practice the Brussels prosecutors developed in wartime: sabotage of their own judicial investigations. In a way never seen before, these legal professionals willingly abandoned their duties regarding law enforcement to protect Belgian patriots from German justice. This strategy was eventually successful, thanks to the relative position of power the judiciary occupied relative to the occupier.

After these analyses devoted to professional bodies, **Dimitri Roden's** chapter narrows the focus to one individual performing a singular mission that is rarely associated with the criminal justice system: Otto Gramann, head chaplain to the German military administration in occupied Belgium. Responsible for the spiritual assistance of detainees at the Saint-Gilles prison (Brussels), Gramann assisted during their last hours hundreds of Belgian inmates sentenced to death for acts of resistance against the occupier. The recent discovery of Gramann's personal archive is a unique source of information. The detailed records of his encounters with the executed not only allow an insight into the execution of the death penalty in occupied Belgium and northern France but also offer a starting point for a fascinating investigation on the chaplain's motivations. The comparison of Gramann's experiences with those of other chaplains who had been in charge under the Nazi regime highlights the inherent tension in the military chaplaincy, marked by the duality between the spiritual mission and membership in an army. Such a duality can lead to loyalty conflicts.

The next chapter explores other judicial confrontations between Belgians and Germans, this time in an entirely different judicial scene at the very heart of the German Empire: the hundreds of thousands of foreigners, including numerous Belgians, who lived in Berlin during the war as forced or voluntary workers. The archives of the common-law courts, up to now less explored than archives of the more impressive special courts, offer access to their individual war trajectories, trajectories that, for the most part, still escape our knowledge. With the help of those documents, **Julia Albert**, **Herbert Reinke** and **Michael Wildt** provide a captivating illustration of the potential of a grassroots approach for the judicial history of the Third Reich. Indeed, study of the judicial files invites us to challenge our vision of the repressive Nazi system as exercising efficient and total control of populations. The grid of the criminal net in fact proved to be looser than generally imagined. The Berlin police and justices had great difficulty controlling the large numbers of foreign workers they considered as a threat. The few cases discussed here help us rethink the image of the Western forced workers. Instead of being disciplined by the national socialist regimes, they appear in fact to have enjoyed a surprising freedom of movement and autonomy—the authors use Lüdtke's concept of *Eigensinn*—within the German capital city.

Back to Belgium, **Lawrence Van Haecke** and **Christoph Brüll's** contribution is devoted to a small border region that experienced a very troubled war history: the East Cantons. It has known no fewer than three changes of nationality during the first half of the twentieth century. Part of Germany before 1914, the population of the German-speaking districts of Eupen and Saint-Vith and the French-speaking district of Malmedy became Belgian in 1920 following the Treaty of Versailles, were annexed by the Third Reich between 1940 and 1944 and became Belgian again at the liberation. These transitions provoked processes of adaptation and conflicts of loyalty. The liberation constituted a specific acute crisis time, with a quarter of the Cantons population facing legal proceedings for military, political or economic collaboration with the Germans. This massive judicial confrontation left lasting marks in the regional collective memory of the war. Focusing on the judicial actors—the central and local military jurisdictions in charge of the repression—Van Haecke and Brüll's study aims to provide a more nuanced view of the legal treatment of the East Cantons population. Their thorough analysis outlines the key role performed by the judicial actors during the transition period. Far from being strictly retributive, the judiciary played an important political role in guaranteeing the future loyalty of the border population towards Belgium and contributed to the economic reconstruction of the region. In 'After the Big Show', **Clive Emsley**, who was the keynote speaker at the conference and unfortunately passed away in 2020, brings the book to a close with a fascinating essay. In fact, it is less a closure than an opening, both geographical—leaving Belgium for the European scene—and thematic—describing the role played by the English police in the post-war reconstruction of former Axis countries. In a colourful account of the Central European journey of two British policemen, members of the brand new Civil Affairs organisation in charge of the reconstruction of the civil society liberated from the Axis powers, the British crime historian gives us an insight into the variety of tasks incumbent upon such a police agency. More generally, the two policemen's story introduces the reader to the challenges and opportunities posed to law enforcement agencies in post-war Europe, during the transition from war to peace, in the emerging Cold War context.

Mélanie Bost
CegeSoma (Belgian State Archives)/Royal
Military Academy (Law), Brussels, Belgium

Antoon Vrints
History Department, Ghent University
Ghent, Belgium

References

Abbott E (1918) Crime and the War. J Am Inst Crim Law Criminol 9(1):32–45

Abbott E (1943) Juvenile Delinquency during the First World War: notes on the British experience, 1914–1918. Soc Serv Rev 17(2):192–212

Cornil P (ed) (1951) The effects of the war on criminality: select papers on penal and penitentiary affairs. Bull Int Penal Penitentiary Comm 15

De Koster M, Leuwers H, Luyten D, Rousseaux X (eds) (2012). Justice in wartime and revolutions, Europe 1795–1950 (Justice and society). Belgian State Archives, Brussels

Eggens A (2005) Van daad tot vonnis. Door Drenten gepleegde criminaliteit voor en tijdens de Eerste Wereldoorlog. Van Gorcum, Assen

Emsley C (2013) Soldier, sailor, beggarman, thief: crime and the British armed services since 1914. Oxford University Press, Oxford

Emsley C (2017) Future themes and research agendas on crime and police in wartime. Crime, Hist Soc 21(2):77–86

Exner F (1927) Krieg und Kriminalität in Österreich (Wirtschafts-und Sozialgeschichte des Weltkrieges. Österreichische und Ungarische Serie 9). Hölder-Pichler-Tempsky, Vienna

Habermas R (2008) Diebe vor Gericht. Die Entstehung der modernen Rechtsordnung im 19. Jahrhundert. Campus Verlag, Frankfurt

Leeson C (1917) The child and the war, being notes on Juvenile Delinquency. P.S. King & Son, London

Liepmann M (1930) Krieg und Kriminalität in Deutschland (Wirtschafts-und Sozialgeschichte des Weltkrieges. Deutsche Serie 10). Deutsche Verlags Anstalt, Stuttgart, Berlin and Leipzig

Mannheim H (1941) War and crime. Watts & Co, London

Mannheim H (1955) Group problems in crime and punishment and other studies in criminology and criminal law. Routledge & Kegan Paul, London
Muncie J (1999) Youth and crime. A critical introduction. Sage, London
Rousseaux X (2013) A history of crime and criminal justice in Europe. In: Body-Gendrot S, Hough M, Kerezsi K, Lévy R, Snacken S (eds) The routledge handbook of European criminology. Routledge, Abingdon, pp 48–51
Rousseaux X, Campion Jonas, Berlière J-M, Lacchè L (eds) (2013). Justices militaires et Guerres mondiales (Europe, 1914–1950)/Military justices and world wars (Europe, 1914–1950).Presses Universitaires de Louvain, Louvain-la-Neuve
Tham H (1990) Crime in Scandinavia during World War II. J Peace Res 27(4):415–417

Contents

Juvenile Delinquency, War and the Food Crisis: A Judicial Response to Delinquent Subsistence Strategies (Belgium, 1914–1918)

Aurore François

Abstract Economic crises, particularly those inherent to war situations, represent privileged moments for understanding the functioning of regulatory institutions often obliged to redefine their priorities and constrained to adapt their functioning to the urgencies certain situations demand. Instituted by law only in 1912, Belgian juvenile courts almost immediately faced a transformation of the juvenile delinquency reported: incidences clearly and directly linked to subsistence during wartime. These specific incidences testified to the economic vulnerability of the offenders as well as of their victims. This contribution examines jurisdictions in direct contact with families plunged into poverty precisely from the angle of the judicial response made to behaviours more or less directly related to the crisis of subsistence: pilfering, gleaning, theft, vagrancy and begging. During the war and in the immediate post-war period, these actors in child protection provided a well-delineated analysis of the delinquency of subsistence, exhibiting a relative degree of tolerance of theft while firmly condemning begging, and *a fortiori* when it formed part of a family strategy. Evaluation of these various behaviours, as well as of the families implementing them in a more or less strategic manner reveals that the actors in the judicial protection of children held a relatively complex interpretation of the contexts of war and economic crisis, as well as their effects on juvenile delinquency and, more generally, on the morality of families.

Analysing World War One's effects[1] on the civil populations of the countries involved invites historians to establish nuances: adjusting for material conditions and living standards in various periods and territories, the effects can be seen to have been quite contrastive (Winter and Wall 1988). By the end of 1914, Belgium found itself confronted with severe problems of provisioning. The country's occupation

[1] This research was first published in François (2015).

A. François (✉)
UCLouvain, Institute for the Analysis of Change in Contemporary and Historical Societies (IACCHOS), Louvain-la-Neuve, Belgium
e-mail: aurore.francois@uclouvain.be

M. Bost and A. Vrints (eds.), *Doing Justice In Wartime*,
Studies in the History of Law and Justice 19,
https://doi.org/10.1007/978-3-030-72050-6_1

by German troops led to requisitions, price increases, unemployment, shortages and famines that lasted nearly 50 months, affecting the country's demography (lower birth rates, a rise in mortality in certain cities) and generating social strains (Scholliers and Daelemans 1988; De Schaepdrijver 2004).

Recent historiography invites us to go beyond an exclusively victimization-oriented interpretation of the populations' sufferings during the war, which clearly prevailed from the conflict's outbreak. Far from being passive recipients of the decisions of the occupying or occupied authorities, some non-elitist social groups acted as true co-producers of public policies for managing the food question, in particular by means of collective actions (riots and strikes, among others) and revindications (Vrints 2015; Trentmann and Just 2006). For this reason, due to its character, at once intense and prolonged, the subsistence crisis that affected Belgium during World War One constitutes a privileged moment of observation of not only the survival strategies—individual or collective, legal or illegal—but also the responses or adjustment of the political and juridical authorities to those behaviours.

The practices of children's courts shed light on the link between delinquent behaviours and the penury context. A jurisdiction primarily centred on childhood perceived to be the product of the family environment, the children's court in fact provides an observatory for seeing tensions emerge between, on the one hand, a concern to maintain law and order in times of crisis and, on the other, what is known as the *protective* dimension of this jurisdiction, one that instead of punishing took 'custody, safeguarding and educative' measures with regard to certain young delinquents (Loi sur la protection de l'enfance 1912, 3457–3467), based on the ideological presupposition that 'committing an act becomes the symptom of a "moral risk of perdition" and its author, still a malleable child, a minor to be "treated"' (Cartuyvels 2001). Possibly requesting a double expertise (social and medical-pedagogical),[2] the court abandoned 'the punishment fits the crime' principle in favour of re-educational action centred on the minor and her/his family, possibly diagnosing the latter's inability to educate the child and the need to pursue the re-educational task in another milieu, usually institutional.

Does the crisis context lead the actors in child protection to renegotiate the ramifications and interpretation of certain behaviours, particularly those linked to subsistence? Having become survival reflexes, do these offences remain heralds of future criminal trajectories in the eyes of decision makers? How, finally, does the work of expertise and the resulting decision integrate the 'familial' dimension into certain cases? This study relies on analysis of the official statistics, the memories of contemporary actors and the 341 files of the Brussels children's court remaining from that period and, more particularly, on files presenting an obvious connection with the question of subsistence: marauding, gleaning, falsifying foodstuffs, as well as theft, vagrancy and even begging.[3] This quantitatively and qualitatively rich material will facilitate a two-stage analysis: based on a restitution of the behaviours and familial

---

[2]On the rise of recourse to social surveys in Belgium, see François (2008a) and François et al. (2014).

[3]Case studies on prostitution have already been the object of an analysis (François 2008b).

dynamics they set in motion, it will then focus on the juridical system's response, as much from the viewpoint of the decisions as the values underlying and justifying them.

1 The Transformation of Juvenile Delinquency Recorded During the War

Possible transformations in the recording of juvenile delinquency and its repression are hard to observe for the 1914–1918 period, for lack of benchmarks. Passed in May 1912, the law had in fact only recently come into force. Admittedly, there was an upswing in the number of files introduced but also and above all a particular configuration in the nature of the files transmitted. The relative share occupied by certain types of cases (vagrancies and begging, property offences) appears very high, more than during the inter-war period. To take an even closer look at this, at the very heart of the files, these behaviours are not only more prevalent than usual but they moreover present particularities characteristic of the penury context. Offenses in the category of robberies have clearly undergone a transformation, with a surge in thefts of food (fruit, vegetables, animals), cash, and also of metals and fuels.

From the outset, the magnitude and rapidity of the penury striking the country affected the most fragile, including children, with full force. If a broad mobilization gradually gained momentum, particularly via international effort (Jacques and Piette 2005) benefiting Belgian children, nevertheless certain elements of the population remained on the margins and suffered considerably from the conflict.

1.1 The Recrudescence of Vagrancy and Begging

The court archives abound in these sorts of cases linked to subsistence, such as vagrancy and begging. With the war, the phenomenon changed and expanded, reaching unusual proportions. Begging is present in many files as a family survival strategy, often initiated by the parents, who then try to come to the rescue—usually rather unsuccessfully—once their little tots have been arrested. Thus on 31 December 1914 in Brussels centre, a police officer apprehended Charles D., only 13 years old, while he was soliciting alms from passersby. At the police station, he said:

> It's mama who told me 'Go out and beg so the three of us can eat: your mama, your little sister and you (…)' the Molenbeek municipality only gives us soup. Mama gave me a little slice of bread for lunch. I'm hungry. Mama kept part of the bread she had so we'd have something for supper.[4]

[4]State Archives in Anderlecht—Archives de l'État à Anderlecht (AEA), Brussels Children's Courts—Tribunal des enfants de Bruxelles (TEB), File 117/15, a Brussels Police Pro Justitia (3rd div.), 31/12/1914.

Whether peddling matches, postcards or bootlaces … the pretexts for going from door to door, accosting passersby or even the occupant are myriad. If certain cases, considered trifling, describe a minor's occasionally soliciting alms to get some pocket money unbeknownst to his/her parents, most are the acts of children issuing from very poor milieux and beset with serious difficulties. The little beggars, moreover, are rather young: the youngest arrested was six years old, with most of them under 14, which already contrasts with the court's habitual clientele, on the average older.

Most of the time, the families of these young beggars and vagrants are clearly identified. But certain files, admittedly rarer, reveal paroxystic situations, like that revealed by the individual who alerted the king's prosecutor to the extreme situation endured by the children of a neighbouring house: motherless and abandoned by their father, forsaken by the usual social or charity services. Living exclusively from begging and plundering, sunken into utter destitution, they burned everything in the house they could lay their hands on to keep warm: doors, hatches, woodwork and even staircases. The judge separated them for lack of space in nearby institutions and sent the oldest to Forest prison.[5]

1.2 Theft, Plundering and Petty Thievery

The percentage of thefts linked to subsistence increased considerably during the conflict, as foodstuffs and fuels became real survival issues. Thus depositions for theft testify to a displacement of the geography of 'crime scenes'. Whereas in periods of peace, businesses of all kinds, and to a lesser extent those run by private individuals, were in the majority among plaintiffs, the war in part moved such behaviour outside: fields, forests, public parks and private gardens were thenceforth also concerned. Forests in the Brussels area were regularly stormed by groups of whole families invading them to scavenge wood and kindling for heating. In addition to thefts targeting cash, food or fuel, we note the pillaging of abandoned houses. Some families carried off everything they could find, sometimes returning again and again. Finally, the objects stolen by children acting alone show the point to which they remained children: they stole whatever piqued their curiosity or amused them, regardless of its value (bicycles, toys, wireless accessories, road signs and marble crucifixes …).

2 Adjusting Tolerance Thresholds in Wartime

Whether it involved predatory behaviour or begging, this particular configuration of juvenile delinquency in wartime reveals at once certain children's development of survival strategies in a context of deprivation, as well as their integration into family or neighbourhood strategies aimed at reducing the effects of penury. Concerning

[5] AEA, TEB, Files 6–7/18, Report by the child protection delegate, undated (Winter 1917–1918).

thefts of foodstuffs, the response of these families' environment (the entourage, the wronged neighbours, victims of plunder) shows a modification in social relationships in wartime, whereas the juridical response was largely coloured by the version the actors provided of the particular context in which they were evolving.

2.1 *Tensions Over Rarefied Resources*

Staples, which saw an increase in worth, henceforth became a privileged target of thefts committed by children, with many more cases being brought to the authorities' attention. This phenomenon, which certainly reveals the misery of those who committed those thefts, moreover reveals the point to which the war also weakened those who still had certain resources, reducing their tolerance, including respect for those even weaker than themselves. In periods of easy access to resources, subsistence offences committed by children issuing from more vulnerable milieux usually evoked attitudes of relative tolerance, even of complacency on the part of those injured, who were little inclined to complain to the police or judge over this type of theft (De Koster 2003).[6] Likewise, the children's tribunals and courts regularly received requests for withdrawal of the victim's complaint after they learned that the perpetrator was a child: most of them simply wanted to recover their goods or wanted the damage to be made good, explicitly announcing that they did not want to press charges (François 2011).

In wartime, that climate gives way to an obvious tension over resources, in turn seen in the children's court files by complaints concerning very minor thefts: raspberries from the end of a yard, cabbages from a family garden or turnips or potatoes marauded in a field.[7] This observation corroborates Catharina Lis and Hugo Soly's (2001) remarks on 'social crime', pointing out a series of factors sometimes favouring, sometimes inhibiting tolerance towards subsistence offences: if the needy families' integration into the community and how they were seen in it would usually play in their favour, an unfavourable socio-economic context pushes the victims of those offences to go to the police and denounce behaviour they would normally close their eyes to or, at least, straighten out between one another, thus preserving a certain form of social peace.

At the outbreak of war, the emergence of a vast and privately initiated assistance movement—coordinated by the National Committee for Assistance and Food Supply (the CNSA)[8] and internationally co-ordinated by the Commission for Relief in Belgium—deployed in the field thanks to municipal structures and a vast network of private charities existing before the conflict. This made such resource predation

[6]On the Antwerp court's practice, Margo De Koster confirms this in referring to the relative tolerance of wronged owners with regard to the authors of petty crimes where need seems to have been the motivating factor.

[7]That is, the Files AEA, TEB 870/16, 22/18 and 23/18, among other examples.

[8]For an interpretation centred on childhood and the actions of the CNSA, see Marissal (2014).

that much more unacceptable, given that an ever greater part of the Belgian population was resorting to assistance (Scholliers and Daelemans 1988; De Schaepdrijver 2004). In fact, supported in prosperous milieux, these solidarity and charitable initiatives in large measure outgrew their reputation of 'almsgiving to improvident populations' and became instead 'solidarity activities' for the victims of a conflict that reached every social condition (Marissal 2014). In such a context of generalized penury and suffering, theft was a form of treason with respect to this shared misfortune, all the more so as the fear of 'profiteering' appeared on the horizon and was even exacerbated when coupled with the idea that maybe some of the needy were not as poor as they made out to be.

2.2 *Absolute Need or Training in Crime? The Juridical Actors' Response*

The other side of the problem of course resides in the system's response to this sort of behaviour. It appears rather nuanced and above all very different from the assessment of the 'familial' dimension that certain offences took on. It also involves great degrees of variability, depending on the nature of the offence.

In wartime as in peacetime, property offences certainly represent most of the cases treated by the courts but also were the type of act toward which judges showed themselves least inclined to placement. This tendency is confirmed during the conflict, with certain actors maintaining a socio-economic interpretation of the rise in juvenile delinquency. In his memoirs of war, the Brussels children's judge Paul Wets, usually known for his very conservative positions, goes so far as to employ the theories of the Socialist Hector Denis,

> who has shown the impressive parallelism which exists between criminality and the price of bread or wage rates: when the price of bread goes up, or wage rates go down, crime increases. Thus there is a close link between criminal reaction and the economic crisis (…). The war will surely go far in proving that truth. Thefts committed by children are multiplied in an enormous proportion: fuel theft: coal, wood (several hectares of the Forest of Soignes were completely stripped by those neighbouring the forest, among whom many children employed by their parents), food theft: potatoes, bread, etc. (Wets 1928, 116)[9]

Faced with these situations, most of the judges adopted a strategy of compromise: acquittal remained extremely rare, while measures of reprimand, allowing a symbolic sanction more or less inconsequential for the family, were numerous. Only minors presenting family profiles judged to be problematic incurred placement measures. Certain actors nevertheless expressed their fears as to the long-term effects of these wartime survival strategies. Once the conflict is over and the situation has improved, they feared, such automatic reflexes may thenceforth transform themselves into

---

[9]Wets, Paul. 1928. *L'enfant de justice. Quinze années d'application de la Loi sur la Protection de l'Enfance*. Brussels, 116. Wets does not specify which writing of Hector Denis he is referring to here.

vicious practices. Accordingly, persons in charge of placement institutions made a real effort to sort out their boarders, as in the example of the Moll establishment's director, who in 1920 reports the conversation he had with a young boy:

> H. is not vicious, he did what other children did who, more skilful or more favoured by the circumstances were not that threatened. He was hungry, he was cold, he stole … A good many others have been pardoned. His principles today are not those he had during the war—by contagion: he explains quite well that stealing food was less serious than now; wrongheaded morals, perhaps, but it was the masses' morals. 'I took potatoes in a field because we had no bread; I cut wood in the forest because we had no more coal'. Quite light offences if we think back to the unspeakable sufferings of almost all large families during the torment.[10]

Begging—*a fortiori* when it fits into a family dimension—for its part falls under a diametrically opposed dynamic. Classified among the plagues that already threatened childhood well before the war, in the eyes of the actors in child protection, vis à vis the society, it symbolised an eminently immoral posture for anyone who succumbed to it. Begging, asserts the king's prosecutor of Brussels, Charles Collard, teaches idleness and ruins the child's project for a life honestly earned by hard labour: 'Once he's learned that you can live and live quite well by holding out your hand instead of working, in loitering around, how can you then expect he will acquiesce to being locked up long hours in a workshop, at the age of fourteen or fifteen, where he will have to toil to earn meagre wages (…)?' (Collard 1914, 27).[11]

After the arrest of children found begging, the investigation carried out by the services of order sought to define the state of need the family finds itself in and, above all, to establish the degree to which the parents could be implicated. The files do not always allow us to determine whether the information was to be used for any further proceedings against the families who exposed their children. But that was indeed the case in certain extreme situations, such as that of the H. sisters, fatherless, with the mother throwing them outside barefoot morning till night. The mother was deprived of her parental rights:

> (…) it appears that the mother made her three children beg from 8 in the morning until 11 at night; when her children did not manage to bring home a tidy sum, the individual with whom the mother lived had no qualms about hitting them [*sic*], that money serving to maintain that individual; evenings, once her children were in bed the mother left to spend the night at that individual's, returning the next morning around 6 or 7 a.m. to send her children unfed and barefoot—to move people to pity (…).[12]

Both dimensions—the parents' responsibility and the family's economic situation—were taken into consideration in the subsequent evaluation of the minor's familial situation, notably by the judge's delegates, often to legitimize the court's

---

[10]AEA, TEB, File n°7/18. Moll: Central Establishment for Observation. Report on medical-pedagogical observation, 12 May 1920.

[11]The remarks are not, strictly speaking, Collard's, but he reproduces them with the sole qualification that they were uttered by a 'voice more authorized than his own (…)'. It seems that Collard may have been inspired, among others, by the work of Fernand Dubief (*La question du vagabondage*, Paris: Fasquelles).

[12]AEA, TEB, File n°55/18. Child Protection. Inquiry on the subject of (model child J), 11/09/1918.

intervention. If, in the context of repressive type legislation, the fact of being induced by another or in a state of absolute destitution attenuates a given behaviour's reprehensible dimension, those same circumstances plead rather in favour of a placement measurement in the *protective* model enshrined in the law of 1912. Because the parents, or institutional services, did not—or could not—fulfil their duties with respect to the child, the juridical power took over, under constraint, via an intervention centred on the child.

Moreover, the war memoirs of Judge Wets reveal very little indulgence for such family strategies of peddling or begging. Childhood relief organisations multiplied during World War One, manifestly alleviating a catastrophic situation (Jacques and Piette 2005; De Schaepdrijver 2004). In hindsight, the magistrate finally concluded that he had seen 'an extremely limited number of minor beggars before his bench who truly inspired pity. Most of them were simply the little victims of their parents' negligence, sluggishness, indifference and cupidity' (Wets 1919, 21). As José Cubero (1998) noted in his analysis of French practices, the child welfare movement's success corresponded to an increasingly manifest intransigence among adults who used their children to benefit from more generous alms.[13] And Wets denounced the 'eternal excuse of invincible misery', a *leitmotiv* of all the parents, most of whom were cynical traffickers in charity. With regard to the latter, he adopted a resolutely intransigent tone:

> (…) they voluntarily withdraw the child, boy or girl, from his/her school obligations just to serve their shameful personal gain; they expose them to all the material, physical, and moral dangers of the street; they initiate them into all the practices, all the tricks for exploiting charitable sentimentalism; they develop the hypocritical tendencies of simulation and idleness in the unfortunate child; they destroy the concern for human dignity in him; the honest virtue of work, which remunerates and uplifts; they walk along the well frequented streets of rich districts, carrying an infant, often rented, on their arms, trailing at their skirts or coat some poor wretched kid whose instinctive and familiar gesture is to hold out an imploring hand, grimy and chapped with cold (for being physically dirty is an adjuvant to begging which is paraded and makes appeal to the compassion of passersby). They teach the child that contracted and beseeching smile, that significant bending of the head which solicits commiseration. Those people deserve the most rigorous sanctions and we cannot sufficiently discourage the easy gesture of the passersby, which relieves no misery and, in being given, does nothing but encourage drunkenness, idleness and the worst moral degradations. (Wets 1919, 20)

3 Conclusion

This paralleling of the dominant discourses with regard to two types of family behaviours linked to subsistence—theft on the one hand, and begging on the other—reveals a rather clear-cut moral hierarchisation of these behaviours by the actors in protection. Whereas the reformers of the 19th century usually remained attached

[13]Cubero notes the decrease in the repression of vagrancy and begging in the interwar years, with prosecutions being very often limited to cases where children were exposed (278).

to a distinction between habitual beggars and 'those for whom accidental circumstances, or those beyond their control, prevent from working',[14] the nuance, despite the dramatic circumstances of war, is somewhat sacrificed from the moment the parents act as instigators of their children's begging. Thus a relative tolerance reigns with respect to thefts for subsistence, while begging, teaching vice and laziness, is definitively condemned. In the context of a survival economy, where more or less illicit individual and family strategies develop, food thefts such as marauding or gleaning remain perceived as more temporary phenomena, readily associated with the expression of an element of resourcefulness typical of wartime circumstances. Begging, as soon as it is organized within the family circle, was seen as definitively symptomatic of the immorality of the parents, who push the child towards an idleness that will certainly become habitual in the long run. The example is just one additional testimony that the war, like every crisis context, witnesses the renegotiation of a society's tolerance thresholds, but it also reveals a differentiation from one social group to another (Vrints 2013).

Hence if the actors of the juridical world revindicated a relatively tolerant positioning with respect to thefts, a part of the population clearly showed itself much more inclined to denounce them to the juridical authorities, even when the offenses were committed by children coming from vulnerable milieux, and even when the latter are usually the subject of greater tolerance. Examining these juridical practices measured against subsistence offences thus confirms the intensity of the tension that reigned concerning resources. Through the prism of delinquent childhood, an alternate society—strained over access to foodstuffs directly linked to its survival, wherein penury modifies the social ties—appears before us: a society in which—counter to the tendency to increasingly leave the task of feeding the family up to women—that mission again, temporarily, became everybody's business (Vrints 2015)— women, men and children too.

References

Cartuyvels Y (2001) Les grandes étapes de la justice des mineurs en Belgique. Continuité, circularité ou ruptures? Journal du droit des jeunes 207:13–33

Collard C (1914) Une année d'application de la loi sur la protection de l'enfance. Revue de Droit pénal et de Criminologie 5–28 & 81–108

Cubero J (1998) Histoire du vagabondage du Moyen Âge à nos jours. Imago, Paris

De Koster M (2003) Weerbaar, weerspannig of crimineel? Meisjes en jonge vrouwen tussen emancipatie en delinquentie tijdens de eerste helft van de twintigste eeuw. Doctoral thesis, VUB (unpublished)

De Schaepdrijver S (2004) La Belgique et la Première Guerre mondiale. Archives et musée de la littérature, Brussels

[14]*Documents parlementaires*, Chambre, session 1890–1891, meeting of 12 November project of law on the repression of vagrancy and begging: 23. The law was adopted on 27 November 1891 (Dupont-Bouchat 1996, 89).

Dupont-Bouchat M-S (1996) De la prison à l'école. Les pénitenciers pour enfants en Belgique au XIXe siècle (1840–1914). UGA, Courtrai-Heule
François A (2008a) Une phalange de collaborateurs pour 'une tâche de coeur': les délégués à la protection de l'enfance en Belgique (1912–1949). *Histoire et Sociétés: revue européenne d'histoire sociale* 25–26:212–225
François A (2008b) From street walking to the convent: child prostitution cases judged by the Juvenile Court of Brussels during World War One. In: Schmidt-Supprian C, O'Brien J, Jones H (eds) Untold war: new perspectives in first world war studies. Brill, Leiden, pp 151–178
François A (2011) Guerres et délinquance juvénile. Un demi-siècle de pratiques judiciaires et institutionnelles envers des mineurs en difficulté (1912–1950). La Charte-Die Keure, Brussels-Bruges
François A (2015) Délinquance juvénile et crise de subsistance: les familles belges à l'épreuve de la pénurie (Belgique, 1914–1918). Revue d'Histoire de l'enfance irrégulière 17:137–148
François A, Mazzochetti J, Willemen N (2014) L'évaluation des familles par les acteurs de la protection de l'enfance en Belgique (fin XIXe/début XXIe siècles): pratiques et discours experts. In: Merla L, François A (eds) Distances et liens. Academia, Louvain-la-Neuve, pp 105–124
Jacques C, Piette V (2005) Une grande bataille: sauver l'enfance. In: Jaumain S, Amara M, Majerus B, Vrints A (eds) Une guerre totale? La Belgique dans la Première Guerre mondiale. Nouvelles tendances de la recherche historique. Archives Générales du Royaume, Brussels, pp 171–182
Lis Catharina, Soly Hugo (2001) Jeugd, criminaliteit en sociale netwerken, veertiende-twintigste eeuw. In: Lis Catharina, Soly Hugh (eds) Tussen dader en slachtoffer: jongeren en criminaliteit in historisch perspectief. VUB Press, Brussels, pp 11–47
Loi sur la protection de l'enfance (15 mai 1912) Le Moniteur belge. Brussels: Imp. Moniteur belge, 148:2467–3457
Marissal C (2014) Protéger le jeune enfant. Enjeux sociaux, politiques et sexués (Belgium 1890–1940). Editions de l'Université de Bruxelles, Brussels
Scholliers P, Daelemans F (1988) Standards of living and standards of health in wartime Belgium. In: Winter JM, Wall Richard (eds) The upheaval of war, family, work and welfare in Europe: 1914–1948. Cambridge University Press, Cambridge, pp 39–158
Trentmann Frank, Just Flemming (2006) Food and conflict in Europe in the age of the two world wars. Palgrave Macmillan, New York
Vrints A (2013) Verschuivende tolerantiedrempels: de morele codes van het leven in bezet België (1914–1918). Volskunde 114(3):317–339
Vrints A (2015) Beyond victimization: contentious food politics in Belgium during World War I. Eur Hist Q 45(1):83–107
Wets P (1919) La guerre et l'enfant. Ecole de Bienfaisance de l'Etat, Moll
Wets P (1928) L'enfant de justice. Quinze années d'application de la Loi sur la Protection de l'Enfance. Office de publicité, Brussels
Winter JM, Wall R (eds) (1988) The Upheaval of war, family, work and welfare in Europe: 1914–1948. Cambridge University Press, Cambridge

Judges, Lawyers, 'Vultures' and 'Butchers': Actors and Stakes of the Rental Crisis in Occupied Brussels, 1914–1918

Mélanie Bost

Abstract Like several other European belligerent countries, Belgium faced significant difficulties in regard to housing during World War One. In particular, the drop in household income caused the multiplication of rent disputes and the polarisation of relations between two classes of citizens with conflicting interests: tenants and landlords. If most countries at war took measures to resolve the crisis—e.g., instituting a moratorium on rents or setting rent price controls—the Belgian case was different and unique in Western Europe because the country was then governed by the German occupier. Likely influenced by lobby groups created within occupied Belgium, the occupier established new authorities—the arbitration tribunals—charged with resolving disputes between landlords and tenants. This essay explores the judicial dimension of the rent issue during World War One. Indeed, beyond its social effect and its impact on judicial organisation, the rent problem questioned the legality of the occupier's decrees and their applicability by Belgian judges. The debate around the legitimacy of those arbitration tribunals provoked the question of the judges' patriotism and generated strong internal divisions amongst them.

1 Introduction

Like several other European belligerent countries, Belgium faced significant difficulties in regard to housing during World War One. Widespread material destruction in war-torn areas, the need to address the refugees' problem but also provide lodging for German soldiers or public servants combined with inactivity in the building sector to create a housing shortage. Moreover, the drop in household income caused the multiplication of rent disputes and the polarisation of relations between two classes of citizens with conflicting interests: tenants and landlords.

M. Bost (✉)
CegeSoma (Belgian State Archives)/Royal Military Academy (Law), Brussels, Belgium
e-mail: melanie.m.bost@gmail.com

M. Bost and A. Vrints (eds.), *Doing Justice In Wartime*,
Studies in the History of Law and Justice 19,
https://doi.org/10.1007/978-3-030-72050-6_2

If most countries at war took measures to resolve the crisis—e.g., instituting a moratorium on rents or setting rent price controls (Voldman 2016; Englander 1983)—the Belgian case was different and unique in Western Europe because the country was then governed by the German occupier. Likely influenced by lobby groups created within occupied Belgium, the occupier established new authorities charged with resolving disputes between landlords and tenants.

This innovation in civil matters provoked a 'shock wave' in the judicial branch. Indeed, beyond its social effect and its impact on judicial organisation, the rent problem questioned the legality of the occupier's decrees and their applicability by Belgian judges. The debate around the legitimacy of those arbitration tribunals provoked the question of the judges' patriotism and generated strong internal divisions amongst them.

This essay explores the judicial dimension of the rent issue during World War One. In doing this it aims to highlight the extent to which civil law cases can be used to study military occupations.

2 The Rent Issue

The drop in household income for a large part of the population as early as August 1914 soon resulted in an increase of rent disputes. Indeed, the social crisis provoked by suspended economic activity along with prices increases became progressively acute. Unemployment grew quickly. Yet most public and private assistance was focused on addressing food needs; there was no relief in the form of *bons à loyer*.[1] Very soon, rents went unpaid and debts threatened to impoverish many tenants, who were also subject to eviction and foreclosure. In France, the decree of 14 August 1914 that would eventually be extended until March 1918, provided a payment extension of 90 days for the low rents (Magri 1997). This measure is known as the 'French moratorium'. Hearing of the French moratorium, many Belgians wondered if they still had to pay, as evidenced by several war publications devoted to the rent issue.

If the crisis hit the working class population directly, traders and manufacturers—already suffering from shortages of goods and raw materials or from German bans on economic activities—also struggled to pay their commercial leases.[2] For their part, numerous smallholders who no longer received rent still had to pay their creditors and their real estate taxes, so they too faced difficulties. The crisis mainly affected cities and industrial agglomerations and was particularly severe in the capital city, where rent prices had already constantly increased before the war (Keunings 2002, 19).[3] The tenancy agreement being an important legal relationship between citizens, a

[1] Such measure would eventually be taken in the city of Ghent in October 1916, inspired by a Dutch regulation (Winsel 1918, 21). In Berlin, in the early stages of the war, a *Mietbeihilfe* had been introduced; it was paid directly to landlords to avoid the accumulation of tenants' debts and to negotiate lower rents (Magri 1997, 378).

[2] Municipal decrees could also be the source of the problem: in Charleroi, for instance, the director of a cinema faced great difficulty paying its lease since the city decided to forbid movie performances for the duration of the war; its demand that the rent be suspended was rejected by the *tribunal de première instance* (Carlier 1915, 30–33).

[3] See the evolution curves produced by Van Den Eeckhout and Scholliers (1979).

large part of the population was directly affected, as tenant or landlord. An increasing number of conflicts therefore inundated the courts.

This, accordingly, raised the question of the juridical tools available to solve the problem.

The Belgian legislation proved to be incomplete and partially unsuitable. Two emergency regulations were taken at the beginning of the war. The Act of 4 August 1914 prohibited prosecutions against men under arms.[4] Another Act of August 1914 allowed judges to grant terms of payment to debtors.[5] However, the latter act ignored the issue of rent exemptions or reductions justified by the war context. The Civil Code (art. 1722) only provided for termination of the lease in the case of destruction of the property; only the physical state of the lodging was taken into consideration. Yet, because of the war, the deprivation of enjoyment of the leased property was often related to personal situations such as, for instance, the deportation or forced exile of the tenant. Belgian law did not cover such situations.

Early on during the occupation period, the German occupier got involved in the rental crisis and its resolution by the Belgian justice system. The German Governor General's Decree of 20 November 1914 extended the conditions for the exemption or reduction of the price of the rent, in favour of the tenant (De Huberich and Nicol-Speyer 1915, 1: 46). In an interpretative circular on 1 January 1915, the chief of the German civil administration justified the decree by the extremely narrow interpretation of art. 1722 by some Belgian judges.[6]

A second decree of the Governor General, dated 10 February 1915, put into place arbitration tribunals in charge of rent cases in municipalities of more than 20,000 people (De Huberich and Nicol-Speyer 1915, 2: 82–86). Justices of the peace who previously judged alone were now assisted by two extrajudicial assessors—one representative of the tenants, one representative of the landlords.[7] Furthermore, the parties involved had to appear in person; Belgians living abroad—hundreds of thousands of exiles were targeted by this provision (Amara 2008)—could not protect their interests. Lawyers and other professional agents were no longer allowed to participate in the debates. Arbitration tribunals could provide for payment delays, forbid expulsions and take other measures favourable to tenants. In addition, the proceedings were more or less free of charge.

The 10 February German decree was directly inspired by another crisis legislation, taken to resolve the rent disputes in Paris during the Franco-Prussian War: the French

[4] Act prohibiting proceedings against citizens at war. *Moniteur belge*, 5 August 1914, 5000. A French law of 1870 inspired it.

[5] Act on granting of grace periods by the courts. *Moniteur Belge*, 5 August 1914, 4999.

[6] *Pasicrisie belge 1915*, II, 14–15.

[7] Twelve assessors (six landlords, six tenants) were chosen for one year by the president of the *tribunal de première instance* on a list drawn up by the justices of the peace of the district. They sat in turns. Whether or not they chaired an arbitration tribunal, their jurisdiction in rental cases was increased.

Emergency Act of 21 April 1871 on rents.[8] Officially, the occupier's decree was motivated by a desire to make the procedures less costly and more efficient. But other aims could explain the occupier's rent legislation: the will to keep social peace in the occupied territory in order to secure its army; and the high number of [...] expelled people, potentially vagrant,[9] was indeed an obvious threat. The will to protect German tenants from patriotic Belgian landlords or judges possibly played a role as well.[10] Beyond this, the solution to rent problems in the occupied society was a political challenge for the German General Governor. He probably aspired to gain popularity among the Belgian population where tenants were in a large majority. Opponents of the decree would actually point out its favouritism to the tenants. There is an interesting parallel with the 1871 French legislation. The rent issue was then the object of strong competition between the French Government and the Paris Commune's authorities to win the favour of the Parisian tenants. The former declared a moratorium on rents during the war while the latter, one big step further, cancelled them. After the war, the arbitration tribunals set up by the government had durable success, which contributed to support for the new regime (Voldman 2016).

3 The Lobby Groups

The German legislation was probably inspired by a pro-tenants lobby. The extent of the social crisis indeed provoked an unprecedented citizen mobilization regarding rents.

Starting in October 1914, some tenants organized themselves into leagues. Collective movements specifically devoted to housing had existed in France during the 'Belle Époque'. The first landlords' organisation was born in Paris in 1872; for their part, before World War One, the tenants' leagues were small-scale (Voldman 2016). In Belgium, some landlords' societies pre-existed the war, but those for tenants were rare. During the war, the first one was created in the capital city and had 10,000 members in June 1916; the national league counted 50,000 members. Founded by

[8] *Dalloz Périodique* (1871, 47–51). In Berlin, 'the city council had established *Mieteinigungsämter*, tenant and landlord arbitrators dealing with accommodation rented at no more than 500 marks per year' (Magri 1997, 378).

[9] Several circulars emanating from the German civil administration and addressed to the Brussels public prosecutor regarding the repression of vagrancy show the occupier's concern about the growing number of vagrants in the capital city. Quite surprisingly, however, the number of vagrants and beggars brought before the police courts drastically dropped during the war years. The difficulties involved in transfering the individuals to specialised detention centres probably offers a partial explanation.

[10] Some German tenants who, in August 1914, temporarily fled their homes to escape the anti-German riots (on the riots, see Vrints 2005), received an unfavorable ruling upon their return. See, for instance, the judgement of the Brussels justice of the peace (3rd canton) of 25 November 1914 that did not award a German woman faced with such a situation—her landlord denounced her to the police as a German spy and threw her out of the house—the applicant damages for being deprived of enjoyment of her property (Carlier 1915, 26–30).

'about fifty bourgeois and tradesmen',[11] the League seemed to represent the interests of the middle class. It was led by tradesmen and 'the most powerful professional unions were represented'.[12] It was successively headed by Elie Nias, the founder of an important Brussels paper mill and a former judge in the commercial court, and by Arthur Boghaert-Vaché, former editor in chief of the liberal newspaper *Petit Bleu* and director during the war of the modest censored newspaper *Le Quotidien.*[13] Apart from them, we know little about the social composition of the league. Such leadership differed substantially from that of the pre-war French associations, led by anarchists and syndicalists like the famous worker Georges Cochon (Kamoun 2000). The Belgian lobby was born out of the desire to prepare a law for the post-war period that would take into account the deteriorated situation of numerous tenants. From April 1915, its bimonthly newsletter—*Le Bulletin*—brought the discussion out in the open.

In its *Bulletin*, the League denounced the magistrates' attitudes. Judges were the accomplices of landlords, whom the League described as 'vultures'.[14] They ordered expulsions when rents went unpaid and authorized foreclosures. 'Bad' judges were also called out by name in the league's journal. However, the lobbyists recognised that ungenerous rulings could not be attributed to the judiciary as a whole. In fact, following a lawyer who in 1915 reviewed the case law on rent, the justices of the peace of the Brussels agglomeration would even have adopted a fair and human jurisprudence (Carlier 1915, 21).

The *Bulletin* also criticised a form of class justice:

> Messieurs les magistrats, sauf les juges de paix, sont si éloignés de la population et n'en connaissent que peu les souffrances et les misères présentes. Ils sont payés. La plupart sont propriétaires et souvent même gros propriétaires. (...) ils doivent sortir de leur tour d'ivoire et faire quelque chose en faveur des locataires.[15]

Because it was hostile to lawyers and agents who purportedly exploited the rent crisis, the League welcomed the arbitration tribunals created by the occupier; furthermore, in its opinion, the new authorities would grant longer terms of payment.

The president of the Brussels bar, Léon Theodor, to whom we shall return later on, accused the League of being the true inspiration for the German decrees. He

---

[11] *Bulletin de la Ligue*, IV, 15 June 1915.

[12] Fédération des ligues de locataires de Belgique, *Les loyers et la guerre*, 13 février 1918, 14.

[13] *Le Quotidien* was heavily criticised in Brussels circles, notably by the liberals. According to the Brussels mayor, Adolphe Max, it was 'a German press medium printed in French' (Gille et al. 1919, 1:47). Yet Boghaert-Vaché was not harassed after the war, his newspaper being intended to answer the economic crisis by gathering job vacancies and applications etc. (Gotovitch 1961, 44).

[14] The term "vulture" when referring to landlords was used widely by the French syndicalists and anarchists during the Second Empire; it was popularized by the cartoonist Honoré Daumier, who created the 'Monsieur Vautour' character. During the war, in Belgium, some landlords would use it in order to distance themselves from the negative figure. A representative of the union of the Brussels landlords once told a journalist that its aim was not to struggle with the League of the tenants: 'Conciliation is our main concern, and M. Vulture mustn't address to us' (Winsel 1918, 17).

[15] *Bulletin de la Ligue*, II, 30 April 1915.

showed great contempt for the members of the League and their belonging to the trade world, as such outsiders of the judicial world that he called 'brave butchers' or 'the honest sellers of haberdashery' who claimed to act as legislators (Théodor 1915, 41). Before the arbitration tribunals were set up, the League had indeed been in touch with some Belgian authorities in order to raise awareness about the tenants' difficulties. It is likely that it did the same with the occupier, the only power with the de facto authority to legislate during the war. If this was the case, the adoption of a system with assessors reflected the wish to reduce the discretion of the justices of the peace, considered hostile to the tenants' interests.[16]

Note that the landlords also had their lobby groups, some of which predated the war. In June 1916, these associations had 9000 members structured into 56 organisations in occupied Belgium. A Federation of landlords was created in 1916 in response to the tenants' one. Landlords also had their own periodic publication papers, such as *De Eigenaar* in Ghent. Unlike their opponents, the landlords' associations did not trust the arbitration tribunals. In their opinion, the assessors were subordinate to the authority of the justice of the peace and did not act autonomously in the proceedings. Both warring sides accused each other of selfishness and anti-patriotism for not having fairly contributed to the 'collective sacrifice'.

4 The Attitude of the Belgian Magistrates

Was the Belgian judiciary really so conservative?

Before the creation of the arbitration tribunals, justices of the peace were very uncertain about which behaviour to adopt. Should they apply the civil code in order to avoid social trouble? Did they have to judge in equity? They did not succeed in adopting a consistent policy but were unanimously in favour of all forms of conciliation between parties. The decree of 20 November 1914 failed to provide further consensus. Some judges behaved patriotically in the presence of German tenants: the *Nieuwe Rotterdamsche Courant* of 1 February 1915 reported that Belgian magistrates who had both texts in front of them—the Belgian code and the German decree—choose to apply the former and were reluctant to release the German tenants from their obligations.[17] As soon as the 'rent decree' of 10 February 1915 was published, parties in pending court cases raised the issue of the legality of the German decrees before the Belgian justice for the first time. This issue caused a huge controversy in the judicial world, dividing it between supporters and opponents of the legislative power of the occupying forces.

---

[16]Even today, such model of a 'mixed' court appeals to those who would like to bring the justice system closer to the people: 'the presence within the tribunal of someone able to understand and share citizens' concerns, interests, even language and culture' (http://www.tnova.fr/essai/la-justice-un-pouvoir-de-la-d-mocratie).

[17]Taking into account the pro-German position of the newspaper at the beginning of the war, this information should be considered with caution.

The strongest opponent of the rent decree was certainly the Brussels Bar Council. Its rebellious president Léon Theodor strived to transform the bar into a space of moral resistance against the occupier. The decree of 10 February 1915 that excluded lawyers from proceedings acted as a catalyst. From that moment, the Brussels lawyers systematically fought against the occupier's legislation. It is plausible that the lawyers' exclusion from the arbitration tribunals was a German retaliation measure against the 'rebels'.[18]

The case of widow Piron-Derrider pending before the Brussels *tribunal de première instance* gave them the opportunity to publicly express their point of view and provoke a judicial decision.[19] The defendant, being prosecuted for non-payment of his rent, was referred to the arbitration tribunal. The plaintiff refused, using the argument that the rent decree was illegal. The case was heard in March 1915, shortly after the publication of the litigious decree, before the first chamber of the *tribunal de première instance*, chaired by Vice-President Benoidt. On 18 March 1915, President Théodor himself defended the bar's position in court. The case was pled in 'an unusually solemn atmosphere. The president of the bar was supported by the bar council and numerous lawyers' (Jofé 1927).[20] He challenged the constitutionality of the decree[21] and argued that the occupier's legislation violated the provisions of the 1907 Hague Convention on War on Land, which prescribes that the authority of the legitimate power having in fact passed into the hands of the occupant, the latter shall take all the measures in his power to restore, and ensure, as far as possible, public order and safety, while respecting, unless absolutely prevented, the laws in force in the country' (art. 43). Theodor argued that with regard to the rent decree, this condition was not met and that Belgian law and the conciliation bodies (see Sect. 4 below) were sufficient to respond to the crisis. The German decree was therefore a serious interference in judicial organisation. After the legal argument came a strong patriotic conclusion: the judges could not abdicate their responsibilities in favour of the occupier. It would be treason against the country (Théodor 1915, 34).

One month later, on 22 April 1915, the *tribunal de première instance* followed Theodor's opinion and declared that it would be impossible to apply the rent decree without violating the law and justice; as a result, the *tribunal* declared that it had

[18]The Brussels bar was accused of defending German clients only with reluctance (Brussels Courthouse, archives of the Court of cassation's public ministry, 3, II).

[19]The Brussels Bar Council reserved a part of its budget to pay the plaintiff's advocacy work and the eventual legal cost of the process, regardless of the outcome of the judicial proceeding (Brussels Courthouse, archives of the Brussels Bar Council, minutes of meetings).

[20]The Ghent Bar president Ligy attended the audience to assist his Brussels colleague (*Bulletin de la Ligue des Locataires*, n°2, 30 April 1915). Theodor could also rely on the Brussels *Conférence du jeune barreau* and on several studies to prepare his opinion. The lawyer Charles Resteau, in his pamphlet *La Belgique sous la griffe allemande*, published in Paris in 1915, devoted one chapter to the decree of 20 November 1914. He would later apply the same reasoning to the arbitration tribunals: the decree's indispensable necessity not being demonstrated, the courts do not have to apply it.

[21]According to the lawyer, the German decree violated two articles of the Belgian Constitution (article 8: 'No one can be reassigned, against his will, to a court other than that designated by law' and article 94 prohibiting special courts).

jurisdiction to hear the case. The 'Benoidt ruling', as it was called,[22] had a major impact in the judicial world (Gille et al. 1919, 1:322). This constitutes an interesting example of the instrumentalisation of justice in wartime; lawyers forced the judges to position themselves and used this precedent as a weapon against the Germans.

If, as we will see, the ruling inspired the *tribunal de première instance* of Liège, the Brussels ruling was not approved unanimously. Even within the court some magistrates disagreed. Under the rent decree, setting up arbitration tribunals in the capital city involved the collaboration of the president of the *tribunal de première instance*, who had to select assessors on the lists compiled by the justices of the peace. Which he did.

With the Brussels *tribunal*, the Liège *tribunal* (ruling of 26 May 1915[23]) is the only court of first instance that refused to apply the German decree. The Liège Court of appeal, with its ruling of 31 May 1915, confirmed the *tribunal*'s ruling.[24] However, the Liège magistrates were more in line with the 1907 Hague Convention than their Brussels counterparts. If they therefore accorded some legislative power to the occupier, they found it not completely arbitrary. It had to be limited, and the court had to assess whether these limits were respected. For practical reasons, this assessment had to take place during the war and could not expect to be submitted to the 'tribunal of the nations'. The main argument of the Liège Court of appeal was based on the preparatory works of the 1899 Hague Conference and, in particular, on the discussions that resulted in the adoption of article 43 of the 1907 Hague Convention. Relying on the comments of the famous Belgian negotiator Auguste Beernaert[25]—a key referee for opponents of the legislative power of the occupier—the Court could not accept the notion that a state that had signed the Hague Convention had abdicated in advance its power in favour of a potential enemy.[26] Interpreting the legality of the German decrees was a right—even more, a *duty*—that the Court enjoyed. In this case, according to their review, the rent decree was not legal: the reforms that it had introduced in the judicial organisation were too important and unconstitutional. Moreover, the Liège high magistrates determined that the absolute impediment to respecting the legislation in force in the occupied country as provided by article 43 only concerned military matters and not civil ones.

---

[22]The personality of Vice-President Benoidt was so identified with the judgement that the two other judges composing the *tribunal*—Leclercq and Oliviers—have been forgotten.

[23]*Belgique judiciaire* 1919, 236–245.

[24]*Belgique judiciaire* 1919, 130–138.

[25]Auguste Beernaert (Ostende 1829–Lucerne 1912): lawyer, Catholic politician. Former Prime Minister and Minister of State, President of the Parliament. After his Belgian political career, Beernaert turned to international politics. He represented Belgium at the Hague Peace Conference (1899) and was awarded the Nobel Prize in 1909 for his investment in international law. See Verwaest (2011).

[26]'Comprendrait-on que, d'avance et pour le cas d'une guerre, celui qui sera battu attribue des droits chez lui à son vainqueur et organise le régime de la défaite? Ce pourrait-il être du consentement anticipé et écrit du vaincu que le vainqueur établisse des impôts et des amendes et prenne à son service des fonctionnaires dont le premier devoir est d'être fidèles à leur pays?' (Verwaest 2011, 25).

But what was the opinion of the justices of the peace, those most affected by the new tribunals? The justices of the peace were directly accused of betrayal by Vice-President Benoidt. They had effectively agreed to set up the new tribunals in almost all cantons by the end of March 2015.[27]From a legal standpoint, they believed that they had to apply the occupier's decrees. As local judges confronted daily with dire situations, the justices of the peace were probably sensitive to their opportunity.

Tribunals of first instance outside the capital city and Liège also applied the German rent regulations. By strictly applying the law, courts did what they had always done: refrain from assessing the laws' legality or even their constitutionality (Dumont 1983).

In the appeal division, the jurisprudence diverged even more. Indeed, a few weeks after the Court of appeal of Liège's ruling rejecting the application of the 'rent decree', the Brussels Court rendered, on 19 July 1915, a judgement that was diametrically opposed to it. In his speech, the Brussels first advocate general Jottrand delivered a political and pragmatic analysis of the situation. During the country's military occupation, he said, power and law were mixed up. Jottrand considered it superfluous to assess whether or not the occupier had complied with article 43. Seemingly, he said, the Court of appeal had to give a decision on the widow Piron-Derrider case. Actually, it had to rule on a conflict of powers between Belgium and the occupying forces. The judges, however, were not supposed to tolerate everything. If they disagreed with the occupier's legislation, they should temporarily step down. It is a matter of conscience for them. In this case it is unnecessary: the suspension of the national justice would be much more harmful for the Belgian citizens.[28] Ignoring the public prosecutor's opinion, the Brussels Court assessed the legality of the German decree. Aware of the important social crisis created by the rental issue, it held that the German measure was justified and hence consistent with international law:

> L'organisation actuelle des juridictions ne suffirait pas à assurer sans retard les solutions indispensables; que la question du logement pourrait devenir aussi urgente et aussi impérieuse que celle du pain et se transformer en agitation et désordre (...). Qu'il y avait donc flagrante nécessité, pour tout administrateur un peu prévoyant, de faire résoudre aussitôt et aussi amiablement et pratiquement que possible, la multiplicité des contestations inévitables dans un grand nombre de localités.

The Court concluded that the decree was legal; it therefore overturned the judgement of the Brussels tribunal and referred the case back to the arbitration tribunal. This opposition between the two courts fed the controversy and led to major legal uncertainty. The League of the tenants, though satisfied by the ruling of 19 July, deplored the juridical insecurity and suggested in its *Bulletin* that the case be brought up to the Supreme Court (*Cour de cassation*).

---

[27] 'Réunion régionale. Arrondissement de Bruxelles, séance du 21 mars 1915', in *Journal des Juges de Paix* 1915, 1–3.

[28] On the public prosecutor's opinion and the decision of the Court, see *Belgique judiciaire* 1919, 119–130.

Nearly one year later, the opportunity arose. The Court of Cassation, mobilised by two appeals, settled the juridical dispute with its judgement of 20 May 1916.[29] As can be imagined, the moment was decisive for both sides. The lawyers of the Court of Cassation, represented by Eugène Hanssens,[30] produced voluminous appeal documents against the ruling of the Brussels Court of appeal, compiling all arguments against the rent decrees. Beyond the rent issue, admitted the lawyer, what was at issue was the legitimacy of the occupier's legislative power. The future of all Belgian legislation depended of it (Hanssens 1919, 86–87). His adversary, the prosecutor general Terlinden, in favour of the applicability of the German decrees, presented comprehensive conclusions. The question to be decided by the Court, in his words, 'essentially belongs to the international public law, which was given precedence over domestic law'. In this regard, even the national constitution must bow to international law. The prosecutor general defended the Hague heritage: the legislative power of the occupier is necessary. In the high magistrate's eyes, the modernity of the juridical notion of 'occupation'—'one of the most beautiful conquests of contemporary international law'—consists in this duty given to the winner to administer the occupied country and in the acceptance by the defeated government that it temporarily cannot exercise its powers. Considering this, citizens and, amongst them, magistrates must apply the occupier's measures. The intervention of the public international law makes it impossible for the courts to interpret the occupier's decrees. Otherwise they would be arrogating the right to impose their decisions on a foreign nation, in other words, to encroach on a state's sovereignty. Must the judicial power therefore totally submit itself to the occupier's rules? No, answered the prosecutor general. The magistrate still has his conscience; he can always refuse to apply a decree. Under this scenario, the occupier should seek other judges.

The Supreme Court followed the reasoning of the public ministry. The occupier's decrees, eventually, escaped the courts' assessment in occupied Belgium.[31] By doing so, the highest Belgian jurisdiction, an institution highly representative of the national sovereignty, provided the occupiers' actions a welcome (and frequently proclaimed) legitimacy. The decision was very controversial and provoked a great deal of concern. The Brussels bar denounced this 'unpardonable failing'. It was only in February 1918, with the judiciary strike, that the magistracy and the bar again formed a common front against the occupier. At that moment, the magistracy had indeed abandoned the prudent stance adopted so far towards the occupiers. In reaction to the political autonomy of Flanders proclaimed by the Flemish activists—who were political collaborators of the Germans—the Brussels Court of appeal urged the chief public prosecutor to prosecute the main activists's leaders as initiators of an

---

[29] *Pasicrisie belge* 1915–1916, I, 375–418.

[30] Eugène Hanssens was not only a judicial personality. He represented the Liberal Party through the National Relief and Food Committee, a powerful national charitable organisation in occupied Belgium that was considered to be the effective government of occupied Belgium.

[31] In contrast, the Brussels and Liège's Courts of appeal considered themselves competent to evaluate the German decrees.

attack against the form of government. Following this demand, the Brussels prosecutor's office arrested two activist leaders, who were freed by the Germans a few hours later. On orders of the latter, the Court of appeals' first president and two presidents of the chambers were deported to Germany, whereas all the counsellors were suspended *sine die* for having participated in a political demonstration. A few days later, the Belgian Supreme court, condemning this flagrant violation of the independence of the judiciary, decided to suspend its functions. Following this example, numerous jurisdictions gradually went on strike, with the support of the lawyers, a protest movement that lasted until the Armistice. The Germans were forced to install German jurisdictions to ensure the security of their armies in the occupied territory (Bost and François 2008).

5 The Multiplication of Paralegal Organisms Dedicated to the Conciliation of Landlords and Tenants

Whereas the occupier increased the competencies of the justice of the peace, certain groups tended, in contrast, to direct rental disputes away from canton courts. The agreements between landlords and tenants, which were part of the traditional jurisdictions of the justice of the peace, then became a matter of competitiveness. The League and the Brussels bar faced each other as adversaries.

The League organised conciliation gatherings in order to avoid legal proceedings and evictions. It claimed to have dealt with more than 10,000 cases. The Brussels lawyers, although excluded from the operations of the justices of peace, remained involved in rental affairs through a charitable organisation. Angry with the League that officially took a position in favour of the arbitration tribunals, the Brussels bar had joined forces with the powerful National Relief and Food Committee to bypass the 'German' jurisdictions and the League's conciliation offices. The department of Aid and Protection to Homeless People that had been set up within the Committee in January 1915 also sought to play a role in the conciliation between landlords and tenants. Moreover, when conciliation did not succeed, the department searched for buildings in which to host the indigent tenants. The emergency social assistance served a charitable purpose and also had patriotic considerations: providing housing to those in most need helped them avoid working for the enemy. The League claimed that the composition of the National Relief and Food Committee's conciliation bodies was questionable, since its members were lawyers, judges, dignitaries and landlords ... but not tenants. 'The decisions rendered by these committees were always extremely in favour of the landlords. The League warns the tenants: only arbitration tribunals feature the needed guarantees of impartiality for both parts'.[32] The bar, in contrast, reported the plans of the tenants: 'they wish to get exonerated

[32] Les Comités de conciliation et l'œuvre du barreau, *Le Bulletin de la Ligue des Locataires*, 30 juin 1915: 1.

from paying rents as much as possible, even with dishonest behaviour and flagrant injustices'.[33]

In this sense, even though the preliminary conciliation abolition was agreed upon in 1911, the practice of conciliation became an asset during occupation. Its importance was both patriotic (the resolution of rental difficulties had to remain a Belgian duty) and part of social control (to satisfy the interests of social classes who benefited from the settlement of rental disputes).

Regardless of the controversies and competitions, the different tools experimented with during the occupation to solve the rental disputes met great success. The quick and toll-free proceeding of the arbitration tribunals attracted a significant number of tenants and landlords. According to the official statistics from the Ministry of Justice, 18,766 affairs were considered in 1915–1916 alone, being the year they were launched.[34] For their part, the numerous extra-judicial conciliation bodies had to manage tens of thousands files. These impressive numbers and the range of stakeholders involved demonstrate the magnitude of the crisis and the multiple stakes of the rent issue in occupied Belgium: socioeconomic but also juridical, political and of social control. The question did not become less acute in the post-war period. A number of laws passed between 1919 and 1925 tried to solve the problem of debts accumulated during four years of occupation. The solutions devised were sometimes far removed from classical civil law: capping of rents, automatic renewal of some leases or debt write-offs in favour of the most vulnerable tenants. These solutions, as in other former belligerent countries, initiated state interventionism in rent matters (Fourcaut and Voldman 2013; Magri 1997, 377–387).

6 Conclusion

Covering multiple aspects and comprised of several categories of actors, the question of rent in Belgium during World War One deserves special attention.

The case law concerning the German decrees related to rent is interesting in more than one way. The variety of interpretations of the Hague Convention is striking. The state of knowledge partly explains the discrepancies. The occupation law had only recently been enacted before the war and had almost no practical application. Furthermore, the perception of social, political and patriotic issues certainly affected the action taken by the judiciary.

In the context of the occupation, during which different social groups engaged in a patriotic competition, tensions were high. Brussels lawyers did not hide their stubborn resistance to any German legislative initiative that aimed to assist, in the courtroom, the struggle of German Belgian soldiers at the front. Even among the magistrates, tensions were palpable. Proponents of pro and contra views to the occupier's orders actually formed two hostile camps.

---

[33] *Conférence du jeune barreau 1914–1918*, s.l., 1919: 82.

[34] Unfortunately, we lack statistical data for the next years.

The controversy concerning rents clearly shows the exceptional situation of the justice system during the occupation: in the absence of the national legislature, jurisprudence gained importance as a source of law. The judiciary remained one of the last expressions of national sovereignty. Judges had to respond to the lack of legislation and had to determine which issues were most important. The impact of their decisions was great, which explains the virulent criticism against some judicial decisions and also attempts at manipulation. The controversy concerning rents certainly weakened the 'patriotic front'.

Finally, the magnitude of the rental crisis illustrates the dynamism of occupied society. Pressure groups emerged. Bringing together several thousand members, the influential League of the tenants debated in public and got the occupier to establish courts of arbitration. This example shows that public life in Brussels was not completely 'padlocked'. Thus the rent issue highlights the existence of leeway in occupied territory.

References

Amara M (2008) Des Belges à l'épreuve de l'exil: les réfugiés de la Première Guerre mondiale: France, Grande-Bretagne, Pays-Bas. Editions de l'Université de Bruxelles, Brussels

Bost M, François A (2008) La grève de la magistrature belge (février–novembre 1918). Un haut fait de la résistance nationale à l'épreuve des archives judiciaires. In: Rousseaux X, Herbaut D, Wijffels A (eds) Histoire du droit et de la justice: une nouvelle génération de recherches. Presses universitaires de Louvain, Louvain-la-Neuve, pp 19–43

Carlier A (1915) La question des loyers et la guerre. E.V. Pasque, Charleroi

De Huberich CH, Nicol-Speyer A (1914–1918) 21 vols. Législation allemande pour le territoire belge occupé (textes officiels). La Haye: Martinus Nijhoff

Dumont H (1983) Le contrôle de la constitutionnalité des lois et des décrets en Belgique: fonction juridictionnelle ou politique? In: Gerard P, Ost F, Van De Kerchove M (eds) Fonction de juger et pouvoir judiciaire. Transformations et déplacements, Facultés Saint-Louis, Brussels, pp 71–174

Englander D (1983) Landlord and tenant in urban Britain, 1838–1918. Clarendon Press, Oxford

Fourcaut A, Voldman D, eds (2013) Les crises du logement en Europe au XXe siècle. Le Mouvement social 245

Gille L, Ooms A, Delandsheere P (1919) Cinquante mois d'occupation allemande, 4 vols. Albert Dewit, Brussels

Gotovitch J (1961) Contribution à l'histoire de la presse censurée, 1914–1918. ULB, Brussels

Hanssens E (1919) Le pouvoir législatif sous l'occupation allemande en Belgique. Larcier, Brussels

Jofé B (1927) L'occupation ennemie et la Loi. Du droit des tribunaux belges d'approuver la légalité des dispositions impératives de l'occupant. In Le Journal des Tribunaux (2 January 1927, reprint)

Kamoun P (2000) V'la Cochon qui déménage. Prélude au droit au logement. Vauchrétien: Yvan Davy

Keunings L (2002) Les 'bras armés' de Thémis. Les policiers bruxellois à la Belle Époque. Cahiers de la Fonderie 27:17–23

Magri S (1997) Housing. In: Winter J, Robert J.-L. (eds) Capital cities at war: Paris, London, Berlin. 1914–1919. Cambridge University Press, Cambridge, pp, 374–418

Resteau Charles (1915) La Belgique sous la griffe allemande. Fontemoing, Paris

Théodor L (1915) Lettres aux autorités allemandes et plaidoiries relatives à l'Arrêté allemand du 10 février 1915. s.l

Van Den Eeckhout P, Scholliers P (1979) De Brusselse huishuren, 1800–1940. VUB, Brussels

Verwaest Rik (2011) Van Den Haag tot Genève: België en het internationale oorlogsrecht (1874–1950). Die Keure, Bruges

Voldman, Danièle. 2016. Locataires et propriétaires. Une histoire française XVIIIe–XXe siècle. Paris: Payot et Rivages

Vrints Antoon (2005) 'Moffen buiten!' De anti-Duitse rellen in augustus 1914 te Antwerpen. In: Jaumain Serge, Amara Michaël, Majerus Benoît, Vrints Antoon (eds) Une guerre totale? La Belgique dans la Première Guerre mondiale. National State Archives, Brussels, pp 47–64

Winsel E (1918) La question des loyers pendant la guerre 1914–1918. Le projet de loi Vandervelde. Le contre-projet de la Ligue générale des propriétaires et créanciers hypothécaires de la Flandre orientale. Gand: E. De Laere

'I Swear I Am a True Patriot!' Rhetorical Defence Strategies of Suspects During the Prosecution of Denunciation to the Enemy in Belgium in the Wake of the First World War

Gertjan Leenders

Abstract In the wake of the First World War, the Belgian judiciary prosecuted Belgian civilians for various kinds of collaboration with the former German occupier. This chapter examines how Belgian civilians suspected of having denounced others to the German occupier defended themselves against such accusations during the post-war judicial investigations. To this end, a corpus of judicial case files of cases of denunciation was scrutinized. Besides analysing the suspect's defence strategies, this chapter also reflects on the nature of cases of denunciations. It is argued that due to the distinctive interpersonal character of the underlying conflicts, the difficulties to prove a denunciation in court and the lack of material evidence, suspects were given ample opportunity to develop various rhetorical strategies to defend themselves against accusations of denunciation to the enemy.

1 Introduction

The First World War and the German occupation of Belgium put serious strain on social relations between Belgian citizens in the occupied country (Vrints 2014). Tensions rose on several issues, for example regarding material deprivations in the occupied country, or between those who had fled the country and those who remained in the occupied country. Another major point of contention was the relationship with the German occupier and German rule over the occupied country. These conflicts intensified during the occupation and culminated in the first days after the Armistice in popular violence against Belgians suspected of having collaborated with the occupier (Rousseaux and Van Ypersele 2005; Van Ypersele 2004). The post-war trials against suspected *inciviques* was another way to vent those tensions in the longer run (Rousseaux and Van Ypersele 2005).

Among those susceptible to prosecution were Belgians who were accused of having denounced others to the German occupier. Denunciation to the enemy was

G. Leenders (✉)
History Department, Ghent University, Ghent, Belgium
e-mail: Gertjan.Leenders@ugent.be

M. Bost and A. Vrints (eds.), *Doing Justice In Wartime*,
Studies in the History of Law and Justice 19,
https://doi.org/10.1007/978-3-030-72050-6_3

problematised by social groups within the population, and already immediately after the Armistice, Belgian citizens started to file complaints to the Belgian judiciary against suspected denouncers in order to see them punished. These prosecutions were based on article 121bis of the Belgian penal code. This piece of legislation was created during the occupation itself by the Belgian government in exile and allowed prosecution of Belgians who had 'maliciously, by the denunciation of a real or imagined fact, exposed a person to the investigations, pursuits or rigour of the enemy' (Cassiers et al. 1967, 249).

Suspects had a chance to defend themselves against the accusation of denunciation to the enemy during the post-war investigations by the Belgian judiciary. This chapter will focus on these suspects and the rhetorical defence strategies they used. How did they try to defend themselves during the investigations, and how effective were their strategies in influencing the outcome of the judicial process? In addition to exploring these judicial cases from the suspect's point of view, this perspective will also allow us to gain insight into the nature of cases of denunciation to the enemy in general.

Although all suspected denouncers were treated by this single article of the penal code, closer observation of the individual cases requires a distinction between occasional denouncers, who just about always had denounced people with whom they were acquainted, and denouncers who were in the occupier's service, who had regularly denounced people they did not know. The latter will be treated as a category of its own, because of some unique characteristics: they were often accused of espionage as well, their modus operandi during the war had been different, the post-war investigations were less likely to start with a complaint from another citizen and they generally received higher penalties. Because of these differences, this chapter will focus on occasional denouncers and will treat denouncers in the occupier's service separately.

2 Sources

A broad range of denunciation case files that reconstruct the post-war judicial investigations are examined. Looking at how the prosecution of denouncers was carried out in Belgium after the First World War, two phases can be distinguished (Leenders 2016, 215–230).

In the first few months after the Armistice, the military courts and tribunals were empowered to investigate and prosecute all kinds of incivism, including denunciation to the enemy. In preparation for the post-war prosecution of *inciviques*, the Belgian government in exile already decided in October 1916 to give the military courts an important role in the post-war prosecution of incivism. Article 7 of the special decree of 16 October 1916 stipulated that suspected *inciviques* were to be brought before the military courts for as long as the—legally determined—state of war and state of siege would endure (Horvat 2009, 63–67; Monballyu 2011, 35–47). Consequently, the Military Prosecutor's Office, established on a provincial level, carried out judicial investigations from the end of the occupation in November 1918 onwards. If the

Military Prosecutor decided to further prosecute a suspect, the Courts Martial were empowered to sentence in the first instance. Higher appeal was possible at the Military Court in Brussels. The Military Prosecutor-General decided in mid-November 1918 to centralise all investigations in the so-called Military Prosecutor's Office of the 'Grand Quartier Général' of the army in Brussels, which would carry out all investigations against *inciviques* and would also judge in the first instance. However, denunciation to the enemy was excluded from this rule already on 6 December 1918, meaning that, once more, the provincially organised Military Prosecutor's Offices and Courts Martial were empowered with the investigations against denouncers (Monballyu 2010, 315).

A second phase in the prosecution of incivism starts when, for various reasons, the authority of the military courts ended in May 1919, when article 7 of the special decree of October 1916 was retracted. As a result of this, ordinary penal courts became empowered with the prosecution of *inciviques*, and all existing files were transferred from the military courts to the Public Prosecutor's Offices in the judicial districts, which thereupon continued all investigations (Monballyu 2011, 37). From May 1919 onwards, all cases were investigated by the Public Prosecutor or the Investigating Magistrate and were judged by either the court of assizes or the correctional tribunal. Because article 121bis of the Belgian penal code specified that correctional penalties should be imposed on convicted denouncers, cases of denunciation were eventually judged by the correctional tribunal of first instance, unless there were aggravating circumstances.

Archival research for this study focused on the judicial district of Antwerp, which at the time comprised both the city of Antwerp itself as well as the surrounding countryside. When examining the archives of the above-mentioned courts and tribunals, it became clear that the military courts were vital during the judicial investigations but did not play an important role in the conviction of denouncers. Not a single civilian was brought before the Antwerp Court Martial on account of denunciation to the enemy. Therefore, this research builds on the archives of the Public Prosecutor's Office and the Correctional Tribunal of Antwerp, which contains files of dismissed cases and cases judged in the first instance. The archives of the Court of appeal of Brussels contained additional files of cases of denunciation that were judged in the first instance in Antwerp but were transferred to Brussels because either the Public Prosecutor or the convicted denouncer entered an appeal.[1]

Investigations against suspected denouncers started when the Military or Public Prosecutor's Office received a complaint (either through a letter of complaint or through a *procès-verbal* [PV] from the local police or gendarmerie nationale) or when the judiciary drew up a PV on their own accord. As for denunciation, however, a

[1]Consulting these archives resulted in a diverse corpus of 391 files that considered a total of 420 suspected denouncers (cases dismissed, cases judged in the first instance and cases sentenced in higher appeal put together). A random sample was taken for this research, resulting in a total of 159 files (196 suspects) scrutinised thoroughly. State Archives Beveren (SAB), Public Prosecutor's Office Antwerp, R527, nr. 138–141; SAB, Public Prosecutor's Office Antwerp, R600, nr. 6053–6058; SAB, Correctional Tribunal Antwerp, R20, Dossiers 'Activisten', nr. 1–548. State Archives Brussels 2—Dépot Cuvelier (SAB2), Court of appeal Brussels, Dossiers incivisme.

complainant was the most likely source of information that initiated a case. In addition to these documents that started a case, a denunciation case file also contained the PVs of the interrogations of suspects, complainants or witnesses, both *à charge* and *à décharge*. These interrogations were conducted by the local police, the *gendarmerie nationale*—at the Military or Public Prosecutor's request—or by the investigating magistrate, depending on what phase in the judicial process the investigation was in. In addition to this, judicial files of denouncers often contain letters from persons involved in the investigation with additional information on the case, reports of experts (often medical reports or documents resulting from handwriting analysis, when an anonymous writer of a letter of denunciation needed to be uncovered) or letters with the interventions of a lawyer. Finally, files contain many procedural documents (with biographical information of the suspect, the conclusions of the Public Prosecutor or Investigating Magistrate, a warrant of arrest, the judgement of the court etc.).

Opting for these sources carries important implications. For instance, it is crucial to realize that the accounts of the persons involved are part of a judicial investigation. As a result, each person will create a personal and therefore fictional narrative that best defends his or her interests. Through their accounts, witnesses and suspects were able to, consciously and unconsciously, influence the impression they left in order to enforce their own credibility and undermine their opponent's legitimacy. The 'fictional' character of these sources does not, however, reduce their value as a historical source: if one is aware of their subjective character, these accounts can give an insight into how and with what goals in mind the individuals involved constructed their own narratives. These sources, therefore, are interpreted similarly to the study of sixteenth-century pardon tales by Nathalie Zemon Davis, who decided to 'let the fictional aspects be the centre of the analysis' (Zemon Davis 1987, 3). With these methodological implications in mind, this paper focuses on the argumentation and implicit discursive strategies of suspected denouncers.

3 Rhetorical Defence Strategies of Suspected Denouncers

Suspects had a whole range of possible positions and discursive strategies at their disposal to defend themselves against accusations of denunciation to the enemy. The two most straight-forward positions suspects could adopt was either to deny all accusations without any further explanation or to make a full confession. However, it is surprising how rarely suspects completely denied or confessed all accusations without any further statement. Suspects most often combined a denial or confession with some other kind of rhetorical strategy.

3.1 *Minimizing Accusations*

Although full confessions were rare, many suspected denouncers admitted some elements of the accusations against them, especially when the complainants were supported by several witnesses *à charge*. In order to defend themselves in such circumstances, many suspects decided to point out elements that downplayed their personal accountability in the case or disputed the punishable character of the denunciation itself.

When disputing the punishable character of a denunciation, suspects most often pointed to their lack of malicious intent. According to the legislation on denunciation to the enemy, proving the malicious intent of the denouncer was necessary in order to convict a suspect (cfr. supra). However, this malicious intent was both difficult for the judiciary to prove and relatively easy for the suspect to contradict. Suspected denouncers often claimed that they had been forced by the occupier to denounce someone, or they claimed that they only denounced because they feared German reprisals if they did otherwise. For instance, Maria Van D. was accused by her neighbours of having denounced them for participating in a Belgian espionage network and smuggling letters across the border with the Netherlands. Van D. admitted that she frequently invited a German officer into her house and that she had denounced both of her neighbours. In a letter to the Military Prosecutor she wrote from prison, she claimed, however, that she only did so out of fear: 'Charel F. [the German officer] and another spy dressed as a civilian came to my house and asked if Mrs. De B. [her neighbour] was smuggling letters. After I said that I did not know, they asked me where her husband [=her neighbour's husband] was, and I said that he was in Holland. Charel F. wrote this on a piece of paper and then I had to sign it. Charel F. forced me to do it, and I did so out of fear, because I had already been imprisoned for three months before [by the Germans, for smuggling letters herself]. Then he put down 20 mark on the table and left'.[2] In her letter Van D. attempted to show that she only denounced because she feared being imprisoned again.

In a similar case, Gabrielle O. was accused of having denounced a fellow *passeur*, someone who helped people cross the border with the Netherlands. At that moment, O. was imprisoned as well. In her defence she stated: 'I cannot remember which confessions I was forced to make during the manifold interrogations I was subjected to during my imprisonment by the Germans'. Her case was dismissed when a witness *à charge* admitted that it was doubtful that O. would have deliberately denounced a fellow *passeur*.[3]

Still other suspects confessed a denunciation but asserted that they originally intended to file a complaint about something else and that German interrogators elicited a denunciation from them during the interrogation. In much this way, barmaid Eugenie Van L. argued that she went to the German *Kommandantur* in Antwerp to

---

[2]SAB, Correctional Tribunal Antwerp, R20, Dossiers 'Activisten', nr. 293, *Case against Maria Van D.*, Letter from Maria Van D. to Military Prosecutor, 16/7/1919.

[3]SAB, Public Prosecutor's Office Antwerp, R527, nr. 141, *Case against Gabrielle O.*, PV from Military Security, 5/3/1919.

complain about her employer stealing from her, but that the German officer steered the interrogation in another direction. Apparently her interrogators were not interested in the theft and asked her instead if she knew of any forbidden goods her employer was hiding. Van L. answered that she only knew he had a woollen mattress.[4] Wool, like several other goods such as rubber or copper, were requisitioned by the German Army, particularly during the second part of the occupation. As almost everyone kept these goods hidden inside their homes, it was very often the subject of a denunciation to the occupier (De Schaepdrijver 1997, 216–217; Zuckerman 2004, 142–143). During her post-war trial, Van L. explicitly denied that she wanted to damage her employer but was sentenced nevertheless to six months of imprisonment and a fine, a penalty that was reduced to three months in higher appeal. It seems therefore that the judge was persuaded of her malicious intention, despite Van L.'s claims. Additionally, one might wonder if Van L. would have received the same penalty if she only had denounced the theft and if the forbidden goods had never been brought up. The denunciation eventually may have been problematised because it made Van L. appear as an unpatriotic traitor and not as a legitimate complainant and victim of a theft.

Casting doubt on the malicious intent of an alleged denouncer was also a proven defence strategy for a group of suspects with a distinctive social profile: government officials or police officers. Sometimes what they conceived of as their routine tasks or professional duties were problematised by others as acts of denunciation to the enemy.[5] Policemen or town mayors probably could not avoid contact with the occupier and transferring some information about citizens from time to time. This sometimes led to a complaint to the Belgian judiciary after the occupation. In one such case, a merchant who wanted to sell his products in an Antwerp market was fined after a Belgian policeman drew up a report about his price policies, arguing that the merchant was not allowed to sell those goods in the city market and that he attempted to sell his wares at a price at least 20 times the fixed maximum price. The police officer suspected usury and communicated his report to the German *Kommandantur*. After the occupation, the farmer sought restitution and claimed that the police officer was overzealous; it had not been his task to denounce the farmer to the Germans. The police officer defended himself vehemently in a letter to the Military Prosecutor: 'Besides the fact of usury, we were already forced to communicate the violations to the German authorities; otherwise we would have exposed ourselves and the local government to heavy penalties. Since the fact of usury added to the violation, we were not only legally but even more so ethically forced to report this, in order to end the disgraceful exploitation of the population, already tormented by the war'. He continued by emphasising that he only did what he was ordered to do: 'Suppressing usury and inspecting the enforcement of the maximum fixed prices was strongly recommended by our superiors, and police officers were even specifically assigned for this task'. He also claimed that he had done what he thought was best for the common good by asking the rhetorical question: 'Who of us both

[4]SAB2, Court of appeal Brussels, Dossiers incivisme, *Case against Eugenie Van L.*, PV police Schelle, 27/1/919.

[5]See also Jan Julia Zurné's chapter in this volume.

served the enemy most? Me, whose reports revealed the acts of a usurer and thereby involuntarily provided the enemy with the usurer's merchandise; or the complainant, who collaborated to force our population to choose between two conditions: slowly withering away from starvation, or having to go to work for the enemy in their munitions factories'.[6] After he had sent this letter, the case against the police officer was dropped without any additional interrogations. As interactions between government officials and the German occupier were intensive and relatively commonplace, it is surprising how rare these cases are in our sample of files. In only seven out of 111 cases was a police agent or town mayor accused of denunciation. In all seven cases, the charges were dismissed by the Public Prosecutor. Possibly, both social groups within the population and the Belgian judiciary took into account the often difficult position and daily dilemmas of police and mayors, which led to few of their actions being problematised as acts of denunciation and few complaints being filed to the Belgian judiciary after the occupation (Naert 2015, 240–254). Following this logic, the judiciary seemed to have been susceptible to the argument that police and mayors did not act maliciously but were merely following orders and performing their professional duties. However, it is equally possible that complainants did not consider complaining against their mayor or against police officers because they did not believe the judiciary would take any measures against individuals in their position.

Partly admitting a denunciation but denying malicious intent was an important defence strategy of suspected denouncers, because it proved to be accessible for many suspects in many situations. The punishability of a certain case was also put into doubt when suspects admitted that they denounced someone but claimed that their denunciation had not caused any damage. If article 121bis of the penal code is taken literally, a suspected denouncer could only be punished if the denunciation damaged the denounced person in one way or another. Suspect Sophia J. defended herself using this line of thought against accusations from her neighbour, who claimed to have been denounced for publicly insulting the Germans and J.'s sons, who voluntarily worked for the Germans. J. confessed but pleaded not guilty because 'she was not punished in any way as a result of my complaint'.[7] J. was acquitted by the correctional tribunal. In much the same way, merchant Herman P. admitted to having denounced a fellow merchant of usury as a result of a business dispute, but he maintained his innocence by emphasising that the Germans never responded to his letter of denunciation. Although P. was convicted by the correctional tribunal and sentenced to two months of imprisonment and a fine, his penalty was reduced in higher appeal after his lawyer highlighted that his client's denunciation remained without effects.[8]

---

[6]SAB, Public Prosecutor' Office, R527, nr. 138, *Case against Van Den P*, Letter from Van Den P. to Police Antwerp, 17/12/1918.

[7]SAB, Correctional Tribunal Antwerp, R20, Dossiers 'Activisten', *Case against Sophia J. & Antonia Van Den E.*, PV Military Prosecutor Antwerp, 18/2/1919.

[8]SAB2, Court of appeal Brussels, Dossiers incivisme, *Case against Hermann P.*, Letter lawyer P. to Public Prosecutor-General, 12/12/1919.

3.2 *Extenuating Circumstances*

If suspected denouncers partially confirmed the accusations of denunciations, some pleaded extenuating circumstances to defend themselves. Suspects hoped that a judge would show his understanding when they pointed to elements that were external to the case of denunciation itself but that might explain their past actions.

Suspects attempted to point out extenuating circumstances, by claiming that they were beside themselves with anger when they decided to denounce their opponent. August B., for instance, explained that he had been so enraged by the quarrel he had had with his neighbour—apparently about a small wooden shack his neighbour allegedly had built on his property—that 'in my utmost excitement, I told a *Feldgendarm* that he [his neighbour] was hiding wool and copper in his garden'. He explained: 'I only acted the way I did out of excitement and rage, not to help the enemy'.[9] B. was punished with six months of imprisonment and a fine of 300fr.

Similar reasoning was extended by another suspect's lawyer, who asked in a letter to the Public Prosecutor 'for the sake of humanity and finding truth, to start an investigation into the mental health and accountability of my client. The hereditary mental diseases also diagnosed in his parents, ancestors and other relatives, seem serious enough that I feel compelled, in good conscious, to call the attention of the court on to this matter'. The lawyer described the alleged mental illnesses of five of the suspect's close relatives and continued by explaining that his client had suffered from 'cardiac and nervous disorders, and several mental crises since a young age'. He concluded that his client should be acquitted and subjected to a profound medical examination.[10] Apparently the judge did not follow this rationale, and the suspect was condemned to one year of imprisonment, which was reduced by the Court of appeal to nine months.

3.3 *Impression Management and Counteraccusations*

In almost all examples above, suspected denouncers at least partly admitted and confessed their involvement in a case but attempted to defend themselves by either minimizing the accusations or by pointing to extenuating circumstances. In many cases, however, suspected denouncers denied any involvement and contradicted the accusations against them entirely. This denial was often combined with an attempt to persuade the judiciary of their innocence by influencing the impression they left with their interrogators. Interpreted this way, the PVs of the interrogations in the judicial file document the role the suspect was playing in order to sway the investigators from his guilt and thus increase his chances of a positive outcome. The suspect's

[9]SAB, Correctional Tribunal Antwerp, R20, Dossiers 'Activisten', nr. 278, *Case against August B.*, PV Investigating magistrate Antwerp, 24/3/1919.

[10]SAB2, Court of appeal Brussels, Dossiers incivisme, *Case against Maurice V.*, Letter from lawyer to Public Prosecutor General, 9/10/1919.

statements were therefore distinctly performative and were part of their 'impression management': a strategy to elicit a positive perception, proving their innocence or a least casting doubt on their guilt (Goffman 1959, 250).

In order to make a better impression on their interrogator, suspects attempted to put the social fault line between 'good' and 'bad' Belgian citizens to use. They actively tried to shake off the label of 'traitor' by instead depicting themselves as good and loyal patriots. In some cases, their representations were entirely detached from the accusations against them. Prudent F., for instance, was accused of having denounced his former employer for hiding wool in the city hospital where he worked. In a letter F. wrote from prison to the Military Prosecutor, he not only claimed to regret his denunciation but also explicitly denied being a traitor:

> One day, when I clearly lost my reason, I did this horrible act of denouncing the wool and copper to the Germans. I had lost all common sense, and I begged the Germans not to punish him [the hospital's manager]. It had even made me really sick, and I had to stay in bed for several months. […] I have not received any money from the invaders for doing these bad things. I swear I am a true patriot! I even followed military training between the ages of 12 and 15, and I made great progress, but unfortunately I was declared unfit because of bad eyesight. Now that my eyes are fully cured, I hope to serve in our army again and make great progress there.[11]

The suspect's self-depiction as a true patriot was separated from the alleged denunciation itself, which shows that it was used purely as an isolated defence strategy. This is slightly different in some other cases, in which a suspect entirely shifted the accusations. Valentina G., for instance was charged with having denounced fellow prisoners to the German investigators, but she argued after the occupation that she instead warned them not to confess anything and claimed that by doing so she was responsible for the liberation of several prisoners.[12] Still others elaborated on their self-depiction as a good patriot by claiming to have been themselves victims of the occupation.

In another strategy involving impression management, suspects painted a picture of themselves—deservedly or not—in which the behaviour of a true denouncer, regarded as treacherous and objectionable, would not fit. In this line of argument, suspects identified themselves not as patriots but, rather, as generally trustworthy and having a good reputation in the neighbourhood. An act of denunciation to the enemy would not match with the generally good reputation of the suspect, thereby explaining the latter's innocence. Irène Van P. and Joseph C., for instance, were defended by their lawyer who remarked that his clients had a good reputation in the neighbourhood: 'People told me that Germans *never* frequented this tavern, which would have definitely been the case if she would have become an informer'.[13] The suggestion was examined by the local police, who reported that 'according to the

[11] SAB, Correctional Tribunal Antwerp, R20, Dossiers 'Activisten', nr. 473, *Case against Prudent F.*, letter from F. to Military Prosecutor, 23/3/1919.

[12] SAB, Correctional Tribunal Antwerp, R20, Dossiers 'Activisten', nr. 266, *Case against Valentina G.*, passim.

[13] SAB2, Court of appeal Brussels, Dossiers incivisme, *Case against Josef C. & Irène Van P.*, Letter from lawyer to Investigating Magistrate, 13/2/1919.

collected intelligence, there were no German soldiers or agents or Belgians in German service in that tavern during the past period. We cannot confirm if at some point a German soldier or agent or Belgian in German service visited to drink a beer; this is even probable. However, this tavern was never ill-reputed or deemed objectionable'.[14] Despite all this, both C. and Van P. eventually were sentenced to six months of prison and a fine, which for Van P. was reduced by the court of appeal to four months. Although possibly unsuccessful in this example, the aforementioned case at least shows that invoking a reputation mattered. By examining the reputation of suspects through interrogations within their neighbourhood and devoting a separate report on it, the local police gave relevance to the argument. By claiming high standing in their neighbourhood, the suspects showed that they believed it could improve their defence as well.

While suspects attempted to defend themselves by eliciting a positive impression, this also worked the other way around. Suspects often tried to undermine their opponent's credibility with counteraccusations or slander and questioned the latter's moral-patriotic or ethical background. By casting doubt on the legitimacy of their opponents, suspected denouncers implicitly questioned the accusations themselves, even if their counteraccusations were completely unrelated. Most counteraccusations focused on the alleged motives of complainants to file a complaint against them. Claiming that the complainants were only seeking revenge for some allegedly meaningless dispute or conflict that existed between them, suspects tried to weaken the complainant's position and his accusations, without tackling the heart of the matter. This went one step further in some cases, when a suspect accused the opposing party of more precise wrongdoing or of having a bad reputation in the neighbourhood. In a case of denunciation that is clearly part of long-existing conflict between two neighbours, Maria C. described in a letter to the minister of Justice, with which she tried to obtain clemency, how she was tormented by her opponents for a long time:

> For reasons I never really understood, the family of S. was at odds with me [...]. I had to endure many nightly assaults on my house. I lived next to them, alone as a widow with my children and imagine, Minister, the fear I had to endure, when with jangling noise, the glass window of my front door was shattered! As a result of these persistent and barbarous harassments, my heart revolted and quarrel arose between us.[15]

It is possible that C.'s counteraccusations had some effect, as she was only sentenced to a fine of 500 fr. Such counteraccusations were also used to claim that a denunciation was nothing more than a reaction to a mistreatment the suspect had suffered. Louise F. claimed that she only denounced her neighbours to receive compensations and to protect her honour and reputation:

> I went through their insults for almost four years, and then she broke one of my windows, cracking its pattern. [...] Then, in the end, I—as people call it—denounced her and her family, but I asked if they could search their houses and make them say that their accusations

[14]SAB2, Court of appeal Brussels, Dossiers incivisme, *Case against Josef C. & Irène Van P.*, PV police Antwerp, 17/2/1919.

[15]SAB, Correctional Tribunal Antwerp, R20, Dossiers 'Activisme', nr. 276, *Case against Marie C. and Jan De M.*, Letter from C. to Minister of Justice, 3/12/1919.

> [i.e., the previous insults] were false and to make them repair my window, which cost me 6 fr.[16]

By highlighting the insults and vandalism she had to suffer because of her neighbours, F. claimed that her denunciation—although she only reluctantly called it that—was nothing more than a legitimate reaction to past injustices and an attempt to receive damages and restore her honour that was harmed by the insults. Maybe the Public Prosecutor followed her line of thought, as F.'s case remained without consequences.

3.4 *Material Evidence*

The strategies explored above were applicable in one way or another in the majority of the cases, albeit with varying degrees of success. As several of the examples above have shown, strategies could also be used together by one suspect. Strategies overlapped and complemented each other. In a few cases, however, these strategies potentially lost their effect, as the judiciary possessed letters of denunciation confirming the suspect's guilt. Marie Van T., for instance, wrote a letter to the German *Kupferzentrale* in which she denounced her former employer for hiding copper in his house. She ended with her signature but asked 'not to misuse my name'.[17] Van T. admitted all charges and was sentenced to six months of imprisonment. In two similar cases, material evidence was available as well, although handwriting analysis was necessary to match the handwriting of the suspect with the one used on the unsigned letter. However, these cases, in which suspects had little chance of successfully defending themselves, were exceptional in our sample.

3.5 *Defence Strategies of Denouncers in German Service*

Denouncers who were suspected of having been formally employed by the occupier generally had their own characteristic defence strategies. In the occupier's service, these denouncers had been responsible for a variety of tasks, ranging from supressing smuggling and usury, to intercepting *passeurs* and others who tried to cross the border with the Netherlands (Leenders 2017; Bost, Horvat and Rousseaux 2014; Bernard 2010; Rousseaux 2009; Naveau 2005; Resöhazy 2014, 2015). Whereas material evidence was mostly nonexistent in cases against occasional denouncers, German documents or lists of employers often served as a basis for judicial investigations after the occupation in cases against denouncers who had been in German service. How these documents passed into the hands of the Belgian judiciary is never specified. The

[16]SAB, Public Prosecutor Antwerp, R527, nr. 140, *Case against Louise F.*, Letter from F. to investigating magistrate, 14/4/1919.

[17]SAB2, Court of appeal Brussels, Dossiers incivisme, *Case against Marie Van T.*, Letter of denunciation, undated.

case against Henri R., for instance, started with the simple remark that 'upon their retreat from Antwerp, the Germans left a file in which are mentioned the names and addresses of those who have worked for them during the occupation. Among these names we find a certain Henri R.'.[18] The actual investigations started immediately with the interrogation of R., who confessed all charges, and the German documents were never even included in the judicial file.

Full confessions were not uncommon in cases against these denouncers, also in the absence of material evidence against them. Karel S., for instance, was accused of being employed by the German *Zivilkommissar* to conduct searches and confiscations in the houses of Antwerp merchants and wholesalers suspected of usury. After the occupation he was accused of denouncing 31 merchants in this way. S. confessed all accusations, gave more information about his work, and listed the names of the fellow agents with whom he had worked during his time in German service.[19] With these confessions, S. not only played an important role in the investigations against these other agents (although most of them fled the country after the Armistice and were never found or interrogated by the Belgian authorities) but also pointed out the existence of a larger network of Belgian agents in German service, who assisted the occupier in counteracting usury, rounding up networks of anti-German espionage or arresting Belgians who helped others to cross the border with the Netherlands, either for smuggling or to join the Belgian Army. S. himself was immediately imprisoned after his confessions, but he apparently was provisionally released in June 1919. He probably fled the country before the actual trial one year later, as he was sentenced by default to three years of imprisonment and a fine of 4.000 fr.[20]

The participation of such professional denouncers and their knowledge about the existing networks of Belgian agents in German police services could also lead to new findings in other cases. Former police officer Camiel De C., who was accused of taking service with German police forces after he was fired during the occupation, was formally recognised by another Belgian professional denouncer. Although De C. vehemently denied ever having denounced anyone or ever having worked as an agent for the Germans, another prisoner, Jozef W. is very clear in his accusations:

> I joined the German *Uberwachungsstelle*, which was subjected to the *Ölzentrale*, from 28/7/1917 until 8/5/1918. When I took service, the former police officer Camiel De C. was already active as an informant. By the end of March 1918, De C. formally joined as an officer which was still the case when I left. It was his task to search for copper supplies, to act as a potential buyer and to confiscate these goods at the delivery, often in cooperation with German agents or soldiers. As an informant he received commissions; as a formal agent he received a fixed wage.

When De C. kept denying his involvement, W. continued: 'Before this interrogation, I was locked up with De C. in the same cell. He asked me to act as if I did not know

---

[18] SAB, Correctional Tribunal Antwerp, R20, Dossiers 'Activisme', nr. 475, *Case against Henri R.*, Note from Belgian Military Security Service, 7/1/1919.

[19] SAB, Correctional Tribunal Antwerp, R20, Dossiers 'Activisten,' nr. 458, *Case against Karel S.*, PV police Antwerp, 6/3/1919.

[20] SAB, Correctional Tribunal Antwerp, R20, Dossiers 'Activisten,' nr. 458, *Case against Karel S.*, Sentence of the correctional tribunal, 26/6/1920.

him and not to accuse him of anything. I therefore ask, in order to avoid any problems, not to be locked up with him in the same cell anymore'.[21] Possibly because of this testimony, De C. was sentenced to one year of imprisonment by the Correctional Tribunal of Antwerp, which was confirmed by the Court of Appeal of Brussels when De C. entered an appeal. It is unlikely that his cooperation with the authorities helped W. in any way in his own case, as he was convicted to three years prison.[22] The confessions of these professional denouncers result in some overlap between cases, which points out that a network of professional denouncers, who worked as agents and informants for different German services, indeed existed during the occupation.

4 The Outcome of Judicial Investigations: How Effective Were Rhetorical Defence Strategies?

It has now become clear that suspected denouncers had a whole range of possible defence strategies at their disposal. However, the question remains whether suspects who employed these strategies were able to successfully influence the outcome of their case. In fact, it is virtually impossible to determine the effectiveness of each of these strategies individually. Not only were they presented above as ideal types and was their use different in every single case but also suspects established their defence through a combination of several strategies. Furthermore, numerous other elements in the case obviously determined its outcome as well, such as the severity of the accusations or the support of witnesses. The deliberations of judges or Public Prosecutors were also never recorded on paper, which means that we remain ignorant of the exact reasons for a conviction or an acquittal and that we can only guess whether the suspect's strategy was decisive or not.

Yet, when examining the outcome of cases of denunciation, the conviction rate, the severity of the penalties and the impact of appeal procedures stand out (1919–1922).[23]

First of all, suspected denouncers had a relatively high chance of being acquitted in court. Figure 1 shows that of a total of 153 suspects brought before the correctional tribunal for denunciation to the enemy, 42 were acquitted. It is not surprising that cases judged by default resulted in higher conviction rates and much higher penalties than those judged in a defended action (Deckers 2003, 23). However, the restrained severity of the penalties for convicted denouncers are remarkable. Compared to the penalties prescribed in the legislation, these penalties were notably low. For a denunciation that had exposed the denounced person to the 'investigations, pursuits or rigour of the enemy', the legislation prescribed a fine and an imprisonment of maximum five years. Article 121bis also foresaw the need to consider aggravating

[21]SAB2, Court of appeal Brussels, Dossiers incivisme, *Case against Camiel De C.*, PV police Antwerp, 18/12/1918.

[22]SAB, Correctional Tribunal Antwerp, R20, Dossiers 'Activisten', *Case against Karel C., Primus di L., Emmanuel Van H., Jozef W.*, Sentence of the correctional tribunal, 18/9/1919.

[23]SAB, Correctional Tribunal Antwerp, R20, Dossiers 'Activisme'.

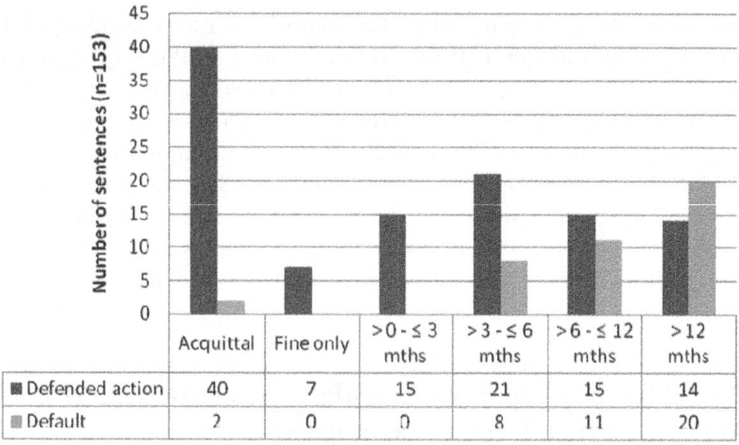

Fig. 1 Outcome of cases of denunciation sentenced by the correctional tribunal of Antwerp

	Denouncers	Sentences	Acquittals	Avg. penalty (in months prison)	Avg. fine (in fr.)
Defended action	In German service	13	4	11	555
	Occasional	44	17	674	252
Default	In German service	14	1	22.62	4.923
	Occasional	8	1	14.29	429

Fig. 2 Outcome of cases of denunciation sentenced by the correctional tribunal of Antwerp (1919–1922), difference between occasional denouncers and denouncers in German service (SAB, Correctional Tribunal Antwerp, R20, Dossiers 'Activisme')

circumstances: if a denunciation caused the denounced person to be detained for at least one month, the law prescribed criminal penalties of more than five years; and if a denunciation caused the death or serious mutilation of the denounced person, the denouncer ran the risk of being sentenced to 15 to 20 years of forced labour. Figure 1 shows that the penalties pronounced by the Antwerp correctional tribunal were not even close to the ones prescribed in the legislation.

Closer examination of the sentences of 79 denouncers in Fig. 2 allows us to distinguish between the penalties received by occasional denouncers and denouncers in the occupier's service. Again, those convicted by default generally received higher penalties. Default judgements were rendered more often for denouncers who had been in the occupier's service than for occasional denouncers, because the nearly half of the former had fled the country (Leenders 2017). Nevertheless, even when judgements by defended action and by default are only compared with each other, this table shows that occasional denouncers generally received lower penalties. This could be

Fig. 3 Sentences of the Court of appeal of Brussels in cases of denunciation, compared to the judgement in the first instance (1919–1925) (SAB2, Court of appeal Brussels, Dossiers incivisme)

	n	%
Confirmation	176	47%
Decrease	137	37%
Increase	50	13%
Others	11	3%
Total	**374**	**100%**

explained by the availability of material evidence in such cases, which would make prosecutions easier. Maybe courts felt pressure from social groups within the Belgian population to be more severe with denouncers in German service and be more lenient with occasional denouncers. However, another explanation lies in the availability of material evidence, which would make prosecutions much easier. Indeed, when hard evidence proved the suspect's guilt, rhetorical defence strategies were of much less use. Conversely, occasional denouncers, in the absence of material evidence, could more successfully employ the defence strategies explored above, which might explain their generally lower penalties.

Figure 3 shows the outcome of the appeal of cases of denunciation judged by the Court of appeal of Brussels in relation to the sentence pronounced by the correctional tribunal (Protin 2014, 20–22).[24] About half of the 374 judgements pronounced in appeal confirmed the original sentence. No fewer than 137 suspects (37%) saw their sentence decreased or completely discarded, while only 50 judgements (13%) eventually increased the penalty for the convicted denouncer. Probably, the Court of appeal was less severe because, by the time it pronounced its sentences, the occupation had already been over for several years and the judiciary felt less pressure, both from the government and from the population, to punish the *inciviques* severely. The figures show that from the suspects' point of view, the chance of a successful procedure before the Court of appeal (i.e., a decrease of the original penalty) was high. This becomes even more important when keeping in mind the relatively low penalties in the first instance in relation to penalties prescribed by the penal code.

The official published statistics displayed in Fig. 4 allow for a comparison of the conviction rates of cases of denunciation and other kinds of incivism such as espionage, trafficking with the enemy and activism–the political collaboration with the German occupier of a minority within the Flemish Movement. It is striking how suspects in cases of espionage and activism had a much lower chance of being acquitted before the court compared to suspected denouncers or traffickers (Rousseaux and Van Ypersele 2008, 143–144; Deckers 2003, 27–28). It is important to note, however, that different courts were authorized to judge on different kinds of incivism. Denunciation to the enemy was judged by the Courts Martial or the

[24] At the time, the Court of appeal of Brussels had jurisdiction for appeal procedures of cases judged in the first instance by the correctional tribunals of Antwerp, Mechelen, Turnhout, Leuven, Brussels, Nivelles, Tournai, Mons and Charleroi.

	Convictions	Acquittals	n
Espionage (art. 116)	82%	18%	116
Activism (art. 104, 115§5, 118bis)	85%	15%	313
Trafficking with the enemy (art. 115§4)	65%	35%	1049
Denunciation to the enemy (art. 121bis)	65%	35%	2366

Fig. 4 Rate of convictions and acquittals for the main kinds of incivism, based on official published statistics (1919–1928) (*Statistique Judiciaire de la Belgique. Gerechtelijke Statistiek van België (1919–1928).* Brussel, 1924–1934)

correctional tribunal, while suspects of espionage, activism or trafficking with the enemy were brought before the Courts Martial or the court of assizes. This might have influenced the rate of acquittal, even though trafficking to the enemy, judged by the court of assizes, had a similarly high rate (Driessen 2012; Delang 2012).

These figures show that something complicated the prosecution of denunciation to the enemy. However, the relatively low penalties (in particular for occasional denouncers), the rare increase of a penalty after an appeal and the high rate of acquittals compared to other kinds of incivism are not easily explained. Several possible hypotheses come to mind. Maybe judges received directives from their superiors (Military Prosecutor-General, Public Prosecutor-General, the minister of Justice) not to overemphasise the prosecution of denunciation to the enemy but to focus on certain specific problematic cases. Maybe social groups within the population insisted more on the prosecution of *inciviques* whose acts they might have perceived as more objectionable (war-profiteers, activists, etc.) and the judiciary was pressured from below to be more severe in those cases than against suspected denouncers. Maybe the investigators did not prioritise the investigations against denouncers, resulting in poorly prepared cases that left judges with no other choice than to discharge the suspect or to pronounce a relatively low penalty (Rousseaux and Van Ypersele 2008, 144). Beyond these possibilities, this chapter has suggested that the rhetorical defence strategies used by suspects have to be factored in as well, even though it is hard to put a finger on their specific effectiveness.

5 Conclusions

This chapter explored the arguments and rhetorical strategies Belgian citizens used to defend themselves against accusations of denunciation. The possible responses were examined in three clusters. Firstly, suspects who only partly admitted the accusations against them questioned the punishability of their case. Suspects often cast doubt on their alleged malicious intent by claiming that they had been forced to pass on certain information to the occupation or that they had only acted out of fear.

Sometimes suspects argued that the denunciation they were accused of had not caused any damage to the denounced person, which should legally lead to an acquittal. Secondly, suspects suggested that extenuating circumstances (social and economic circumstances and poverty, mental illness, a sudden frenzy of rage, etc.) should be considered. In this way, suspects explained the context in which they had denounced their opponent, trying to justify their deeds. Finally, suspects who for the most part denied any involvement in a case of denunciation tried to manage the impression they made on the judiciary by emphasizing their good deeds during the occupation, for instance by depicting themselves as 'true patriots' or by touting their good reputation in their neighbourhood. This also worked the other way around: suspected denouncers actively tried to undermine the legitimacy of their opponents, either with accusations of their own or by calling attention to the latter's low social standing.

Although it is virtually impossible to determine the effectiveness of each of these strategies, it seems clear that they played a role in the complicated prosecution of denunciation to the enemy. The reason for this lies in the specific character of these cases.

First of all, a case of denunciation to the enemy generally was, unlike other kinds of incivism that were prosecuted after the First World War, the settlement of an interpersonal conflict in which two civilian parties opposed one another. When Belgian citizens were suspected of espionage (art. 116 of the Belgian penal code), having supplied the enemy with goods, money, weapons or provisions (art. 115§4) or having assisted the enemy in the transformation of Belgian political institutions and organisations (art. 118bis), suspected *inciviques* were accused of having harmed the Belgian State or its allies. Suspects of denunciation (art. 121bis) were accused of having damaged other Belgian citizens by transferring possibly harmful information about them to the German occupier. Not the Belgian State but another civilian was the direct adversary. This interpersonal conflict was continued during the judicial investigations, when both parties presented competing versions of the same events, refuted each other's arguments and undermined each other's legitimacy and credibility. This distinctly personal character of the judicial investigations allowed suspects to use counteraccusations as a defence strategy.

Secondly, the fact that suspects used extenuating circumstances and ways to minimize the accusations against them shows that denunciation to the enemy, as described in article 121bis of the Belgian penal code, was difficult to establish in court. It was sometimes difficult to establish the damage a denounced person had suffered as a result of a denunciation, and some suspects were acquitted because they successfully claimed that their denunciation had never had any consequences. Also the malicious intent of the suspect, a necessary requirement for the punishability of the denunciation, was particularly difficult to prove. Suspects exploited these issues with the legislation in their defence strategies. Probably because it proved difficult to establish that a suspect had acted maliciously, this requirement was cancelled in 1942, and suspected denouncers judged after the Second World War were already liable to punishment if they had acted 'knowingly'.[25]

[25] See also Jan Julia Zurné's chapter in this volume.

Finally, prosecution of denunciation to the enemy was complicated by the lack of hard material evidence. With the exception of a handful of cases that were decided with letters of denunciation that proved a suspect's guilt, the large majority of cases depended on the testimonies of complainants, suspects and witnesses of both parties. Denunciation to the enemy was already difficult to verify, because it was often only a verbal practice and because it was frequently shrouded in secrecy by the denouncers themselves. This did not change after the occupation: the argumentations between all parties involved during the investigations were almost exclusively oral, in the absence of any material proof. Such 'my word against your word' cases not only vested an investigating magistrate or a judge with important discretionary powers but also put much emphasis on the argumentations of all persons involved.

These three elements, inherent to almost every single case of denunciation, complicated the prosecution of denunciation to the enemy. Although other elements certainly contributed, they can be considered as important factors to explain why the prosecution of denunciation to the enemy after the First World War proved to be such a complicated matter.

References

Bernard L (2010) La cour militaire et l'incivisme. In: Baclin G, Bernard L, Rousseaux X (eds) En première ligne. La justice militaire belge face à l'incivisme au sortir de la Première Guerre mondiale. Algemeen Rijksarchief, Brussels, pp 113–197

Bost M, Horvat S, Rousseaux X (2014) Les espions civils au service de l'ennemi, au prisme de la justice militaire. Belgisch Tijdschrift voor Nieuwste Geschiedenis 44(2/3):37–75

Cassiers P, Debroux F, Gilissen J (1967) Crimes et délits contre la sûreté de l'Etat. *Les Novelles. Droit Penal* 2:112–319. Larcier, Brussels

Deckers M (2003) De strafrechtelijke omvang van het aktivisme. Deel 3: De omvang, Besluiten. Wetenschappelijke tijdingen 62:22–31

Delang N (2012) De repressie van de economische collaboratie door het Hof van Assisen van Antwerpen, 1921–1927. Unpublished Master's thesis, Leuven, University of Leuven

De Schaepdrijver S (1997) De Groote Oorlog. Het Koninkrijk België tijdens de Eerste Wereldoorlog. Atlas, Antwerpen

Driessen E (2012) De repressie van de economische collaboratie door het Hof van Assisen van Antwerpen in 1919–1920. Unpublished Master's thesis, Leuven, University of Leuven

Goffman E (1959) The presentation of self in everyday life. Anchor Books, New York

Horvat S (2009) De vervolging van militairrechtelijke delicten tijdens Wereldoorlog 1. De werking van het Belgisch krijgsgerecht. VUB Press, Brussels

Leenders G (2016) De rol van het militair gerecht in de vervolging van verklikking aan de vijand na de Eerste Wereldoorlog. Studie van de bronnen. In: Bost M, Drossens P, Horvat S (eds) Ressources et usages des archives de la justice militaire/Bronnen en onderzoeksperspectieven in verband met het militair gerecht. Algemeen Rijksarchief, Brussels, pp 215–230

Leenders G (2017) Verklikkers in Duitse dienst in Antwerpen en hun gerechtelijke vervolging na de Eerste Wereldoorlog. Belgisch Tijdschrift voor Nieuwste Geschiedenis 47(2–3): 41–72.

Monballyu J (2010) Het uur van vergelding. Vlaamse activisten voor de krijgsraad van het Groot Hoofdkwartier van het Leger (23 jan. tot 30 juni 1919). Deel 1. *Wetenschappelijke Tijdingen* 69(4):306–330

Monballyu J (2011) Slechte Belgen! De repressie van het incivisme na de Eerste Wereldoorlog door het Hof van Assisen van Brabant (1919–1927). Algemeen Rijksarchief, Brussels

Naert J (2015) Burgemeesters en activisme tijdens en na Wereldoorlog I (1914–1921). *Wetenschappelijke tijdingen* 74 (3):220–257

Naveau B (2005) L'affaire Douhard: méfaits, procès et condamnation d'un collaborateur liégois durant la Première Guerre mondiale. Liège: unpublished Master's thesis, University of Liège

Protin C (2014) La répression des dénonciations à l'ennemi pendant la Première Guerre mondiale à traers l'activité de la Cour d'assises de Brabant et de la Cour d'Appel de Bruxelles (1919–1926). Unpublished Master's thesis, Université catholique de Louvain, Louvain-la-Neuve

Rezsöhazy E (2014) Les agents du contre-espionnage allemand en Belgique occupée durant la Première Guerre mondiale: contexte et première approche. Unpublished Master's thesis, Louvain-la-Neuve

Rezsöhazy E (2015) Entre vraisemblable et faux-semblants: Leopold Wartel, agent du contre-espionnage allemand en Belgique occupée durant la Première Guerre mondiale. In: Lanneau C (ed) La Grande Guerre à Mons et dans sa région. Avant-propos, Waterloo, pp 165–185

Rousseaux X (2009) Spionne of verklikster? Anna-Maria D. en de krijgsraad van het Hoofdkwartier van het Belgisch leger (november 1918-juli 1919). In: Coppens EC, et.al (eds) Fabrica Iuris: opstellen over de 'werkplaats van het recht', aangeboden aan Sjoerd Faber. Gerard Noodt Instituut, Nijmegen, pp 255–275

Rousseaux X, Van Ypersele L (2005) Leaving the war: popular violence and judicial repression of 'unpatriotic' behaviour in Belgium (1918–1921). Eur Rev Hist 12:3–22

Rousseaux X, Van Ypersele L (2008) La Patrie crie vengeance! La répression des 'inciviques' belges au sortir de la guerre, 1914–1918. Le cri, Brussels

Van Ypersele L (2004) Sortir de la guerre, sortir de l'occupation. Les violences populaires en Belgique au lendemain de la Première Guerre mondiale. Vingtième siècle. Revue d'histoire 83: 65–74

Vrints A (2014) Eenheid in verdeeldheid: spanningsvelden in België tijdens de Eerste Wereldoorlog. Belgisch tijdschrift voor nieuwste geschiedenis 44(2/3):11–35

Zemon Davis N (1987) Fiction in the archives: Pardon Tales and their tellers in sixteenth-century France. Stanford University Press, Stanford

Zuckerman L (2004) The rape of Belgium: The untold story of World War I. New York University Press, New York

Prosecuting Food Profiteers After the Armistice: A Transitional-Justice Perspective, 1919–1923

Martin Schoups

Abstract Food was a particularly tense issue in Belgium during the German occupation in'14-'18. This experience left a lot of bad blood between customers and merchants. Consumers accused sellers and producers of "profiteering", i.e. making good money out of the food shortages. The prosecution of this group after the war proved to be a very difficult operation, due to complex legal restraints. This article argues that the Belgian government did try to hit this group by introducing stricter food regulation after the Armistice. A study of the Judicial Statistics demonstrate that this was not a mere legislative propaganda exercise, since food offenses were also massively prosecuted. Only the accusation of theft would bring more people to the correctional courts in the first post-war years. Prosecution was not very severe however. Court records show mostly smaller infractions being prosecuted and quite mild sentences given. On the other hand, the law targeted a group that was largely 'new' to the justice apparatus, namely: farmers, retailers and butchers. Thereby, the Belgian state was thus forced to take up a new role in a market that it had largely left free before the war. The Food Profiteering Law should therefore be considered as a non-retroactive form of transitional justice.

1 Introduction

At the end of the First World War, the Belgian State was confronted with a fierce 'demand for vengeance' by a large part of its population. Contrary to the claim of Belgian's most famous historian, Henri Pirenne (1929), Belgium's *sortie de guerre* was particularly rowdy and 'retributive' (Van Ypersele and Rousseaux 2005; Rousseaux and Van Ypersele 2008). All over the country, civilians took the law into their own hands. War wrongdoers were subjected to rituals of public shaming: their heads were shaved, property damaged and shops plundered. The ways in which the Belgian State dealt with this public demand for justice has in recent years been

M. Schoups (✉)
History Department, Ghent University, Ghent, Belgium
e-mail: martin.schoups@UGent.be

M. Bost and A. Vrints (eds.), *Doing Justice In Wartime*,
Studies in the History of Law and Justice 19,
https://doi.org/10.1007/978-3-030-72050-6_4

studied through the lens of 'transitional justice' (Rousseaux and Van Ypersele 2008; Monballyu 2012; Grevers 2012). This relatively new field of study deals with the question of 'how justice is served' in the aftermath of regime change, after a violent conflict or authoritarian rule. This question also pertains to the Belgian case after the First World War, as most of its territory had been occupied by an authoritarian ruler, and the national executive and legislative powers had been absent during the war. When the occupier left the building, a period of transition set in.

Scholars for this transitional period have focused primarily on 'violations of state security'. These concern the gravest war crimes, such as espionage, collaboration and denunciation to the enemy. Thus focus has been almost exclusively on the activities of the criminal and military courts. Such studies have documented that economic collaboration was by far the most prosecuted crime (Massin and Rousseaux 2008). These findings confirm the thesis of Belgian historians who have in last decennia come to the conclusion that food was by far the most important and contentious political problem during the war, and that the traditional focus on the divisions between the Flemish and the Walloon and labour and capital is not entirely justified (Scholliers 1994; Vrints 2011, 2015).

In this article I will demonstrate that post-war prosecution of economic perpetrators was even far larger than assumed. Thereby, I take issue with the claim that the small war villains—for example shopkeepers—were completely spared after the war (Van Ypersele and Rousseaux 2005, 8). The sole focus on 'violations of state security' is too narrow to fully grasp the transitional policies of the Belgian government. The decree-law of 5 November 1918 'concerning the alimentation of the civilian population' (*Moniteur belge* 8–9/11/1918) clearly formed part of the same transitional strategy. To demonstrate this, I will analyze the law on three levels: the level of the legislator, that of the correctional courts, and the individual level of the judicial arrondissement of Malines. Three questions structure the argument. Firstly, how was the law intended by the different actors on the legislative level? This question can be analysed through the *Parliamentary Acts, Chamber* (PAC) and Senate (PAS), which are the literal transcriptions of the parliamentary debates on the law. Also the *Parliamentary Documents, Chamber* (PDC) and *Moniteur belge* (MB) provide further information on motivations. Secondly, how was the law actually applied throughout the kingdom? That the law was not merely a discursive phenomenon can be shown through the Judicial Statistics, published annually by the Belgian Ministry of Justice. These statistics contain abundant data on the prosecution activity of the different courts, the conviction rates and the nature of the pronounced sentences. Thirdly, how was the law actually 'used' on the streets? Which practices were prosecuted, which groups were targeted and which groups took the initiative in putting the law into practice? This question will be answered through a thorough case study of the judicial arrondissement of Malines. The judgment books and individual judicial records are very rich sources, providing information on the practices that were actually prosecuted, the socio-economic profile of the groups against whom the law was used, and which agencies took the initiative in putting the law to work. This three-level analysis will allow a more full-scope image of the decree-law.

2 La Volonté Du Legislateur: MPs Dealing with Popular Anger After the War Towards War Profiteers

During the first year after the war, MPs continuously denounced the impunity towards economic collaborators. Their affluence was juxtaposed with the deplorable living conditions of the war veterans. On the occasion of a demonstration of war veterans in Brussels, socialist MP Nikolas Berloz cited a rallying cry oft heard in their circles:

> Voyez ce qu'ils ont fait pendant que nous exposions notre vie au front, pendant que nous devions aller dans les tranchées! Et ces gens, dans leurs automobiles, éclaboussent tout le monde! (PAC 24/9/1919: 1677)

Their cars, an exclusive means of transport at the time, symbolised the fortunes they had shamelessly acquired during the war.

The prosecution of economic collaboration was indeed provided for in the Belgian Criminal Code, more particularly under paragraph 4 of article 115. In the actual application of the article, the Belgian State was confronted with many problems however (see Monballyu 2012). There were interpretative issues, on the meaning of 'munition', for example, as the article dated from the time of the Napoleonic code of 1810. There was great uncertainty as to whether 'special intent' (the specific aim to hurt the Belgian State) was required for a conviction, or if 'general intent' was enough (knowingly committing an offense). The gathering of sufficient financial evidence on wartime collaboration also caused many problems. Finally there was the matter of how the war profits could be confiscated. Therefore, some MPs proposed to resolve the issue by passing 'interpretative laws'. These laws would then clarify the intent of the legislator and eliminate all ambiguities. The Belgian political class, however, was very reluctant to embrace the idea of *penal retroactivity*, i.e., applying new laws to old facts, committed *before* the issuance of the law. Even the socialist minister of Justice, one of the three first socialist ministers in Belgian history, Émile Vandervelde, who was very sympathetic to the public discontent with the 'nouveaux riches', strongly opposed the idea of a retroactive law. He saw this as a violation of one of the fundamental principles of the Declaration of the Rights of Man (1789), which he considered the cornerstone of a just and democratic legal system. The Declaration stipulated that 'no one can be punished but under a law established and promulgated before the offense and legally applied' (PAC 24/9/1919: 1677). However, as law historian Jos Monballyu has demonstrated, Vandervelde tried to pursue the same end by many other means. This was done, for example, through the extraordinary tax on war benefits and the right of the state to bring civil proceedings in cases of economic collaboration (Monballyu 2012, 476–479).

There was one more measure that formed part of the same strategy, however. This was the law 'regulating the alimentation of the civilian population' and its associated decrees. This law had already been voted upon in October 1918, more than a month before the Armistice, by the council of Belgian ministers in exile in Le Havre. From the summer of 1918 onward, this council-in-exile was busy preparing for the return of the Belgian government. The availability of food supplies figured high on their agenda, as food security was considered vital for a calm and peaceful transition of power (Deneckere 1994, 425). This decree-law enabled the creation of a *Service du Ravitaillement* (Department of Supplies) under the Ministry of Labour. This department was led by one of the other three socialist ministers, namely, the Hesbayian Joseph Wauters. In the first three war years he would intervene in the trade of 'primary necessities' such as bread, meat and sugar, unseen before in Belgian history. The decree-law authorized the state to impose price caps, requisition supplies and restrict exports.

Alongside this interventionist component, the law also contained a strong repressive component. Articles 3, 4 and 5 of the decree-law defined punishable food offenses and stipulated the punishments. Certain offenses were directly related to the interventionist component. The law's authority to impose price caps made infractions against those price caps a punishable offense, for example. There were also some *new* offenses, however, like the act of voluntarily spoiling food, l'*accaparement* (the act of withdrawing supplies to drive up the prices) and the usurious pricing of primary necessities. This repressive component catered to warnings already issued during the war by, inter alia, Joseph Wauters himself, who already in September 1916 had written:

> Il sera prudent de donner satisfaction … au sentiment … du peuple en frappant les éléments heureusement rares qui n'ont pas hésité à trafiquer au détriment de la nation ou qui ont spéculé sur la misère générale… Un peu partout on s'apprête même à faire bonne et prompte justice populaire .. ce qui peut hélas dériver en de cruelles méprises. (cited in Deneckere 1994, 425)

Some of these offenses were actually already introduced with the emergency law of 4 August 1914 'concerning the emergency measures required by the war', voted by the Belgian Parliament on the day of the German invasion, which enabled the king to take extraordinary war measures. The law was barely applied during the war, however, as the German occupier appropriated this authority already in September 1915 (Bost 2013). A comparison of the 1914 emergency law and the 1918 decree-law is instructive because it exemplifies how punishments for the *same* offenses were drastically changed in 1918. The maximum penalty for the offense of hoarding was increased from eight days imprisonment to two years. The maximum fine of 500 francs was raised to 10,000 francs, which was a drastic multiplication, even if one takes inflation into account. Food offenses clearly were considered much graver after four years of war than they had been at its beginning. The decree-law was thus partly the continuation of the legislation voted on the day of the invasion (emergency law of 4/8/1914). The post-war legislation had a moral and 'retributive' dimension that the emergency law had not possessed, however. Therefore, the law would go through life as the Food Profiteering Law.

However, even these punishments were considered too light in peacetime Belgium. During a parliamentary discussion in August 1919 on the difficulty in prosecuting economic collaborators, socialist minister of Justice Emile Vandervelde declared that he would therefore submit a new legislative proposal together with minister of Industry, Labour and Supplies, Joseph Wauters. He related this new proposal explicitly to the issue of retroactivity.

> Il est impossible de faire rétroagir (la loi) pour le passé. Mais, d'autre part, pour l'avenir, en matière d'accaparement par exemple, il est possible de renforcer la loi. Nous l'avons fait, mon ami Wauters et moi. Nous demandons à la Chambre de hâter le vote de notre projet, qui permettra de frapper énergiquement et rapidement les accapareurs, ceux qui vendent à des taux usuraires, ceux qui, par le fait même, augmentent la misère des massses et rendent ainsi difficile la reconstitution morale et matérielle du pays. (PAC 24/09/1919: 1678)

Even though Vandervelde remained averse to penal retroactivity, he intended this proposal explicitly as compensation for the difficult prosecution of *economic collaborators*. The proposal concerned extension of the aforementioned decree-law of 5/11/1918 for one more year, during which the penalties and fines were once again increased for all offenses (*Parliamentary Documents* 8/8/1919, nr. 306). The proposal included other innovations as well. Firstly, a new offense, namely, that of usurious pricing, was added to the law. Secondly, the investigating judge was therefore enabled to provisionally shut down the shop of a suspect *before* a conviction. Thirdly, the buyer could from now on be penalized in this new bill (in practice this part was only applied to wholesalers, not to consumers). Finally, new emphasis was put on the *extra* sanction already prescribed in the decree-law, namely, the obligation to display the verdict on the windows of the convicted and publish it in the local papers. This complementary sanction was intended as nothing less than a very severe form of public shaming.[1]

On the basis of the Parliamentary debates and documents that clarify 'the intent of the legislator', two things can be concluded about this proposal. Firstly, the aggravation of the penalties for food offenses was directly motivated by the war experience. The proposal was intended as redress for the impunity towards the grand majority of economic wartime collaborators, whose number, due to a strict interpretation of the pre-war laws, increasingly shrunk to only a few big shots. At a reunion of the socialist party, Minister Vandervelde explicitly stated that his proposal was intended primarily to give *moral satisfaction* to the country and was 'only secondary from a material point of view' (Records Meetings Belgian Workers Party 28/7/1919: 407). Secondly, post-war resentments were actually not restricted exclusively towards those groups that had economically collaborated with the German occupier. In reality, anger was towards all those who had, even without collaborating, materially enriched themselves during the war: the so-called *war profiteers*. This group was accused more generally of not having paid their fair share of the war's burden and to have jointly caused the material misery suffered by their compatriots.

The Vandervelde/Wauters bill could count on wide cross-party support. It was unanimously voted for in the two Chambers (PAC 1/10/1919: 1810; PAS 9/10/1919: 837). Since it was a 'war law', it only stayed in effect for another year, and the government had to submit every extension to the Chambers. Until the end of 1921, not one member of Parliament would vote against extensions of the unaltered law (PAC 12/8/1920, p. 2436; 30/6/121: 1855).[2] From 1920 on, opposition in the Senate

---

[1]Minister Vandervelde declared in Parliament that the law would require shopkeepers 'to display their infamy in front of their windows', PAC, 17/10/1916: 1610.

[2]Two catholics and two liberals would vote against the partial extension of the law on 29/11/1921: 11. PAC.

was more outspoken, as its membership had a more elitist and conservative character (PAS 13/8/1920: 979; 30/12/1921: 48; 5/7/1921: 671). However, in contrast with the prolonged discussions on the laws regarding the eight-hour workday and house rents (Gerard 2006, 930), which were endlessly amended and sent back and forth between Parliament and Senate, the *pensée unique* in the first years after the war concerning this law is remarkable. After the war, all political parties would indeed severely condemn *the enriched, war profiteers, and the Barons* '*Zeep*'.[3] This condemnation was in early years never explicitly contradicted in Parliament. As the war had forged a strong, 'holy' National Union between the three political parties, it had also created extreme hostility towards a new public enemy number one.

The Food Profiteering Law would stay in effect until the first of March 1923. The law was extended five times by the Chambers. However, a distinction should be made between the period before the first of January 1922 and after. The general elections of 20 November 1921 heralded the definitive end of the governments of National Union. The new government led by the Catholic Georges Theunis, now without socialists, liquidated the Department of Supplies and withdrew its powers to ration food, requisition supplies, impose price caps and regulate agricultural production (Law of 31/12/1921, MB 1/1/1922). Whilst it is tempting to interpret this as an ideological change of direction, this was, above all, the continuation of a process already set in place by Wauters in the summer of 1921. This process was established because the normalisation of the economic situation made the Department and its authority obsolete. However, the repressive articles and associated decrees of the decree-law remained in place longer than its interventionist component. As such, the ban on usurious pricing, the ban on hoarding, and the obligation for retailers to keep books and to clearly display the prices of 'goods of prime necessity' on the goods and on their windows remained in place until the first of March 1923.

Remarkably enough, on two occasions after this date the conservative Theunis government would try to transform the ban on usurious pricing into a permanent law (PDC 16/3/1923, nr. 225; PDC 26/3/1924, nr. 179). Twice this effort was frustrated in Parliament. This is not to be understood as a conflict between the economic left and right, as the Theunis government was itself on the economic right. Rather, it represented a conflict between the executive and legislative powers of the Belgian State. The Belgian political class remained very devoted to the liberal principles of its founding fathers. It was very reluctant to introduce any legal uncertainty that might potentially harm individual liberties. Even the socialist MP Jules Destrée explicitly opposed the law because of its ambiguous definitions: 'je n'entends pas mettre dans les mains du gouvernement un texte pénal aussi élastique' (PAC 30/4/1924: 1027). These discussions did result in two *other* laws, however, which are still in force today: the obligation for retailers to display the prices of goods on sale; and the law

[3]Baron Zeep, often abbreviated to Zeep, was a typical Belgian war epithet, designating those who had received a permit from the Germans to sell soap. They were accused of driving up the prices and making large profits at the expense of their compatriots. The meaning of the epithet was later expanded to all sorts of war profiteers.

'on illegal speculation in food and consumer goods', which is still in our penal code today.[4]

3 The Actual Application of the Profiteering Law: A Massive Intervention

The Britannica of 1922 mentions that from 1919 on, 'the majority of European countries, including Belgium, France, Germany, Italy, Norway, Poland, Portugal, Rumania and Sweden, passed some form of legislation with a view to checking profiteering or speculation in the necessities of life'. Even though this sort of legislation was ubiquitous in the post-war period, studies on the topic are few. The few historical studies focus mainly on the political decision-making, i.e., on how and why the legislators introduced such legislation. As a result, these laws are often characterized as merely a 'political propaganda exercise' (Morris 1991, 185). German historian Martin Geyer speaks of a populist strategy with 'politisch-taktischen intentionen' (1990, 201). To dismiss the 'profiteering laws' as merely a futile palliative is not unproblematic either, however. It entails the risk of reproducing a political discourse that is as partisan as the uncritical echoing of wartime denunciations against profiteers (see Bouloc 2008). These characterisations do indeed not differ that much from the words of some Belgian MPs in 1924, who denounced the law as *poudre aux yeux* (Jules Destrée, PAC, 30/4/1924: 1027) or a *palliatif d'ordre purement psychologique* (Arthur Pater, PAC 11/4/1924: 981). It is important to recognise that 'profiteering' was not solely an imagined public opinion phenomenon. Economic circumstances did favor certain social groups and did alter market power relationships to the disadvantage of the consumers. To avoid the self-confirming loop of analyses on a merely discursive level, the judicial level should thus be taken in account. These sources allow for an empirical investigation into how the law was actually applied on the street level.

Infractions against the decree-law and its associated royal decrees fell under the jurisdiction of the correctional courts. These courts dealt with misdemeanors. This was the category of violations considered graver than petty offences (judged by the police courts) but less grave than felonies (judged by the criminal courts). Judges in correctional courts could issue punishments from 25 francs on up, and imprisonments from six days up to five years. The judicial statistics show that from 1919 to 1923 (the year the law ceased to exist), 27,122 people were brought before a correctional court for a misdemeanor related to the Food Profiteering Law, its extensions and associated decrees.[5] Looking at the *relative* share of this type of offense in the total prosecution

---

[4]The law of 30 July 1923 'concerning the display of goods and basic necessities', MB 18/8/1923; and the law of 18/7/1924 'on illegal speculation in food and consumer goods, public papers and effects', MB 24/8/1924.

[5]Ministry of Justice, *Judicial Statistics of Belgium*, Brussels: Larcier. For the year 1919 (issued in 1922), 1920 (issued in 1924), 1921 (issued in 1925), 1922 (issued in 1926) and 1923 (issued in

Year	Total of defendants, decree-law 5/11/1918	Conviction rate, decree-law 5/11/1918	Share of defendants food offenses in total of defendants in correctional courts
1919	6,060	72.3%	11.3%
1920	9,147	82.7%	13.5%
1921	7,245	81.4%	11%
1922	3,123	86.4%	5.5%
1923	1,547	87.1%	3.6%
TOTAL	27,122	80.72%	9.2%

Fig. 1 Prosecution decree-law 5/11/1918 in correctional courts, 1919–1923

activity of the correctional courts, the prosecution's large-scale character becomes clear (Fig. 1). In the five post-war years, almost *one-tenth* of all people brought before a correctional court were judged in a case relating to the Food Profiteering Law.

Figure 1 shows that only the accusation of theft would bring more people to court in the first three post-war years (1919: 11,921; 1920: 10,745; 1921: 7999). The relatively high numbers for the second period, 1922–1923, are also remarkable, considering the fact that by the first of January 1922, the government had renounced most of its authority and that the Department of Supplies had ceased to exist by then. These numbers demonstrate two things. Firstly, the access to food remained a relevant and contentious issue in the post-war years. Secondly, contention about food issues resulted in a large-scale state intervention. These numbers are even higher if the prosecution of food adulteration is included. The number of defendants in food adultery proceedings in the five post-war years almost tripled in comparison to the five pre-war years. The steep rise in defendants related to the sanitary condition of domestic animals provide further evidence that food was increasingly policed by the state after the war.[6]

The Food Profiteering Law thus was not the only form of food legislation. However, other types of legislation were primarily motivated by *qualitative* considerations. They also had a more permanent character and predated the war. The legislation under scrutiny in this essay was primarily motivated by scarcity concerns, thus *quantitative* considerations. In order to make a clear distinction, I will speak about food supply offenses from now on to designate all offenses related to the Food Profiteering Law.

1929). Due to the wartime disorganisation, statistics for 1918 are missing. As the law only entered into force in November 1918, this does not account for a great lacuna.

[6]This broader approach towards food offenses is taken by Janssens 2012.

Of the 27,122 defendants in food supply offense proceedings, 21,892 were actually convicted. The conviction rate (ca. 80%) for these type of offenses was as high as the general conviction rate by the correctional courts in those years. It was slightly higher than the conviction rate for 'violations against state security' (ca. 74%), which also concerned cases of economic collaboration (Baclin et al. 2007). In absolute terms too, the number of accused was almost seven times higher. Undoubtedly the penalties were much lower. In those five years, only one person was sentenced to an effective imprisonment longer than six months, and only 357 (1.6% of all sentences) to an effective imprisonment shorter than six months. Compared with the other offenses judged by the correctional courts, fining was a much more common sentence for this type of offense (97% in comparison to 68%). Even though the legislator left judges with the choice, the judges clearly preferred the fine as the most appropriate penalty for this type of offense. This could be explained by the economic nature of the crime. Economic collaboration was also more often punished with solely a fine than other forms of collaboration (Massin and Rousseaux 2008).

The statistics do not provide any information on the actual amount of the fines. This can only be established on the level of the individual court. In the correctional court of Malines, the case studied in this essay (cf. infra), fines ranged from 4 francs to one maximum fine of 1800 francs. More than half of the sentenced fines were lower than 80 francs. On average a fine amounted to 121 francs. This was a considerable sum, equalling at the time 71.5 working hours of an unskilled labourer. From a penal point of view, however, this is a relatively light sentence. The lightness of the sentences is proportional with the gravity of the offenses that were actually prosecuted under the law. As mentioned above, the decree-law criminalized a whole variety of practices, ranging from usurious pricing to not obeying requisitions. The practices actually prosecuted were mostly small business infractions, such as, for example, not displaying or not clearly displaying prices on the consumer goods (cf. infra). The lightness of the sentences is also proportional with the profile of the targeted groups. In contrast to the cases for economic collaboration, which primarily implicated large and medium-sized firms, the decree-law targeted small business owners, mostly farmers, butchers and street vendors. Moreover, in the correctional court of Malines, 40% of the accused in a large sample size were considered to be financially 'not capable to pay a fine' by the local police. A relatively small fine could thus have considerable effect on these groups. Nevertheless, it can be convincingly concluded that on the judicial level, the soup was not eaten as hot as it was served by the legislator.

The judicial statistics also allow an analysis of the different regional levels. At the time, Belgium was divided into 27 correctional districts. Figure 2 demonstrates considerable differences among the different correctional courts. Conviction rates are constant all over the country, but prosecution activity in the different districts diverges significantly. Prosecution activity is calculated by looking at three variables. First is the relative share of defendants in food supply proceedings that appeared in court, i.e., how many of all the defendants in food supply proceedings were judged in this specific court. These numbers show, for example, that about 12% of all defendants in food supply proceedings appeared in the correctional court of Brussels. The second

	Defendants, food supply offenses	Share of the court in total of defendants, *food supply offenses*	Total of defendants in correctional court	Share of the court in total of defendants, *all offenses*	% Food supply offenses/% total	Share of defendants in food supply proceedings in the correctional court
Brussels	3,376	12.44%	35,608	12.08%	1.03	9.48%
Mons	2,936	10.82%	16,933	5.74%	1.88	17.34%
Antwerp	2,424	8.93%	29,393	9.97%	0.90	8.25%
Liège	2,166	7.98%	23,287	7.90%	1.01	9.30%
Nivelles	1,428	5.26%	8,552	2.90%	1.81	16.70%
Charleroi	1,423	5.24%	22,016	7.47%	0.70	6.46%
Dendermonde	1,374	5.06%	14,449	4.90%	1.03	9.51%
Namur	1,184	4.36%	12,344	4.19%	1.04	9.59%
Ghent	1,150	4.24%	21,659	7.35%	0.58	5.31%
Tongeren	998	3.68%	7,598	2.58%	1.43	13.14%
Bruges	979	3.61%	13,886	4.71%	0.77	7.05%
Kortrijk	916	3.38%	11,606	3.94%	0.86	7.89%
Turnhout	868	3.20%	6,113	2.07%	1.54	14.20%
Hasselt	846	3.12%	6,875	2.33%	1.34	12.31%
Dinant	702	2.59%	4,604	1.56%	1.66	15.25%
Oudenaarde	676	2.49%	7,952	2.70%	0.92	8.50%
Tournai	670	2.47%	6,167	2.09%	1.18	10.86%
Verviers	661	2.44%	6,303	2.14%	1.14	10.49%
Leuven	497	1.83%	8,378	2.84%	0.64	5.93%
Malines	479	1.77%	6,276	2.13%	0.83	7.63%
Huy	444	1.64%	5,842	1.98%	0.83	7.60%
Veurne	341	1.26%	4,326	1.47%	0.86	7.88%
Ypres	236	0.87%	7,807	2.65%	0.33	3.02%
Neufchâteau	185	0.68%	2,763	0.94%	0.73	6.70%
Marche	119	0.44%	1,717	0.58%	0.75	6.93%
Arlon	56	0.21%	2,378	0.81%	0.26	2.35%
TOTAL	27,134	100.00%	294,832	100.00%	1.00	9.20%

Fig. 2 Prosecution activity, regional correctional courts, 1919–1923

variable is the comparison with the total share of defendants in all proceedings, i.e., how many of all the defendants judged in correctional courts were judged in this court? This comparison demonstrates that the share of food supply offenses in Brussels is in line with its 'total' contribution of defendants. The third variable is the share of food supply proceedings in the total of cases judged in the correctional court, i.e., of every ten defendants judged in this court, how many were judged in a food supply proceedings. In the case of Brussels it is then shown that in the period from 1919 to 1923, about one in ten defendants in Brussels were judged in a food supply offense proceeding.

The numbers displayed in Fig. 2 show that the courts of Mons and Nivelles were significant outliers. Food supply offenses were notably more intensely prosecuted in these judicial arrondissements than in others. The relative importance of the food supply offenses in these courts amounts to almost double their 'total' contribution. On the other side of the spectrum loom the correctional courts of Ypres and Arlon, where this proportion amounts only to one-fourth. It might be tempting to explain this difference by socio-economic factors. Mons was one of the country's most industrialized arrondissements of the country, encompassing the industrial basin of the Borinage and le Centre. Ypres and Arlon were two of Belgian's most rural arrondissements. The district of Nivelles does not fit this picture, however, as it was only average from a national perspective. The share of the population active in the primary sector was almost as high as in the district of Malines (one-fifth). Furthermore, not one correlation could be identified by matching the judicial numbers on the aggregate level of the province with the socio-economic data of the census of 1920 (Ministry of Interior 1926).

Closer examination of the data in Fig. 3 demonstrate that on the level of the provinces, another cleavage seems to be running through the country. This was the one between the two different occupation areas during the war: the *Etappengebiet*, the rear army area, and the *Generalgouvernement*, the rest of the country. A different occupation regime applied in each of the two areas. The *Etappengebiet* circumscribed the area behind the frontline and encompassed almost the whole of the two Flanders provinces. (As the war went on, and the frontline moved westward, also the extreme western part of Hainaut and the extreme southern part of Luxembourg came to lie in the rear area.) Here a more strict military regime applied, whereas the *Generalgouvernement* was ruled by a civil administration, the *Zivilverwaltung*. However, these numbers seem to confirm the hypothesis that the food situation was actually less tense in the rear army area (Vrints 2011, 37). In the area of the *Generalgouvernement*, it was generally believed that the *Etappengebiet* was more well-off in material terms (Vrints 2012, 236). This was partly due to its rural character, but not only. The province of Limburg, for example, had a much more rural character. Instead, it seems to point to the importance of the two different policies pursued by the occupier during the war. Surprisingly enough, the German occupier was more committed to organize a secure food supply in the 'rear area', in order to prevent disturbances behind the frontline. This does not contradict the fact that political liberties, such as the freedom of speech and circulation, were more strictly suppressed in the rear area. A notable exception in this regard is the province of Luxemburg, which was for the largest part

	Defendants, food supply offenses	Share court in total of defendants, *food supply offenses*	Total of accused in court	Share of the court in total of accused, *all offenses*	% food supply offenses/% total	Share of food supply offenses in court itself	Share of the population active in the primary sector	… in the secondary sector	… in the tertiary sector
Brabant	5,301	19.54%	52,538	17.82%	1.10	10.09%	12.89%	40.24%	40.40%
Hainaut	5,029	18.53%	45,116	15.30%	1.21	11.15%	9.68%	58.92%	25.73%
Antwerp	3,771	13.90%	41,782	14.17%	0.98	9.03%	14.40%	32.10%	48.83%
Liège	3,271	12.05%	35,432	12.02%	1.00	9.23%	8.36%	56.00%	29.97%
East Flanders	3,200	11.79%	44,060	14.94%	0.79	7.26%	19.69%	48.89%	27.27%
West Flanders	2,472	9.11%	37,625	12.76%	0.71	6.57%	22.28%	46.71%	26.53%
Namur	1,886	6.95%	16,948	5.75%	1.21	11.13%	19.11%	38.75%	33.02%
Limburg	1,844	6.80%	14,473	4.91%	1.38	12.74%	38.09%	29.62%	28.10%
Luxembourg	360	1.33%	6,858	2.33%	0.57	5.25%	33.27%	25.77%	32.65%
TOTAL	27,134	100.00%	294,832	100.00%	1.00	9.20%	15.63%	45,.85%	32.99%

Fig. 3 Prosecution activity of correctional courts on the level of the province, 1919–1923 + occupation distribution

of the war under the control of the *Generalgouvernment*. Here the rural character of the province is probably the main explanation for the low number of defendants in absolute and relative terms.

Hence it can be convincingly concluded that the law was more than a political propaganda exercise. The law was intensively applied on the judiciary level in the years that the law was in force. It should be noted, however, that the judicial application was notably less severe than intended by the legislator.

4 The Case of Malines: Between Popular and National Justice

Statistics only tell so much, however. As mentioned above, they do not provide any information on the actual practices that were prosecuted under the law. Therefore we have to descend down to the level of the individual court, as only the judgement books and judicial records can provide this information. Judgment books are the collections of all the verdicts delivered by the court. They sum up crucial information on the verdict and the nature of the offense prosecuted and provide essential information on the profile defendant. The judicial records are the collection of all the documents produced in the 'judicial chain' leading up to each verdict. They thus contain the first police record, additional background information on the defendants and further interrogations of witnesses.

These sources allow a more accurate insight into how the law was actually used. This focus on 'the uses of justice' is in line with a recent trend in criminal justice history in which the judicial system is no longer considered as a superimposed top-down institute but is seen as being shaped by the constant interactions between citizens and judicial actors. Scholars have pointed out that even though the modern state expanded its powers drastically, it remained almost entirely dependent on the reporting of the victims to enforce its self-proclaimed 'monopoly on punishment' (Churchill 2014). This focus on *Justiznutzung* does not dismiss the fact that in comparison to the early modern area, the state would indeed come to act more autonomously in the domain of penal prosecution. The state would take more firm action towards so-called 'victimless crimes', for example, public drunkenness (Davis 1989).

In this essay, the judicial arrondissement Malines serves as a case study. Crime historian Frédéric Vesentini has designated the arrondissement of Malines as 'a microcosm of Belgium' in respect of penal structures (2006, 219). In socio-economic terms too, the area seems very 'average' from a national perspective. It is situated on the country's urban axis running from north to south, in between the nation's two largest cities, Antwerp and Brussels. It is quite densely populated but includes only two towns, Lier and Malines. Almost two-thirds of the communes of the arrondissement had fewer than 3000 inhabitants. Lier was a fairly average provincial town. At the time, Malines was one of Belgium's largest cities, accounting for half of the arrondissement's population. The arrondissement did not have an exclusively rural or industrial character in professional terms. With regard to the prosecution of food supply offenses, the arrondissement is slightly below average, but it has the advantage that its judicial records are almost integrally preserved, a unicum in Belgium. This allows for a truly serial analysis of prosecution in the first five post-war years.

Looking at the offenses actually prosecuted—specified in the judgment books—a great variety springs to eye. One special case should be mentioned beforehand, namely the slaughter offenses. These concerned infractions against the prohibitions on slaughtering non-adult cattle and pregnant cows, issued with an eye on restoration of Belgian livestock herds. These decrees, like the others, were issued by the Ministry of Agriculture, and not by the Department of Supplies. Officially they were associated with the emergency law of 4/8/1914, not the decree-law of 5/11/1918, but in practice slaughter offenses were judged together and were also aggregated in the statistics. As these prohibitions also concerned the quantitative matter of food supply, the integration of these offenses is justified.

According to Fig. 4, infractions against the obligation for retailers to clearly display the prices from the 'goods of prime necessity' on sale (RD 31/3/1919) was by far the most prosecuted offense. This was a relatively small business infraction, and accordingly the fines for this offense were in general quite low. A typical fine amounted to 26 francs. In the second period in the existence of the profiteering law, 1922–1923, fines were remarkably higher, however. The explanation for this is the fact that in the second period, the non-displaying of prices was actually one of the few offenses that still *could* be prosecuted, as the Belgian State had withdrawn from most of its powers regarding food supply. A female shopkeeper M.M. from Malines was sentenced in January 1923 to a fine of 1500 francs after repeated warnings and run-ins with the local food inspector. The public displaying of the verdict was also

Price display-infractions	145
Non-delivering of requisitioned goods	82
Transport of bread grains without a letter of conduct	69
Slaughter offenses	47
Bookkeeping infractions	46
Usurious pricing	42
Maximum price-infractions (selling)	37
Transport and/or sale of animals illegitimately slaughtered	34
Selling, buying, holding and/or transporting of unauthorized bread grains, flour	31
Grinding the wheat under the minimum	7
Selling of bread under the mandatory weight	4
Supplies not declared	4
No indication of the type of meat put on sale	3
Maximum price infractions (buying)	2
Simultaneously selling meat and frozen meat	2
Using bread grains as feedstuff	1

Fig. 4 Types of food supply offenses prosecuted under the decree-laws, CC Malines, 1919–1923

Non-delivering of requisitioned goods	82
Usurious pricing	38
Maximum price infractions (selling)	35
Price-display infraction	18
Bookkeeping infractions	10
Slaughter offenses	2
Maximum price infractions (buying)	2
Selling, buying, holding and/or transporting of unauthorized bread grains, flour	1

Fig. 5 Types of misdemeanours prosecuted under the decree-laws in the year 1919, CC Malines

more commonly ordered for this offense in the second period, a privilege normally reserved for graver offenses.

This is confirmed when the temporal distribution of verdicts is taken into account. One-third of all the verdicts on non-displaying were delivered in the period from 1922 to 1923, in which it also constituted half of all the verdicts delivered. Furthermore, it is seen that nearly all the verdicts on infractions against requisitions were given in 1919 (Fig. 5). These concerned all the farmers who did not obey the orders from local mayors to deliver milk for childcare and care of the poor in their communes. This observation corresponds to a more general trend in the prosecution activity of the court of Malines. Focus shifted away from infractions on the level of the supplies (slaughter offenses, requisitions, transport of grains) to infractions on the level of the distribution (keeping of the books, displaying of the prices). This shift can be explained by the fact that the most acute scarcity disappeared after 1919, and the economic situation gradually improved from then on.

Based on the data for Malines and the reports of the Department of Supplies (1921, 467), it is thus entirely plausible that the most common offense prosecuted under the decree-law in the whole of Belgium was the non-displaying of prices on consumer goods. The enforcement of the displaying of prices on consumer goods might not seem like a spectacular state intervention today, but for retailers at the time, this interference by the national government was unprecedented. This is exemplified by the many police records in which the interrogated shopkeepers declared that they simply were not aware that such a thing was mandatory.[7] The obligation for shopkeepers to keep books had been non-existent before the war as well. Except for the aforementioned laws on food adulteration and the policing of the sanitation of domestic animals, almost no legal obligations applied to small business owners

[7]Examples given: State Archives (SA) Beveren, Correctional Court (CC) of Malines, R55, 1919: judicial records 1022; 1920: 799, 801; 1921: 59, 200.

before the war. The unprecedented nature of these obligations was consequently met with fierce resistance in middle-class circles (Heyrman 1998).

Another factor causing the high prevalence of price display-infractions was the nature of the offense. Those infractions could be established rather quickly and unambiguously by a police agent on his beat, especially if compared with other offenses. The question of usurious pricing for example, involved long and costly judicial procedures. In a certain way, price-display infractions were the most efficient and quick way for the state apparatus to keep constant pressure on the supplying classes. This is supported by the fact that the acquittal rate for price-display infractions was slightly lower (13%) than the general acquittal rate for food supply offenses (19%). Furthermore, it is important to note that this obligation and the one to keep books were the only elements of the profiteering law that would be eventually transformed in a permanent law in 1923. All Belgian parties regarded the law as an appropriate measure against the high cost of living, as it increased competition and strengthened control by the public. In contrast to other dispositions, this obligation corresponded to liberal as well as socialist ideology. The obligation to display prices on consumer goods could thus be regarded as one of the first cautious attempts at consumer protection by the national government. The government stated that it was their intention that consumers should be able to determine prices independently from the seller (MB 20/10/1923). At the same time it ended all *à la tête du client* arbitrariness on the side of the seller. Seemingly banal today, the obligation was not so in its day.

The judgment books also provide the answer to another question, namely the nature of the products that were policed (Fig. 6).

'Retail goods' concerned all sorts of groceries, such as coffee, sugar, soap and rice. These appeared mostly in later years, corresponding to the general trend of prosecution activity shifting from supplies to distribution. The minimal share of potatoes is entirely logical. The potato trade was one of the first that was deregulated after the war, because of its abundance on Belgian soil. The high share of dairy products and meat, in contrast, is striking. In Fig. 6, I distinguish between 'animals' and 'meat', depending on if the offense concerned a living animal or an already-slaughtered animal. If taken together, though, meat was the most policed staple. These products had only fairly recently become part of the diet of the modal Belgian (and in a pan-European perspective, this share was still relatively low) (Scholliers 1985). This conclusion points to the special status that 'fats' had acquired within the Belgian population. In her book about wartime Berlin, Belinda Davis has pointed to the importance of popular beliefs among the working classes that food should be 'hearty' and 'bodily' warming (2000, 77). In Belgium too it was the shortage of butter that led to heightened emotions (Vrints 2011). Butter bread was a central staple in the labourer's diet. Because of its relatively recent status as an 'acquired need', the scarcity of this hearty food was experienced as a particularly great loss. Tellingly, the potato did not enjoy this status.

Considering that the bread trade was by far the most regulated market in post-war Belgium, the share of bread and its raw materials is in fact quite low. This seems to indicate firstly that the bread intervention of Wauters was relatively successful. Furthermore, it confirms the thesis that it was actually easier for governments to

Fig. 6 Products policed, CC Malines, 1919–1923

Grains and flour	115
Butter and margarine	112
Retail goods	107
Animals	97
Meat	87
Milk	37
Bread	22
Agrarian products	14
Clothing	7
Sugar	3
Melted fat	3
Eggs	2
Gist	2
Saddles	1
Potatoes	1

control the trade of products that were for the largest part imported (Kramer 2014). The potato formed a notable exception as it was so abundant. For meat, however—which was still largely domestically produced— the market was much tighter. To a certain extent, the native farmers formed some sort of unruly internal opposition against the interests of the market-dependent urban classes.

This observation is also confirmed when the socio-economic profile of the defendants is taken into account (Fig. 7). More than one-third of the defendants were farmers. It is well documented that popular anger after the war against the peasants as a group was especially virulent, much more than against activists for example (Demasure 2016). In contrast to the situation of the city dwellers, the war had been a period of growth and affluence for the agricultural sector. In his overview article on 'the fortune and well-being' in post-war Belgium, Ernest Mahaim, a sociologist from Liège, wrote the following on the situation of the peasants in, unusual for him, a compassionate tone:

> Sous l'occupation allemande, nous l'avons vu, l'agriculture a présenté ce paradoxe d'avoir une production déficitaire et cependant de faire des bénéfices considérables … Malgré les réquisitions et parfois les exactions, ils parvenaient à vendre à bon prix—à prix croissant souvent-, le produit de leurs cultures, soit à l'occupant, soit aux compatriotes. Au jour de

General Farmers	187
Working Proprietors (Wholesale and Retail Trade)	129
Butchers and Meat Preparers	102
Bakers, Pastry Cooks and Confectionery Makers	29
Grain Millers and Related Workers	14
Housekeeping and Related Service Supervisors	12
Street Vendors, Canvassers and News Vendors	8
Tailors and Dressmakers	8
Working Proprietors (Catering, Lodging and Leisure Services)	3
Other	11

Fig. 7 Professional profile of the accused, CC Malines, 1919–1923

> l'armistice, il y avait dans les campagnes une accumulation inusitée de numéraire et de capitaux. Aussi, on vit bientôt s'y répandre un bien-être tel qu'on n'en a jamais vu. (Mahaim 1926, 570)

Consequently, the agricultural class came out of the war economically empowered but seriously damaged politically. As stated above, the decree-law formed part of a transitional-justice strategy by the legislature to address the popular demand for justice against those groups that had enriched themselves during the war. This motivation is thus reflected in the actual 'use' of the law, and it clarifies which groups were actually understood to fall under the somewhat vague denominator 'profiteers'.

The numbers in Fig. 7 make clear that shopkeepers (26%) and butchers (20%) had to take the rap. It can be concluded that this was the first time that these professional groups were so massively targeted by the Belgian State. This is even more the case if we take into account the steep rise in the prosecution of the other aforementioned 'food offenses' such as food adulteration and policing the sanitation of domestic animals. This is further confirmed by the judicial statistics. In the first two post-war years, the statistics were especially exhaustive and also mention the criminal records of the convicted. The share of clean criminal records in this type of offense was remarkably higher than for other offenses. The law thus targeted a group that was largely 'new' to the justice apparatus.

These observations confirm the thesis of German historian Jürgen Kocka on the autonomy of the state. In his *Facing Total War* (1984), the first truly social-historian work on the First World War, he argues that the First World War marked the decisive transformation of the modern state. The state was no longer solely the protector of the interests of the dominant classes but gained a substantial degree of autonomy as a third player in the field of socio-economic interests. Kocka saw important proof of this in the growth of 'those state interventions into aspects of the private economic order which those affected regarded as basic to that order' (Kocka 1984, 144). Belgian police historian Jonas Campion described a similar transformation for Belgium in the case of security matters. He designates the First World War as 'la fin d'une conception à la fois bourgeoise et citoyenne de l'exercice de la sécurité, vécue comme la protection de l'intérêt et des biens d'une élite sociétale' (Campion 2017).

This does raise the question of which actors were most assiduous in bringing up cases to the judicial system. The cases were not strictly interpersonal conflicts but formed infractions against a more abstract common interest. Who was the victim then? Did civilians consider themselves victims, and did they formally lodge complaints? Or was it the law enforcement agencies who enforced the law? To answer this question we have to descend to the first link in the judicial chain, namely, the police report. Police reports, preserved in the judicial records, were the written account by a law enforcement agent of what had occurred. In it the offense was established and the parties concerned were heard—namely, the accused, the victims and witnesses. These reports were consequently transferred to the Public Prosecutor's Office, where the decision was made whether to prosecute the case or not. These reports are of particular importance because the 'reporter', often a police officer, also reported how the case came to his attention. Therefore this type of source offers a unique insight into how the interactions between civilians and law enforcement occurred.

From a large sample of the judicial records in the correctional court of Malines (75), it becomes clear that only in 12% of the cases was a police report compiled on the initiative of a civilian. These civilian complaints were, for the large majority, concentrated in the first two years. All were related to butter and meat, which confirms the thesis of Belinda Davis concerning 'hearty goods'. All other reports were drawn up on the initiative of mayors, during police inspections, or by agents 'on the beat'. These numbers do not seem to fully comply with the fact that the law was the judicial translation of a popular demand for justice. Perhaps civilians felt reluctant to bite the hand that feeds them. Distance from the perpetrator and mutual power relations are important variables in the willingness of civilians to file a formal complaint (Churchill 2012). Also, an uneven power relationship is at play between food suppliers and consumers. Proof of this is given by the 38-year-old dressmaker from Lier, L.H., who did lodge a complaint and thereby declared to the police in February 1919 that 'there are many more persons who've bought butter at these prices, but they don't reveal themselves for fear of not getting any more butter'.[8] A 70-year-old widow later regretted filing complaint, because'from now on I don't get any more butter'.[9] This is also confirmed by the fact that in 10% of the cases, agents vaguely referred in their report to the 'general rumour' that had notified them.[10] Indeed, a certain *omertà* seemed to surround the food chain. Many of the accused farmers and butchers refused to name their suppliers, declaring that they had forgotten their names or that they

[8] 'er zijn nog personen die de boter aan dergelijke prijzen betalen doch deze maken zich niet kenbaar uit vrees dat zij geen boter meer zouden krijgen'. SA Beveren, CC Malines, R55, 1919: 140.

[9] 'nu krijg ik geene boter meer'. SA Beveren, CC Malines, R55, 1919: 327.

[10] SA Beveren, CC Malines, R55, 1919: 147, 327; 1920: 52, 267, 550, 552, 691, 777, 819.

did not even know them all, which seems a very implausible assertion.[11] Also the data in the judgment books point to the fact that the accused were mostly established 'insiders' in their community, a factor that probably further hampered the willingness to report.[12]

Law enforcement did not form a monolithic unit either. At least four different parties were involved: local police, the national gendarmerie, the newly founded judiciary police and the inspectors of the Ministry of Labour, Industry and Food Supply. Based on the reports, there was a clear division of labor between those different agencies. In the city of Malines, the local and judiciary police was most active. There was even a specialised food inspector in the police force, Arthur van Battel. The police reports reveal the image of an inspector who was especially dedicated, regularly accused of overzealousness by accused shopkeepers. In our sample, he is also responsible for reporting one-fifth of all cases. The presence of such an active individual might thus be a possible explanation for regional differences. The more centralised 'national' police forces—namely, the gendarmerie and the inspectors—were most active in the smaller and rural communes. In rural areas, a distinction could be made between the static and dynamic forces. The inspectors of the ministry were dynamic, as they all resided in the city of Antwerp and had to cover the whole province of Antwerp. Thus even in rural contexts, it was urban actors who enforced the law. The national gendarmerie was more static, as they were quartered in a commune in the arrondissement for a longer time.

As mentioned above, socio-economic variables do not entirely explain the distribution of prosecution activity. However, comparing population data of the arrondissement of Malines with the incidence of food supply offenses, the cities Lier and Malines are disproportionally represented. Together they include 40% of the population but represent 60% of the cases. The use of the Food Profiteering Law was thus primarily urban. The fact that local police were most active in the largest city might spring from the fact that the law corresponded with the interests of the market-dependent city dwellers, whereas in more rural areas the law had to be imposed 'from above'. In Brussels, policy makers expressed great dissatisfaction over the laxity of local elites and local police forces towards economic perpetrators. As a measure, the centralised national police forces were drastically enforced after the war, to the detriment of the civilian militias and local sovereignty in security matters (Campion 2017). Food supply, traditionally *the* local prerogative, was one of the main domains in which the national authorities wanted to assert themselves very strongly after the war.

[11] Examples: SA Beveren, CC Malines, R55, 1919:140, 270; 1920: 777; 1921: 52.

[12] In 58% of the cases, place of birth, place of residence and the place of offense were identical.

5 Conclusion

To sum things up, our three-level analysis provides the following answers. On the level of the national legislator, in spite of its non-retroactive character, the Food Profiteering Law and its consecutive extensions were clearly intended as a form of transitional justice. Secondly, the law did not remain a dead political letter; correctional courts massively prosecuted food offenses after the war. The correctional courts have been largely overlooked in the study of post-war Belgium. On the level of the arrondissement, it becomes clear that certain groups were specifically targeted in the use of the Food Profiteering Law. Through the study of a local case, it becomes clear that food was a crucial domain in the shifting of powers in security matters that took place after the war between the national and local forces.

Hence, can the decree-law of 5/11/1918 'concerning the alimentation of the civilian population', its consequent extensions, associated royal decrees and its actual implementation be considered as a form of a transitional justice? On one hand, the law was indeed a temporary law enabling a transition after a period of *regime change*, answering to a particularly strong 'demand for justice' by large parts of the population, thus corresponding to all the traits of a transitional-justice law. On the other hand, it could be argued that the law did not deal with *past crimes*, that the penalties were relatively low and that it did not target the violent war crimes that are usually studied in a transitional-justice perspective. On the matter of retroactivity, it can be argued that the law and its extensions were intended as exactly a compensation for the fact that the Belgian political class was so reluctant to implement any penal retroactivity. This ingrained liberal constitutionalism was as strongly supported by all parties as their condemnations of war profiteers. As such, it can be concluded that the Food Profiteering Law was a *non-retroactive* form of transitional justice. The relatively light penalties were proportional with the profile of the perpetrators. In contrast to prior statements, the small fries did not go completely free after the war. Regarding the penalties, it can be contended that the relatively low fines can be interpreted as the outcome of the balancing between the different powers in Belgium. The law was, after all, the judicial translation of a particularly strong, but also quite foggy, societal discontent. It is probable that the state agents chose to prosecute in the first place those offenses that could be established most unambiguously, like, for example, infractions against the obligation to clearly display the prices of the goods on sale. A similar balancing of powers took place when the Theunis-government (without socialists) tried to transform the ban on usurious prices into a permanent law but was frustrated by the Belgian Parliament. This pointed to a cleavage that was not ideological but that, rather, ran between the three different powers of the constitutional parliamentary democracy. Finally, the law did not target the suspects usually under scrutiny in the field of transitional justice. But this article confirms the thesis of scholars who have in recent years demonstrated that resentments against economic perpetrators—"*the enriched, the profiteers, the Barons 'Zeep'*"—was actually far larger and more virulent than resentment against political collaborators.

The decree-law thus should be interpreted as part of a transitional strategy by the Belgian State to give political and judicial satisfaction to popular resentments against war wrongdoers. This effort was necessary to preserve its stately monopoly over violence and punishment. Nevertheless, the Food Profiteering Law was *not only* a form of transitional justice. Looking at the steep rise in the prosecution of pre-war food laws, it can be contended that certain dispositions, such as, for example, the obligation to display prices, are part of a development that predated the war in which the national state would increasingly intervene in the trade of consumer goods in favour of Belgian consumers (Nath 2016; Guiot 2016). The law was thus more than solely transitional, but it persists in certain ways to this day.[13]

References

Sources

Unpublished sources

State Archives Beveren. Correctional Court of Malines. R55, judgment books (1919) and judicial records (1919–1923)

State Archives Beveren. Correctional Court of Malines. R478, judgment books and judicial records (1920–1923)

Published Sources

Ministry of Interior (1926) Statistique de la Belgique: population: recensement général, Tome III. Weissenbruch, Brussels

Ministry of Industry, Labor and Food Supply (1921) Rapport Général sur l'activité des Services du Ravitaillement du 11 novembre 1918 au 1er Septembre 1921. Imprimerie Veuve Corneille De Clercq, Jette

Ministry of Justice, *Judicial Statistics of Belgium, 1919–1923.* Larcier, Brussels

Literature

Baclin G, Campion J, Rousseaux X (2007) Les chiffres en guerre. Occupations, justices et statistiques pénales en Belgique (1914–1950). Histoire & Mesure 1:5–44

Bost M (2013) Traverser l'Occupation 1914–1918. Du modus vivendi à la grève, la magistrature belge face aux occupants allemands. Unpublished doctoral thesis, UCL, Louvain-la-Neuve

Bouloc F (2008) 'War profiteers' and 'war profiters': representing economic gain in France during the First World War. In: Jones H, O'Brien J, Schmidt-Suppria C (eds) Untold war: new perspectives in First World War studies. Koninklijke Brill, Leiden, pp 325–356

Campion J (2017) Un nouvel équilibre: le système sécuritaire belge à l'issue de la Première Guerre mondiale. *Revue de la Gendarmerie Nationale*, no spécial 'L'ordre dans la guerre. Polices et gendarmeries européennes face à la Première Guerre Mondiale'

Churchill D (2012) Crime, policing and control in Leeds, c. 1830–1890. Unpublished doctoral thesis, The Open University, Milton Keynes

---

[13]For example, in the obligation to display prices and the law of 18/7/1924 on 'illegal speculation'.

Churchill D (2014) Rethinking the state monopolisation thesis: the historiography of policing and criminal justice in nineteenth-century England. Crime, Hist Sociétés/Crime, Hist Soc 1:131–152
Davis JS (1989) Prosecutions and their context: the use of the criminal law in later nineteenth-century London. In: Hay D, Snyder F (eds) Policing and prosecution in Britain 1750–1850. Clarendon Press, Oxford, pp 379–426
Davis B (2000) Home fires burning: food, politics, and everyday life in World War I Berlin. University of North Carolina Press, London
Demasure B (2016) Een slecht imago? Beeldvorming over boeren en voedselvoorziening tijdens en na de Eerste Wereldoorlog. Het Virtuele Land. Erfgoed van landbouw, platteland en voeding. http://www.hetvirtueleland.be/cag/exhibits/show/beeldvorming_boeren_woi. Accessed 1 May 2017
Deneckere G (1994) Sire, het volk mort. Collectieve actie in de sociale geschiedenis van de Belgische staat, 1831–1940. Unpublished doctoral thesis, Ghent University, Ghent
Gerard E (2006) De democratie gedroomd, begrensd en ondermijnd. 1918–1939. In: Dumoulin M, Gerard E, Dujardin V, van den Wijngaert M (eds) Nieuwe Geschiedenis van België. II 1905–1950. Lannoo, Tielt, pp 867–1118
Geyer MH (1990) Teuerungsprotest, Konsumentpolitik und soziale Gerechtigkeit während der Inflation: München 1920–1923. Archiv für Sozialgeschichte 30:181–215
Grevers H (2012) Voorbij Bijltjesdag? Recente werken over de bestraffing van collaboratie na beide wereldoorlog in de Lage Landen. Low Countries Historical Review 1, webeditions
Guiot F (2016) L'État belge face aux enjeux de qualité alimentaire dans la seconde moitié du 19e siècle. Responsabilisation et institutionnalisation consacrées par les lois des 17 mars 1856 et 4 août 1890 relatives à la falsification alimentaire. J Belg Hist 3/4: 137–163
Heyrman P (1998) Middenstandsbeweging en beleid in België 1918–1940. Tussen vrijheid en regulering. Universitaire Pers Leuven, Leuven
Janssens R (2012) Economische misdrijven in het arrondissement Mechelen in de jaren 1916 en 1919. Unpublished Master's thesis, Ghent University, Ghent
Kocka J (1984) Facing total war: German society 1914–1918. Berg Publishers, Dover
Kramer A (2014) Blockade and economic warfare. In: Winter J (ed) The Cambridge history of the First World War. volume II: the state. Cambridge University Press, Cambridge, pp 460–490
Mahaim E (1926) La fortune et le bien-être. In: Mahaim E (ed) La Belgique Restaurée: étude sociologique. Institut de Sociologie Solvay, Brussels, pp 505–612
Massin V, Rousseaux X (2008) Mesures de la répression: quelques chiffres. In: Rousseaux X, Van Ypersele L (eds) La Patrie crie vengeance!, pp 131–146
Monballyu J (2012) La justice transitionelle en Belgique dans les affaires pénales après la Première Guerre Mondiale (1918–1928). Tijdschrift voor Rechtsgeschiedenis 80:443–479
Morris M (1991) In search of the profiteer. In: Wrigley C, Shepherd J (eds) On the move: essays in labour and transport history presented to Philip Bagwell. Hambledon Press, London, pp 185–293
Nath G (2016) Shaping consumer interests. Belgian consumer movements between technocracy, social democracy and Cold War internationalization (1975–2000). Unpublished doctoral thesis, Ghent University, Ghent
Pirenne Henri (1929) La Belgique et la Guerre Mondiale. Les Presses Universitaires de France, Paris
Rousseaux X, Van Ypersele L (eds) (2008) La Patrie crie vengeance! La Répression des inciviques belges au sortir de la guerre 1914–1918. Le Cri Edition, Brussels
Scholliers P (1985) Oorlog en voeding: de invloed van de Eerste Wereldoorlog op het Belgische voedingspatroon, 1890–1949. Tijdschrift voor sociale geschiedenis 1:30–50
Scholliers P (1994) The policy of survival: food, the state and social relations in Belgium, 1914–1921. In: Burnett J, Oddy DJ (eds) The origins and development of food policies in Europe. Leicester University Press, London, pp 39–53
Van Ypersele L, Rousseaux X (2005) Leaving the war: popular violence and judicial repression of 'unpatriotic' behaviour in Belgium (1918–1921). Eur Rev Hist 1:3–22

Vesentini F (2006) Pratiques pénales et structures sociales. L'État belge et la répression du crime en temps de crise économique. Presses Universitaires de Louvain, Louvain-La-Neuve

Vrints A (2011) Sociaal protest in een bezet land. Voedseloproer in België tijdens de Eerste Wereldoorlog. Tijdschrift voor Geschiedenis 1:31–47

Vrints A (2012) 'All the butter in the country belongs to us Belgians'. Well-being and Lower Class National Identification in Belgium during the First World War. In: Van Ginderachter M, Beyen M (eds) National identification from below: Europe from the late 18th century to the end of the First World War. New York: Palgrave Macmillan, pp 230–249

Vrints A (2015) Beyond victimization: contentious food politics in Belgium during World War I. Eur Hist Q 1:83–107

In the Jails of the Fatherland: The Penitentiary Repression of Disloyal Civilians After the First World War in Belgium

Florent Verfaillie

Abstract Post-war penitentiary repression remains an unexplored angle of the Belgian historiography of the Great War. It was nevertheless a key task of the state when reclaiming its post-conflict authority and legitimacy, as popular violence was rising in a divided and devastated country. How did the state repress its own citizens in the immediate aftermath of the war? How did it manage the detention of the numerous 'anti-patriotic' suspects? Which behaviours were targeted, and which 'bad Belgians' actually ended up in jail? How were the detention conditions experienced by them? This essay aims to provide a first overview of the role played by prisons in the restoration of the post-war political rule of Belgium, to describe its legal boundaries, and to explore the daily-life conditions of prisoners after the war. It reveals how wartime and post-war political decisions impacted the arrests policy of suspects and how those decisions modified the detention conditions of the prisoners.

In November 1918, Belgium was finally freed from an everlasting German occupation. For more than four years, Belgians had been afflicted with mass impoverishment and, furthermore, had to cope with an impressive number of repressive measures. This exceptional—and exceptionally long—situation naturally created important societal tensions among Belgians, as many citizens were struggling to subsist. Smuggling, product falsifications, a black market and robbery had become widespread. Armed banditry even re-emerged from a distant past (Leloup et al. 2014). Close cohabitation with the Germans and their intrusion into the social-economic functioning of Belgium inevitably further sharpened these tensions (Tilly and Deloge 2012). Some Belgians took advantage of the new circumstances to engage in illicit or illegal business with the occupiers, to brusquely solve conflicts by denouncing rivals or to achieve some controversial political goals. Some even spied for the Germans, while some women had intimate relationships with occupying soldiers. When the Belgian Army and government regained power in November 1918, they found a divided and devastated country where popular violence was rising (Van Ypersele and Rousseaux

F. Verfaillie (✉)
CEGESOMA (Belgian State Archives)/Ghent University, Brussels, Belgium
e-mail: florentverfaillie@hotmail.com

M. Bost and A. Vrints (eds.), *Doing Justice In Wartime*,
Studies in the History of Law and Justice 19,
https://doi.org/10.1007/978-3-030-72050-6_5

2005). The spartacist turmoil around the German retreat was soon followed by intra-Belgian violence targeted against 'anti-patriotic' citizens: shops and private houses were assaulted and destroyed and some women were molested and humiliated in public places (Majerus 2007, 132–142; Van Ypersele 2008). Besides such 'patriotic' reprisals, economic revenge played a role as well: individual thefts but also scenes of mass pillaging and armed banditry added to the troubled situation. Unlike in other European countries, a revolutionary scenario never became a serious threat in Belgium. Nevertheless, it was essential for the exiled government to restore its authority rather quickly.

The Belgian penitentiary system was to provide a major tool in this respect. Belgium indeed possessed a large and modern penitentiary network that had been built during the last decades before the war, able to quickly host a large number of prisoners. When the war began, the penitentiary lay in the middle of a large reformatory movement that had occurred across Europe. These reforms, halted by the war, progressed more quickly after 1918. Therefore, disloyal citizens arrested at the liberation experienced several changes in their daily detention conditions. Prior to the war, Belgium had applied a particularly radical version of the solitary confinement regime. While community detention was still widely used in France, the United Kingdom or Germany along with expulsion or chained forced labour, Belgium applied solitary confinement as a generalised standard punishment (Vanhulle 2010, 178–179). The strict Belgian policy mandated that detainees wear hoods on their head as they left their cell—called the 'Belgian hood' in neighbouring countries—in order to prevent any visual contact with other prisoners. Following that policy, prisoners also were separated by partition walls as they sat in the penitentiary classroom or chapel and were constantly forbidden to talk, forced to use sign language instead when talking to the staff. Questioning of this radical policy had started already before the war, but the reforms reached their peak in the inter-war period, particularly under the rule of the first socialist minister of Justice, Emile Vandervelde.[1] From 1920, the radical confinement regime was progressively abandoned. Instead, a systematic medical-anthropological control on detainees was generalised to all Belgian prisons, based on the 1907-founded 'Penitentiary Anthropological Laboratory'. This evolution expressed an important switch in the management philosophy of the prisons, aiming at individualised 'treatment' of the convicts. The moralising approach of the confinement regime, based on the monastic ideal and aiming at the redemption of the convicts, gradually gave way to a scientific methodology based on observation, diagnosis and classification, oriented towards the reintegration of the prisoners into society (De Bont 2001, 75–76).

This essay is partly based on prisoners' files from these penitentiary anthropological laboratories. Yet, rather than examining the anthropological treatment of political prisoners, the focus of this essay is to chart the larger phenomenon of the post-war repression of disloyal Belgians in a penitentiary perspective. Indeed, most studies

[1] Emile Vandervelde (Ixelles, 1866–Brussels, 1938), leader of the Belgian Workers Party, professor at the Free University of Brussels, he was regularly minister of the Belgian government during the interwar period. See Polasky (1998).

so far have focused on the judiciary repression at the liberation (Rousseaux and Van Ypersele 2008; Baclin et al. 2010; Monballyu 2011). We must stress the difference in this regard between the judiciary repression, its penitentiary counterpart, and the actual criminality. As Charlotte Vanneste states:

> Far from reflecting a 'criminality' phenomenon, the detained population statistics are rather the ultimate expression of a 'penalty' phenomenon existing autonomously as a specific social production. A series of empirical studies further shows an important dissymmetry between the pictures given by the so-called criminality statistics, i.e., registered at the police activity level, and statistics related to the imprisonment.[2] (2015, 220)

In order to take those different levels and filters of the repression process into account, this essay proceeds in three steps. Firstly, it exposes the conceptual and legal issues around the phenomenon and discusses their political significance. Secondly, it examines the scope of the penitentiary repression in comparison to the judicial one, and deals with the detention management of the suspects. Thirdly, it enters the prisons walls as to explore what the incarceration experience of the detainees looked like in the early 1920s.

1 Between *Incivisme* and Political Prisoners: The Definition Issue

Belgian scholars of the First World War commonly use the term "*incivisme*" (in both French and Dutch) to point to both legally and socially unaccepted wartime behaviours towards the German occupiers—a term that will be replaced by "collaboration" during the Second World War. From a legal perspective, they mainly refer to the 'crimes and delicts against the state safety' (i.e., Title I of Book II of the penal code, art. 101–136), especially to its chapter II dealing with offences against the 'external state safety' (art. 113–123). This specific chapter includes espionage, denunciation to the enemy and political as well as economic help to the enemy. In fact, most civilians sentenced for anti-national behaviours were indeed prosecuted following that chapter. Yet these legal provisions do not encompass all incarcerated disloyal perpetrators.

On the basis of chapter I and II (art. 101–123 of the penal code),[3] 2607 Belgians were sentenced between 1919 and 1928 (Monballyu 2011, 43–44; see Fig. 1), but this total is not complete. First of all, it excludes other political delicts or crimes from the penal code such as chapter III dealing with 'internal state safety' (art. 124–136), as well as some other provisions.[4] But most importantly, it excludes various

[2]Translated by the author.

[3]Chapter I, protecting the king, his family and the shape of the government (art. 101–112), played a marginal role in this repression, as only 16 prosecutions and one condemnation took place (under art. 104 and 109), targeting activist activities prior to 8 April 1917, date of a new law on this matter. See infra.

[4]Such as articles 234–235 and 255 targeting civil servants plotting or abusing their authority.

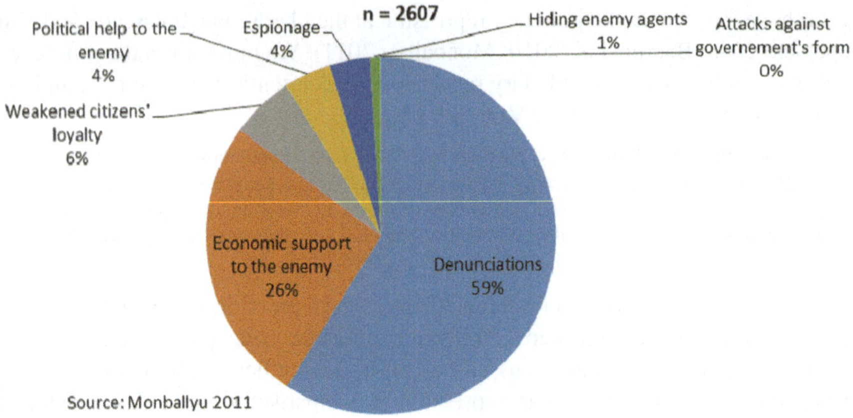

Fig. 1 Proportions of civilians sentenced under articles 101–123 of the penal code (1919–1928) (*Source* Monballuy 2011)

special laws that were adopted in addition to the penal code to repress extra forms of anti-national behaviours. We can mention the laws repressing false news reports regarding military operations[5]; the escape from military recruitment[6]; the diffusion of strategic information or defeatist ideas[7]; economic relations with the enemy outside the occupied country[8]; or help to dispossession and other irregular measures taken by the enemy.[9] All these offenses—albeit not an exhaustive list—were very similar in their nature and could lead to prison penalties.

In his monograph, Monballyu (2011) adopts a broader legal definition of disloyal Belgians than the traditional focus on the penal code and discusses the main problematic issues that lawyers, magistrates and politicians faced when trying to define the exact meaning and scope of the patriotic repression. He includes in his analysis cases from some of the above-mentioned special laws, finding 454 extra cases totalling 3061 convicted *inciviques*, which represents 17.4% more anti-patriotic citizens than found using only the penal code definition (see Fig. 2). This proportion could be even higher if it included other special laws, but Monballyu does not discuss his choices in this regard. He thus provides a larger legal understanding of anti-national behaviours, although the legal extent of that notion remains imprecise. As Monballyu's delimitation remains the most complete on that issue, this article uses it as its working basis.

Since *incivisme* was not a legal concept, it seems indeed illusionary to precisely identify its legal boundaries. In contrast, 'treason' was a well-defined legal notion,

[5]Royal decrees of 25 November 1914 and 12 January 1915.

[6]Law-decree of 5 January 1916.

[7]Royal decree of 11 October 1916 on the state of war and siege, articles 8 and 11.

[8]Law-decree of 10 December 1916.

[9]Royal Decree of 31 May 1917.

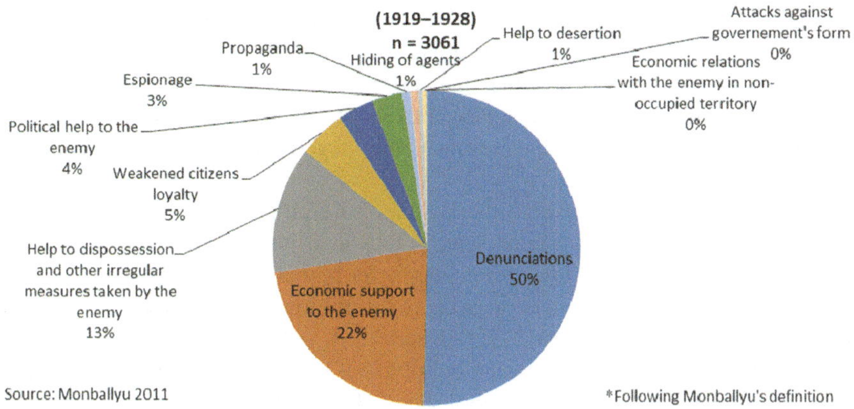

Fig. 2 Proportions of civilians sentenced for "incivisme" (1919–1928) (*Source* Monballuy 2011)

although only for militaries.[10] Regarding civilians, we may rely on the notion of 'political crime', which is directly related to the type of penalty and to the status of the convict inside the prison. While ordinary criminals were sentenced to either 'reclusion' (from five to ten years), 'forced labour' (up to perpetuity) or the death penalty, political criminals were subjected to 'detention' penalties (up to perpetuity as well). The detention regime granted political criminals with privileged incarceration conditions. According to pre-war legal reasoning, political crimes 'suppose less perversity than audacity, less corruption in the heart than anxiety in the mind, in one word, less vice than passion'. For this reason, 'political crimes cannot be compared to other crimes'[11] (Nypels 1878, 35). This rather romantic description of political crimes reflected the certain tranquillity that prevailed in Belgium regarding its political safety before 1914. However, this view was about to be challenged by the experience of the Great War.

Most forms of threat against state safety were considered political crimes and as such were subject to detention penalties. However, the political qualification did not systematically fit with this penal code section (art. 101–136), as some political crimes were to be found in other sections of the code,[12] while those dealing with state safety could lose their political status under certain conditions.[13] Although detention was exclusively reserved for criminals, some delinquents were also considered political—in particular, those threatening state safety—and were granted a similar protection in jail. Formally though, they were exposed to 'imprisonment' (up to five years) or financial penalties, as were the ordinary delinquents. Last but not least, most special

[10]The term "treason" (*trahison* in French, *verraad* in Dutch) is defined in art. 15 of the Belgian military code.

[11]Translated by the author.

[12]Such as articles 234–235 and 255 targeting civil servants plotting or abusing their authority.

[13]Namely, when political motives implied an ordinary crime, usually a violent one such as murder. The political crime was then considered as a mixed crime and exposed to ordinary penalties.

laws also targeted mere delicts, and therefore foresaw imprisonment penalties. The actual political status of this latter category inside the prisons is not very clear, since it was not formally included in the state safety legal section. But if we leave this uncertainty aside, 'crimes and delicts against the state safety', 'political infractions' and 'detention' with privileged conditions were largely overlapping notions before the war.

However, on 11 October 1916 the Belgian government increased the penalties for most crimes and delicts against state safety, as it introduced the death penalty for military espionage (art. 116), for economic or human support to the enemy (art. 115 §3), for weakening soldiers or citizens loyalty towards the state (art. 115 §4) and for hiding enemy agents (art. 121). In addition to more severe penalties for these offences, those changes also affected the political protection of the offenders. The detention penalty was not formally abolished—the death penalty was prescribed for the worst cases only—and in fact the changes allowed the government to commute death penalties into ordinary ones—most often forced labour—as it had been the common practice before the war. The complete exclusion of those offences from the political status was formally established after the war by the Royal Decree of 30 July 1919. Minister of Justice Vandervelde clarified the government's will, arguing that 'the notion of political infraction, under the current circumstances, includes facts that are or may be, in reality, not political at all, such as treason, espionage, trafficking with the enemy, etc.'[14] The government therefore added article 276*ter* to the 1905 General Rules of Procedures of the prisons, stating that:

> Are excluded from the regime established for political convicts, individuals sentenced under §§ 1, 2 and 3 of art. 115 of the penal code [military, economic or human help to the enemy], as well as those sentenced to treason and espionage. Those sentenced under art. 115 §4 of the penal code [weakening citizens loyalty] can only be granted of this regime by means of a special decision of the minister of Justice.

Hence the war had a direct restrictive effect on understanding political offences, as most political criminals became excluded from a guaranteed protected status, the obtaining of which was no longer a regular judicial procedure but had turned to a political one.

Consequently, when the Belgian government created two new categories of crimes and delicts against state safety with the law-decree of 8 April 1917, it denied them the detention regime. Denunciation to the enemy was criminalised by the creation of article 121*bis*[15] and punished by imprisonment, reclusion or forced labour, while political aid to the enemy (art. 118*bis*) was to be punished by 15 to 20 years of forced labour. As clarified in the Royal Decree of 30 July 1919 (art. 276*quater*), both offences could benefit entirely or partly from the detention regime but had to also request a special approval by the minister of Justice. The fact that article 118*bis* specifically targeted 'political' aid to the enemy while being dismissed from the detention regime was not merely ironic; it was paradoxical. The governmental worry about the situation in occupied Belgium had indeed moved since the beginning of the

[14]Royal Decree of 30 July 1919 (translated by the author).

[15]Regarding denunciation I refer the reader to the chapter of Gertjan Leenders in this book.

war from a purely military towards a growingly political concern, which contrasted with the restriction of political protections for convicts.

Back in 1914, the first and paramount focus of the newly at war Belgian State was to further detail and more heavily repress espionage. During its last session on 4 August 1914, as the German troops were crossing the national border, the Belgian parliament hastily adopted six new variants to article 120 of the penal code on the transmission of state secrets and severed other related provisions. This early legislative inflation targeting almost exclusively espionage contrasts with its utility after the war[16] and reflects the importance of the spy mania in that context. But two and a half years after the invasion, the political danger in occupied Belgium had become more prominent. The political division policy of Belgium pursued by the Germans, which consisted in favouring the Germanic Flanders—a policy known as the *Flamenpolitik*—was having some success with the foundation of the Flemish Academy of Ghent (*Vlaamsche Hoogeschool*) in October 1916 and that of the Flemish Council (*Raad van Vlaanderen*) in February 1917, meant to support an autonomous Flanders (Wils 2014, 193–225; Loockx 2013). The Belgian government specifically targeted such political collaboration in April 1917 (art. 118*bis* of the penal code), but the criminalisation of denunciation (art. 121*bis*) in the same decree meant that political loyalty was expected and mandatory for all Belgians, who were forbidden to bypass the Belgian and only legitimate judiciary system to solve their disputes in occupied Belgium. The creation of these two new crimes illustrated a resolute switch from a military and espionage-centred concern towards a deeper, political-oriented and patriotic control by the state over Belgian behaviour. The fact that this evolution led simultaneously to a reduced understanding of political crimes and to their narrower protection is a remarkable paradox. It probably best illustrates, however, how the totalisation process took place during the Great War and how it specifically affected Belgium. It had direct consequences at least on the penitentiary repression after the war.

2 The Post-War Penitentiary Repression

In 1919, the average population in Belgian prisons reached 6230 prisoners, that is, 40.6% more than the average number of prisoners for the year 1914 (see Fig. 3). Although these numbers are merely averages, they emphasise the significance of the 3061 convicted *inciviques* reported above when situated in their penitentiary context. It would take three years, until 1922, for the prison population to gradually shrink to its pre-war level. This sharp rise of the prison population was part of a larger wave starting in 1915 with the increasingly severe German repression, which reached its peak in 1918 and then constantly declined until the mid-1920s to below its pre-war level. In 1915, no less than 20% of the prisoners in Belgian prisons

[16] Only one case would be condemned according to these new articles (art. 120 *quinto* on forbidden photos), on top of the 95 spies sentenced following article 116 of the penal code.

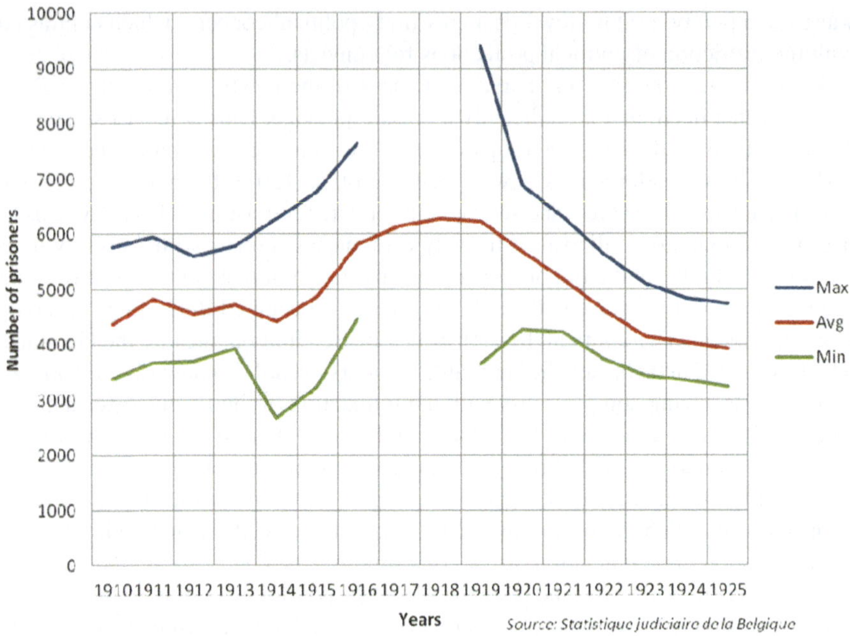

Fig. 3 Yearly Belgian prison population (1910–1925)

were detained under the request of the German authorities, a proportion that is not given for the following war years.[17] This percentage certainly became higher in the next years, however, as the number of prisoners significantly rose from 1916 onwards in an uninterrupted growth until the end of the war. Simultaneously, the number of prisoners committed by the Belgian justice system inside the prisons was reduced—by 14.1% from 1914 to 1915—in order to make more room for the German needs.[18]

As noted by Drossens et al. (2011, 102) in the case of the secondary prison of Ghent, the Germans emptied the sections they had requisitioned before leaving the country in October and November 1918. In Ghent the prison population was even reduced from 667 to 80 prisoners in one month's time, which reveals how some prisons had been almost entirely taken over by the German authority by the end of the war. The registers of the prison of Antwerp show that 5012 prisoners had been incarcerated under German request between 26 October 1914 and 13 February 1916,[19] i.e., during a little more than one year. Given that Belgium at the time

[17]This proportion is based on the number of days of detention in Belgian prisons. *Statistique Judiciaire de la Belgique*, 1915: XXVII.

[18]This drop of 14.1% between 1914 and 1915 is indeed too significant to be explained by natural variations alone.

[19]Belgian State Archives (henceforth BSA), Beveren depot, *Strafinrichting Antwerpen overdracht 1996*, n°776–778.

counted 29 prisons of various sizes, there were probably several dozens of thousands of Belgians repressed by the German authorities throughout the Belgian prisons, even if most stayed in jail only for a few days or weeks. After Ghent prison was emptied by the Germans, it was filled up again by the Belgians in the first months of the liberation: in April 1919, the secondary prison of Ghent counted again almost 600 prisoners, far more than it was built for—officially around 380 places. This number then gradually reduced until October, to stabilise around 330 prisoners (Drossens et al. 2011, 105). The new prisoners of this Belgian post-war repression obviously included many Belgians suspected of being anti-patriotic, but one of the largest groups among the new convicts was actually made of deserters. In Antwerp, no fewer than 236 deserters were counted against only 66 *inciviques* during the same period.[20]

The major rupture in the number of incarcerated prisoners between the German and the Belgian administration was short-lived. From a penitentiary perspective, Fig. 3 gives the impression that the repression by Belgians during the liberation was as severe as the German repression at its peak at the end of the war. However, these penitentiary numbers do not take into account the thousands of civilian prisoners detained in German prisons and camps. Furthermore, however striking at the time, the population increase in Belgian prisons (over 40%) might seem rather small in comparison to the estimated 40,000 to 70,000 detained people suspected of collaboration after the Second World War (Aerts 2013, 85–86). Yet the yearly average number of 6230 prisoners in 1919 says very little about the number of individuals who actually went to jail. It only expresses how many prisoners were kept *at the same time* in prison and gives merely an average. If many citizens were successively kept in jail for a short period in the direct aftermath of the war, the average number of the synchronic population of detainees would not have been much affected. Looking at the maxima and minima of the yearly population gives an idea of the important variations that affected the prison population. Despite the lack of data for 1917 and 1918, we can see an outstanding difference between the minimum and maximum peaks in 1919: from 3644 to 9398 prisoners (Fig. 3). It is tempting to interpret the gap between these two figures as the result of the German evacuation followed by Belgian repression at its highest. However, in January 1919 Belgian prisons were already getting full. If there must be such a minimum peak in 1919, it was probably due more to the Amnesty Law of 28 August, which suddenly released all delinquents who had been sentenced to less than one year of imprisonment. But more fundamentally, those peaks do not give the accurate maxima and minima of the synchronic population in Belgian prisons. They give instead artificially exaggerated sums obtained by the addition of individual prisons peaks that occurred at possibly different moments throughout the year.[21] Yet, despite the dubious methodological provenance of those peaks, they give an idea of the magnitude of the immediate

[20]This count was made on the basis of the penitentiary moral registers, including prisoners sentenced to at least three months of imprisonment, between February 1919 and February 1921. However, the count includes deserters from the trenches, refractory civilians hidden abroad during the war and also post-war deserters, while the 66 disloyal citizens do not include the women detained in Antwerp (BSA, Beveren depot, *Strafinrichting Antwerpen overdracht 1996*, n°316–320).

[21]See the detailed table in *Statistique Judiciaire de la Belgique*, 1919: 274.

post-war repression, the maximum peak being 36% higher in 1919 than in 1920 and 62.5% higher than in 1913.

According to Monballyu's legal scope of the judicial repression of *inciviques*, 3407 civilians were judged in 1919 and 1920 for their non-patriotic behaviour, which partly corresponds to that peak. In 1928, a total of 4645[22] civilians had been judged, 3061 of whom were sentenced (see Fig. 2 and Monballyu 2011, 43–44). This judicial repression, however does not take into account the numerous suspects who were arrested and then released without trial in the aftermath of the war. In March 1919, just for the district of Brussels, civilian prosecutors were investigating around 9000 foreigners to be expelled along with Belgians suspected of disloyal behaviour (Massin and Rousseaux 2008, 131). Two months later, in May 1919, the military prosecutor for the province of Hainaut had collected 5233 cases to be investigated, the vast majority of which seemed to be cases of suspected disloyal civilians (Baclin et al. 2010, 24), while the military prosecutor attached to the General Headquarter had, on a nation-wide basis, collected 4180 more suspect cases—including some militaries—(Baclin and Rousseaux 2008, 105). In the absence of a systematic study on post-war prosecution activity, the extent to which those numbers overlap with each other and the exact proportion of disloyal civilians among them are not entirely clear. However, if we combine all nine provinces and both military and civilian prosecution activity, we could extrapolate that the post-war period probably saw a couple dozens of thousands of citizens being investigated for their allegedly suspect behaviour towards the enemy. Far from all of them were incarcerated, however, and between the crowd of investigations and the 4645 judgements, the actual number of incarcerated civilians for *incivisme* largely remains uncertain. But the discrepancy between the suspected number of investigations and that of the judgements reveals how deeply rooted suspicion and anger had become in society and how eager Belgians were to begin judicial prosecutions, often regardless of legal grounds.

Despite artificially exaggerated peaks, prison population statistics presumably underestimate the actual detained population after the war, as they do not take into account detentions outside of official prison sites. There are few sources to document such extra-penitentiary internment centres, but various testimonies give us some insight. The Flemish activist Rosa De Guchtenaere complains, for instance, about her arrest on 17 November 1918 in Ghent by the Military Security Service (*Sûreté Militaire*)[23] *without judicial warrant* and her incarceration in a camp in Adinkerke.[24] This camp seems to have been erected at the liberation in order to receive suspected German residents or Belgians of German descent who were to be expelled following the law-decree of 12 October 1918 (Caestecker and Vrints 2014, 141). That same law-decree also foresaw the detention in those camps of Belgians on the sole basis that 'their relations with the enemy make them suspect'. Hence, suspected *inciviques*

---

[22]Monballyu gives a total of 4693 judgements, but that number includes 48 militaries judged for treason under art. 15 of the military penal code.

[23]On the Military Security Service, created in April 1915, see Bost (2015).

[24]BSA, Anderlecht depot, *Military Court*. Dossiers 1915–1954, box 163 B, file 2. Mentioned in Monballyu (2011, 181).

were handled in a different way than ordinary offenders: they could easily be detained in extraordinary detention camps, and they were falling under military jurisdictions for their trial and judicial investigations.

In the first months of the liberation, suspected offenders against state safety were indeed subjected to military tribunals.[25] From May until October 1919, only espionage and recruitment for the enemy were maintained under this exceptional regime. During that period, the Military Security Service was a key police force in arresting and investigating suspected 'traitors' (Baclin and Rousseaux 2008, 67–68). Military prosecutors could make arrest decisions without further institutional control, in contrast to the civilian system. Therefore, as the testimony of Rosa De Guchtenaere suggests, arbitrary arrests could take place. Oscar K. also complains of being detained in a prison since the Armistice, although he has never been interrogated (Baclin et al. 2010, 83). Even before making a formal arrest, Mélanie Bost notes that the Military Security Service used 'sorting camps' (*camps de triage*) in order to interrogate all suspects and to decide upon their formal arrest (2015, 177–178). It is unclear whether these camps were of a different sort than the one in Adinkerke, but such precarious arrests left some wounds. Two years after the war, the Flemish Catholic member of Parliament Frans Van Cauwelaert, who was keen to defend the Flemish cause, depicted the situation as follows: 'Respectable people were placed for months behind the bolts without investigations and were liberated afterwards without any trial. Others were freed from their cell after one year and, because of their imprisonment, had lost their wealth and social position'.[26] The exceptional treatment of political suspects came to a definitive end almost a year after the Armistice, in October 1919, with the formal end of the state of war.[27] If, between the Armistice and the end of the state of war, arrests and trial conditions continued to disadvantage political suspects, they were only a minority to benefit from the return of privileged detention conditions.

3 Behind Bars

Once sentenced to jail, the former political suspects became a heterogeneous group of prisoners, enduring various types and lengths of penalties. Moreover, political detention conditions were granted to prisoners by the minister of Justice on a case-by-case basis—except for those automatically excluded in July 1919. It is not possible

[25] By the law-decree of 11 October 1916, the exiled government had extended military judicial authority to judge civilians who were accused of offences against state safety (articles 101–136 of the penal code) as well as against the public security, especially criminal organisations and armed banditry (articles 322–326).

[26] *Annales parlementaires* 1920–1921, *Chambre*, 25 January 1921: 383. Quoted by Monballyu 2011, 181 (translated by the author).

[27] The exceptional authority of the military justice system regarding civilians was ultimately abolished with the end of the state of war on 30 September 1919, as declared by the Royal Decree of 21 September 1919.

to identify clearly who was granted political status and who was not on the basis of the used material. Combining formal judicial penalties and testimonies, however, gives some insight into the various conditions experienced by *inciviques* prisoners. On the basis of a selected sample of 134 prisoners,[28] it appears that the vast majority among them were considered to be mere delinquents, as 93 or almost 70% of them were sentenced to 'imprisonment' penalties (up to five years), often coupled with fines.[29] This penalty includes mainly prisoners convicted for denunciation or for economic help to the enemy, i.e., the two largest categories of *inciviques*, but it also includes some light political activists who worked for the Flemish Academy of Ghent or as pro-German journalists. If economic *inciviques* were banned from the detention regime, it is clear that activists could pretend to the protected status, as the testimony of Wies Moens attests (1980). The situation is less clear regarding those guilty of denunciation, however, since that motive served to condemn some forms of political disloyalty, sometimes even activists. Political activists seem overall underrepresented in Belgian prisons: they comprise only 4% of the sample while they represent 9% of the sentenced *inciviques* (art. 115 §4 and 118*bis* combined). Indeed, the vast majority of the condemned activists (63%) were sentenced in absentia, as most flew to Germany or to the neutral Netherlands at the liberation.

Next to this principal group of *inciviques* delinquents, the second most often applied punishment is the detention penalty (up to perpetuity, but usually between 10 and 20 years), representing 18% of the sample. It includes many prisoners convicted for espionage, as well as those having recruited workers for the enemy industry. Both offence categories were the longest to be maintained under military jurisdictions, until October 1919, and mainly detained offenders in central prisons (i.e., Leuven in this sample). Yet both are excluded from any political protection as from July 1919. In contrast to political activists, pro-German spies are particularly overrepresented, comprising around 12% of the analysed sample, while only 3% of condemned *inciviques* were spies. This overrepresentation is even more striking given that the majority of them also flew abroad after the war: 55% of them were condemned in absentia.[30] However, spies were the most severely repressed offenders in the category of treason, as they often directly led civilian resisters to death before German firing squads. Several spies were even sentenced to death, but their penalty was usually commuted to life at forced labour—no convicts were actually executed after the war. But their penalties were the longest, and they rarely obtained early release,

---

[28]This sample includes all collected individual files of *inciviques* prisoners from the Penitentiary Anthropological Laboratory of the prisons of Forest, Saint-Gilles, Antwerp, Liège and both Leuven Central and Secondary prisons, between November 1918 and December 1925. The total sample is of 145 convicts, but the penalty is indicated in 134 cases.

[29]This proportion of delinquents was probably even higher across the country, since this sample over-represents the heavier cases: it includes the Central prison of Leuven among merely five secondary prisons while there were merely two central prisons and 27 ordinary prisons in the whole country. Yet this sample includes the largest secondary prisons.

[30]In comparison to this, the rate of judgements in absentia for economic traitors is 34%. Since denunciation is a delict, judgements I absentia did not apply except in four aggravated cases that were criminalised. There are no national statistics regarding the judgement of delicts by default.

unlike activists, which explains their overrepresentation in prisons. Finally, only a few traitors were sentenced to reclusion or forced labour, among whom some more vocal political activists or aggravated cases of denunciation can be found.

Wies Moens was one of the lucky few prisoners to benefit from the privileged political status. As a Flemish activist, he played a leading role in the student life of the Flemish Academy of Ghent and participated in the propaganda in favour of an independent Flanders. After the war he was sentenced to four years of imprisonment and was incarcerated at the secondary prison of Ghent, from which he was liberated after fewer than two years (Moens and T'Sjoen 1998). Inside the prison, political prisoners like Moens had a higher status due to their privileges, which were often combined with a social gap compared to ordinary prisoners. Social differences indeed appear from the professions indicated in the penitentiary registers. Moens also mentions his encounter with a 'typical recidivist' during one of his trips between the tribunal of Antwerp and the prison: 'Twice I had to repeat my phrase: "I am a Flemish activist (*Ik ben Flamingant*)". He looked at me surprised, suspicious from the head to the feet … He didn't get a word of it' (Moens 1980, 16). Moens describes his fellow convicts as follows: 'A large number among those men is illiterate, do not know the delight of reading and thinking. Day after day they are bent forward on miserable works: sticking sacks, knitting nets, making mousetraps; going out in the open air for half an hour; staying locked in for the rest of the day' (Moens 1980, 32). Not only convicts condemned to forced labour but indeed all ordinary convicts were forced to work. Political prisoners and detained defendants waiting for their judgement were exceptions in this regard. The main difference regarding the work of ordinary convicts was the salary they received for their work: prisoners condemned to forced labour received only three-tenths of the normal salary, those to reclusion four-tenths and imprisoned delinquents perceived half the salary. Those for whom labour was facultative, like political prisoners and defendants, received seven-tenths of the salary. Moreover, optional workers could get their salary in full, while ordinary prisoners had access to half their total pay only, called *pécule*, at their disposal at the penitentiary canteen.[31] This *pécule* was used by prisoners to buy extra food or various extras, as the detained spy Raoul C. notes in a letter: 'This way I could get for a price that defies all competition, the few books I wanted, also the smoking pipe I missed, and for the cold times, you made me consider the possibility to purchase a fanciful pullover'. Certainly the hierarchy of salary among prisoners had an impact on their daily lives, namely, affecting their negotiating power with the guards and with other prisoners. Emmanuel Debryune notes at least that, regarding Belgian political prisoners detained in Germany as resisters, the relationships were modified after the authorisation for political detainees to receive parcels from their family or charities at the beginning of 1917, as it developed various channels and in turn affected the guards' authority (Debruyne 2015, 164).

Instead of working constantly, political prisoners could receive up to three newspapers a day and order books outside of the (selective) prison library. They could also walk two hours per day in the courtyard instead of thirty minutes and, before

[31] *Règlement général des prisons*, Royal Decree of 30 Septembre 1905, articles 330–346.

their condemnation, were allowed during those walks to remove their hoods, to see each other and talk together. Moens reports that his 'neighbour' was the Professor of the Flemish Academy Lodewijk Dosfel, with whom he chatted and studied poems during their joint walks (Moens 1980, 20). By contrast, ordinary prisoners were not allowed to speak and see each other, as the hood was mandatory at all times for them outside their cell. In December 1919, Moens writes: 'I don't know whether the evil ones have another face than the good guys. Wrongdoers are wearing a hood on their head. I never saw the face of a villain. Even my own face I can't see it' (Moens 1980, 6). This extreme isolation is a recurrent source of complaint from prisoners subjected to the ordinary detention regime, working all day long alone in their cell. The spy Raoul C., as ordinary prisoner, claimed that he was becoming mad 'like a rabbit' in his cell: 'No doubt that nine months of inactivity and isolation, when having weak nerves, results in the complete destruction of the nervous system'.[32] Henri H., detained in the prison of Forest in Brussels for having worked as a food controller for the Germans, also complained about his nerves as he asked the Anthropologist doctor of the prison for some medication, as well as more time in the courtyard and more books: 'if I had some intellectual work to do, I could find there a salutary distraction (…) instead of thinking about things that obsess my mind, since manual work is combined to my dark thoughts'.[33] Raoul C. further reported: 'I miss some conversation, some distraction, fresh air, a better food and more tiredness. I need to exteriorise the unhealthy ideas that haunt me and I can't do that here, seating at my table for 10 hours and busy (…) at a purely mechanic work'.[34]

As a result, if we believe Moens, ordinary inmates could look at political prisoners with some consideration: 'They always have one question ready in their mouth, when they accidentally see one of us coming closer: "Mister, no news about the pardon?"—In their view we are the "Misters", who are reading newspapers, who receive visits and walk long outside', he notes (Moens 1980, 32–33). Indeed, political prisoners could also receive visits every day as political delinquents, twice a week as political criminals. It was only twice a month for imprisoned delinquents, once a month for criminals condemned to reclusion and once every two months for those to forced labour, normally on Sundays. The visits took place in a special room for political prisoners instead of behind the bars of the parlour. Political defendants were even allowed before their condemnation to exchange letters without control and censorship from the prison direction.[35] Yet, in the immediate aftermath of the war, furtive conversations among prisoners as described by Moens were systematically repressed by the penitentiary authorities for political prisoners as well: in 1919, 21% of the disciplinary punishments were repressing communications or attempts at

[32]Belgian State Archives (henceforth BSA), Leuven depot, Central prison of Leuven, Penitentiary Anthropological Laboratory (hencefort PAL), Box 11, file 781 [letter of 10 March 1928 (translated by the author)].

[33]BSA, Cuvelier depot in Brussels, *Prison of Forest*, PAL, box 34, file 1604, undated letter (translated by the author).

[34]BSA, Leuven depot, Central prison of Leuven, PAL, Box 11, file 781, letter of 6 November 1930 (translated by the author).

[35]*Règlement général des prisons*, article 252*bis*.

communication among prisoners, a ratio that grows to 26% in 1920.[36] The majority of disciplinary punishments were fines to repay damages caused to the building or its furniture. But prisoners were also repressed for their communication, for smoking in their cells, for being seen at the cell window, for uncleanliness, for possessing forbidden objects, corruption attempts, fighting, bad will at work or falsification of the work register. In such cases the prisoners were most frequently put under the 'bread and water' regime, but in the most severe cases they were locked in a repression cell (*cachot*), where they could remain officially up to nine days. They could also be deprived of particular advantages (letters, visits, walks etc.) or excluded from the penitentiary school. In some cases, the extreme isolation of prisoners and the mental torture they endured could lead them to commit suicide. In 1919, 39 prisoners attempted to hang themselves in their cell, jumped from the balcony or drank a corrosive substance. Thirteen effectively died. In 1920, 54 attempted suicide and 17 died.

On 24 March 1920, however, the reformatory minister Vandervelde issued a royal decree, which was a first step towards easing the solitary confinement regime. The hood, as symbol of the radical isolation, became optional. Moens testifies that this change was quickly implemented in the secondary prison of Ghent, as he writes on 28 July 1920: 'Every day I see here dozens of shadows of men in their white prison uniform. Pale, gaunt faces; greyish, weakened faces, where the eyes are burning deep and scabby' (Moens 1980, 32). Communication inside the prison was also partially authorised, and the letter received by the Anthropologist doctor from a former inmate who shared the cell of Léon D. in Forest[37] testifies that prisoners were no longer systematically detained alone in their cells. Partition walls in classrooms and chapels were also meant to disappear. However, Drossens, Vanhulle and Velle note that this measure remained a dead letter in the Ghent prison until after the Second World War (2011, 106). The easing of the solitary confinement regime indeed remained dependent upon the local penitentiary management, as the changes were merely 'facultative'. Helen Grevers observes in this regard that solitary confinement remained the dominant option in Belgium until the Second World War: only the huge flow of collaborators in 1944–1945 seemed able to force the definitive transition towards a more humane and more collective detention regime (Grevers 2011, 231–232).

[36] *Statistique judiciaire de la Belgique*, 1919: 282–283 and 1920: 320–321. Unfortunately, disciplinary statistics disappear from the records after 1920, which does not allow comparison as the solitary confinement regime changes.

[37] BSA, Cuvelier depot in Brussels, *Prison of Forest*, PAL, box 34, file 1653, letter probably written in November 1923.

4 Conclusion

The First World War had a paradoxical effect on political control by the state in Belgian society. While this control was intensified through the criminalisation of both political help to the enemy and denunciation in 1917, the very meaning and scope of political offences was simultaneously considerably narrowed, with espionage, treason and economic help to the enemy being excluded from that notion. This revised definition of a political infraction also led to a change in how the protected status of 'political prisoner' was assigned: it was no longer a regular judicial procedure but became a government monopoly. Rather than an automatic status granted according to the nature of the infraction, the status of 'political prisoner' became a political favour granted by the minister of Justice on a case-by-case basis. That transformation had concrete effects on suspects and convicts, as it broadened the scope of criminal political behaviours to include political help to the enemy and denunciation while worsening the detention conditions of most *inciviques*, who henceforth were relegated to the status of ordinary convicts. Thus, both old and new categories of political prisoners preserved a specific status as they all were exposed to precarious arrests in internment centres and to military jurisdictions. But only a smaller and largely new elite among them was elected to the privileged detention condition for the rest of their incarceration.

This deteriorated situation for most political prisoners was simultaneously accompanied by an improvement of the general incarceration conditions, however. The strict solitary confinement regime was liberalised from 1920, as the hood, mandatory silence or solitary detention in the cell underwent some adaptations. However, these changes remained limited until the Second World War. But this parallel evolution nevertheless illustrates the interactions that caused changes in prisoners statuses. In a way, the growing and politicised control over citizens' behaviour by the state went hand in hand with both a more humane consideration of ordinary criminals and a revalorisation and renewal of the political elite. Prisons therefore did not only play a significant role in the restoration of the post-war political rule in Belgium. They also were an instrument of the reconfiguration of the relationship between the state and its citizens.

References

Aerts K (2013) 'Repressie zonder maat of einde?' De juridische reïtegratie van collaborateurs in de Belgische Staat na de Tweede Wereldoorlog. Academia Press, Ghent

Baclin G, Rousseaux X (2008) Les pratiques judiciaires. In: Rousseaux X, Van Ypersele L (eds) La Patrie crie vengeance! La Répression des 'inciviques' belges au sortir de la guerre 1914–1918. Le Cri/CHDJ, Brussels, pp 103–130

Baclin G, Bernard L, Rousseaux X (2010) *En première ligne. La justice militaire belge face à 'l'incivisme' au sortir de la Première Guerre mondiale.* Brussels: State Archives of Belgium

Bost M (2015) Une nouvelle venue dans le paysage militaire et judiciaire belge: la sûreté militaire, produit de la Première Guerre mondiale. In: Cools M, Leroy P, Pashley V, Stans D, Testelmans E,

Van Acker K (eds) 1915–2015, Het verhaal van de Belgische militaire inlichtingen-en veiligheidsdienst; L'histoire du service de renseignement militaire et de sécurité belge. Maklu, Antwerp, pp 155–183

Caestecker F, Vrints A (2014) National mobilization of the descendants of German immigrants in Belgium (1914–1920). In: Panayi Panikos (ed) Germans as minorities during the First World War: An international comparative perspective. Routledge, Ashgate, pp 123–146

De Bont R (2001) Meten en verzoenen. Louis Vervaeck en de Belgische criminele antropologie, circa 1900–1940. *Cahiers d'histoire du temps présent* 9:63–104

Debruyne E (2015) Le réseau Edith Cavell. De femmes et des hommes en résistance. Racines, Brussels

Drossens P, Vanhulle B, Velle K (2011) Het dagelijks leven in de gevangenis voor de Tweede Wereldoorlog. In: Martyn G, Velle Karel, Drossens P, Wyns Nacy (eds) 150 jaar nieuwewandeling: gevangenis Gent (1862–2012). Snoeck, Ghent, pp 70–113

Grevers H (2011) De opsluiting van collaborateurs als proeftuin voor penitentiaire vernieuwing. Het Belgische en Nederlandse gevangeniswezen tussen 1946 en 1950. Journal of Belgian History 24:209–232

Leloup P, Rousseaux X, Vrints A (2014) Banditry in occupied and liberated Belgium, 1914–1921. Social Practices and State Reactions. *Social History* 39(1):83–105

Loockx K (2013) Vlaamsche studenten, komt naar Gent! Prosopografie van de studentenbevolking aan de Vlaamse Hoogeschool 1916–1918. Unpublished Master's thesis, Ghent University, Ghent. Accessible on http://lib.ugent.be/fulltxt/RUG01/002/060/140/RUG01-002060140_2013_0001_AC.pdf)

Majerus B (2004) Bruxelles, 1918: révolution et sortie de guerre. In: Chassaigne P, Largeaud Jean-Marc (eds) Villes en guerre dans le premier XXe siècle (1914–1945). Colin, Paris, pp 196–207

Majerus B (2007) Occupations et logiques policières. La police bruxelloise en 1914–1918 et 1940–1945. State Archives of Belgium, Brussels

Massin V, Rousseaux X (2008) Mesures de la répression: quelques chiffres. In: Rousseaux X, Van Ypersele L (eds) La Patrie crie vengeance! La Répression des 'inciviques' belges au sortir de la guerre 1914–1918. Le Cri/CHDJ, Brussels, pp 131–145

Moens O, T'Soen Y (1998) Moens, Wies. In Nieuwe Encyclopedie van de Vlaamse Beweging, 2066–2068. Lannoo, Tielt

Moens W (1980) Celbrieven. Introductory texts by Arthur De Bruyne and Eric Verstraete, 9th edn. Danthe N.V., Sint-Niklaas

Monballuy J (2011) Slechte Belgen! De repressie van het incivisme na de Eerste Wereldoorlog door het Hof van Assisen van Brabant (1919–1927). State Archives of Belgium, Brussels

Nypels JSG (1878) Le code pénal belge interprété, principalement au point de vue de la pratique. 1. Bruylant-Christophe & Cie, Brussels

Polasky J (1998) Vandervelde. Nouvelle biographie nationale 1:344–354

Rousseaux X, Van Ypersele L (eds) (2008) La Patrie crie vengeance! La Répression des «inciviques» belges au sortir de la guerre 1914–1918. Le Cri/CHDJ, Brussels

Tilly P, Deloge P (2012) Milieux économiques belges et occupation allemande de 1914 à 1918: une stratégie du moindre mal. Entreprises et histoire 68:11–27

Van Ypersele L (2008) Les violences 'populaires'. In: Rousseaux X, Van Ypersele, L (eds) La Patrie crie vengeance! La Répression des 'inciviques' belges au sortir de la guerre 1914–1918. Le Cri/CHDJ, Brussels, pp 33–59

Van Ypersele L, Rousseaux X (2005) Leaving the war: Popular violence and judicial repression of 'unpatriotic' behaviour in Belgium (1918–1921). European Review of History—Revue d'histoire européenne 12(1):3–22

Vanhulle B (2010) Geschiedenis achter de grendel? Bedenkingen over de Belgische en internationale gevangenishistoriografie. In: De Koster M, Rousseaux Xavier, Velles Karel (eds) Sources et perspectives pour l'histoire socio-politique de la justice en Belgique (1975–2005). State Archives of Belgium, Brussels, pp 171–190

Vanneste C (2015) L'usage des prisons en Belgique de 1830 à nos jours. Une analyse en termes d'économie politique de la pénalité. In: De Koster M, Heirbaut D, Rousseaux X (eds) *Deux siècles de justice. Encyclopédie historique de la justice belge*. Die Keure-La Charte, Bruges pp 219–237
Wils L (2014) Onverfranst, onverduitst? Flamenpolitik, Activism, Frontbeweging. Pelckmans, Kalmthout

Policing Occupied Countries: Gendarmes and Populations Facing Security Needs (1940–1944, Hainaut/Nord-Pas-de-Calais)

Jonas Campion

Abstract The German occupation from 1940 to 1944 was a paroxysmal crisis that led to a redefinition of security policies and practices within destructured societies. That situation created the need to reinvent the paradigm of protecting people and property faced with the new security conditions brought on by the multiplication of sources of law and of authors of violence as well as by new regulations. A delicate equation came to be established between the population, civil and military servants, the occupying authorities and those occupied: the boundaries of tolerance, repression and protection were blurred, whereas new behaviours and new categories of the population were criminalised, and living conditions deteriorated. This study concentrates on relations between gendarmes, populations and authorities during the 1940–1944 occupation, by proposing a cross-border approach that involves the Hainaut province in Belgium and the Nord-Pas-de-Calais in France. It aims to understand when and how the gendarmes redesigned their professional practices during the war. The key question is to evaluate the impact of the occupation on relations and interactions between gendarmes and civil populations when the first are policing.

The Second World War, which was marked by a military, political and ideological occupation of a broad part of Europe, was a paroxysmal crisis period, which resulted in a major shift in security-related policies, practices and requirements within societies in disarray. The 'traditional' paradigms of protection and repression fell under the pressure of events. This situation had indeed never been seen before. In democratic states, the shift in the relationship between police forces and populations reveals to us this crisis situation: before the war, the objective of the police was to schematically protect the majority of people by regulating and fighting a minority (of offenders). During the German occupation, the majority came to be seen as an at-risk population that must be controlled.

J. Campion (✉)
Centre Interuniversitaire d'études québécoises, Université du Québec à Trois-rivières, Trois-Rivières, Canada
e-mail: jonas.campion@uqtr.ca

M. Bost and A. Vrints (eds.), *Doing Justice In Wartime*,
Studies in the History of Law and Justice 19,
https://doi.org/10.1007/978-3-030-72050-6_6

The crisis was plural. War led to the multiplication and the acceleration of rules and laws and in numerous domains of daily life, criminalising behaviours that previously had been both legal and legitimate. In broad outline, at the *macro*-level in Western Europe's democracies, war led to a brutal questioning of the central state's structures and of its monopoly over legitimate violence that had gradually developed throughout the 19th century, along with the construction of the centralised state. During the German occupation, there was a competition between several order-keeping and repressive institutions. It was a case of doing justice on the one side (Zurné 2017) and policing on the other. The policing field, for example, was marked by the cohabitation of traditional national institutions, that of the occupants and—later on—of the allied forces, but also by the emergence of new police or military institutions, often unofficial—for example, the French Milice or the Rexist 'brigade A' and the 'bande Duquesne' in the Belgian Hainaut (Maes 1993). Furthermore, various resistance networks with growing revendications developed in the field. The war had other consequences on security matters, such as a *localisation* process that weakened central control (Wouters 2006), blurring traditional and social standards that had been commonly accepted until then. The war was also characterized by an ever-present use of weapons in the context of ever-increasing violence.

Whereas it has been broadly studied at the national and political levels, this phenomenon deserves a more detailed analysis at the local level or in a biographical perspective (Smeets et al. 2014). By means of such a local analysis, this study aims to scrutinise how the security frameworks were redefined between police forces, policemen, controlled/protected populations and tutelage authorities during the war. In this context, security is defined as a mission of public authorities to ensure the protection of property and the people, as well as the stability of institutions and social relations, in the short- and long-run. The study will focus on the Belgian province of Hainaut and the French departments of Nord and Pas-de-Calais. This cross-border and bilateral approach has a clear added value to understand the security stakes within a geographic area comprising many similar aspects (industrial and migration areas, traditions of social conflicts etc.), the same long-term military occupation and attachment to German MBB (Militärbefehlshaber in Belgien) in Brussels[1]—in spite of fundamental differences, starting with the nature of the 'national' authority in power during the war (Durand 1988). In France, the Vichy Regime had a political nature. It was established in June 1940 by a vote of the Third Republic Parliament (Wieviorka 2001). In contrast, the Belgian *Collège des Secrétaires généraux* was firstly an administrative instance: the Secrétaires Généraux were indeed at the head of the national administration. They later played a political role in occupied Belgium, due to the circumstances (Van Den Wijngaert 1975).

[1] We must note that the attachment of Nord-Pas-de-Calais to MBB (Militärbefehlshaber in Belgien) instead of MBF (Militärbefehlshaber in Frankreich) has no consequence on gendarmerie matters. Indeed, the French hierarchy of the institution in Paris will always be involved in the action and organisation of the 1st Gendarmerie Légion, around Lille, dealing with the German administration in Paris (Cazals 1994). About the difference between MBB and MBF related to the Nord, see Wouters (2005).

In other words, this chapter aims to study in a comparative perspective the transformations of security matters and practices on both sides of the Franco-Belgian border. Firstly we will give a general view on order and disorder transformation during the war. Later, we will highlight the consequences of this new order context on policing practices, when gendarmes conduct police work in interaction with the population. We will finally discuss the impact of this new context on the social integration of policemen, by emphasising the place and the role of the gendarmerie (Emsley 1999, 2014; Luc 2010; Luc and Houte 2016).

Present in many European countries since the conquests that followed the French Revolution, the gendarmerie is a full-fledged police institution that carried out administrative, judicial or state-related missions. At the dawn of the Second World War, the Belgian and French gendarmeries were still organised on the same model, sharing similar functions, rationales and values. The gendarmerie police force was always a powerful tool for ensuring the control of territories and populations and for strengthening central authority. Whether as national and military police forces entrusted with the mission to uphold the law through their various functions (protection of public order, crime repression and embodiment of the state sovereignty), the gendarmeries were at the heart of the *État-Nation* (nation-state) building and strengthening process in the nineteenth century. Consequently, they have been fully involved in the reforming and rebuilding process of the Western European states during and after the Second World War.

1 An Uncontrolled Situation: Factors and Chronology of Unrest in Occupied Territories

The study of the gendarmeries' and tutelage authorities' archives throughout the German occupation illustrates the gradual degradation of the security situation during the War. It mainly sheds light on the shift in the stakes related to the defence of property and the people, but also on the corresponding official rationales and discourses. Chronology is an interesting key to understand how the official perception of security was structured.[2] According to gendarmerie documents, the war period started with a phase of 'restoration' that lasted a few months in the wake of the defeats of summer

[2]For the Belgian case, the analysis is made with gendarmerie reports from La Louvière and Mons *districts* to Public Prosecutor of Mons (Mons, State Archives [hereafter AEMons], Parquet du Procureur du Roi, 725–727) and with *Compagnie de gendarmerie de Charleroi* reports (Brussels, Study Centre War and Society [hereafter CEGESOMA], Instruction en provenance du Parquet de Charleroi et du district de gendarmerie de Charleroi 1940–1943, AA 2072). For the French case, we use for the analysis the *registres de correspondance* (correspondence registers) from Nord and from Pas-de-Calais *compagnies* and also registers from the first *légion de gendarmerie de Lille* (Vincennes, Service historique de la défense, département gendarmerie nationale [hereafter SHD-DGN], 59E, 62E and 1D1). We also mobilise archives from the *Direction générale de la gendarmerie nationale*/General Directorate from French Gendarmerie (SHD-DGN, 1A).

1940. It was characterised by the police's will to reinvest territories on the one hand,[3] and by the need to deal with the defeat's consequences on the other hand. Afterwards, there was a period of seeming normality, the duration of which varied in France and Belgium (end 1940–mid-1942). In spite of the occupation and the challenges that it entailed, it was defined by the gendarmes as a period of continuity with pre-war security issues and described as a period of relative calm. Unrest was still limited to some (traditional) at-risk social groups and was only present in some restricted places. Notwithstanding the discourses of 'National Revolution' put forward by the authorities, as was the case in France, it resulted in a situation that seemed 'under control' in terms of order-keeping and consequences, or at least in a discourse that insisted on this image.

From the year 1942 onwards, the situation gradually changed. According to the gendarmerie reports, this year was a real transition period, in Nord-Pas-de-Calais as well as in Hainaut. Factors of tension multiplied. The situation had never been seen before by the policemen. Several kinds of reasons could explain the shift. Firstly there are national reasons, such as the enactment of the STO (*Service du travail obligatoire*/Compulsory Labour Draft). Political changes must also be considered. The come-back of Pierre Laval into office as head of the Vichy French Government in April 1942 or, in Belgium, the rise in power of Gérard Romsée as head of Ministry of Interior in 1941 (Raskin 1995) and of Colonel Emiel Van Coppenolle as head of the Royal General Police/*Police générale du Royaume* in 1941, then of the gendarmerie in 1943, had a major impact on security policies and practices (Fransen 2001). Both Romsée and Van Coppenolle were members of the *VNV* (*Vlaams Nationaal Verbond*), the Flemish Nationalist political movement. They reformed the police and security system in order to increase Flemish influence within it. They also refused to make a distinction between political and common-law criminality. Both continually were asking for strong police action against crimes and disorders.

There are also institutional reasons. The archives testify that in 1942, the turnover in the gendarmerie's management and staff began to produce important consequences in comparison with the 1940 situation, both at the local and national levels. In Belgium, for example, the staff grew more than 30% during the occupation, and more than 30% of pre-war officers were subjected to a political purge between 1940 and 1943.[4] The recruits were trained in new gendarmerie schools and were concentrated in some mobile units. In 1944, the Belgian gendarmerie was often considered

[3]After the 1940 military campaign, some areas in France—such as the Nord Departement—or in Belgium lacked any gendarme presence, due to retreat or military operations. The gendarmerie re-implantation remained a subject much discussed between German and National authorities during the occupation: occupying authorities using the situation to pressure the occupied authorities in order to get better cooperation. The re-implantation of gendarmeries only ended in April 1941 with the 1st gendarmerie legion (AEMons, Parquets du Procureur du Roi, dossier relatif à la réinstallation du groupe territorial de gendarmerie de Mons, n° 730; SHD-DGN, 1D1 1, historique de la légion (1940–1946), [11/1952]).

[4]Brussels, State Archives, Fonds de l'activité du HCSE, AA 1311, n° 2008, corps de gendarmerie. Situation à la date du 15 septembre 1943, s.d.; Brussels, Police Museum, Fonds École de Tervueren, carton n° 1, cadre des officiers de gendarmerie [06/1942].

as divided between a 'new' and the 'old' gendarmerie. Only the new one was seen as trustworthy by the German and collaborationist authorities. The same purges took place in France in order to ensure its 'quantitative and qualitative' turnaround.[5] An estimated 6000 French gendarmes were subjected to disciplinary and/or political measures during the occupation.[6]

So there are international reasons to explain the 1942 security shift, as part of the total war perspective. But there are also very local ones. The 1942 security shift must also be analysed within a local context. It depended upon the regional structures and networks of resistance and collaborationist groups, on people in charge of state functions, on specific industrial and economic stakes[7] and also on regional geographical challenges and particularities.

From 1942 onwards, the reports testify to a multiplication of acts of violence and destruction of private and public properties: attacks on mines and factories, sabotage of roads and railways, arson attacks on farms and crops, ration stamp thefts, robbery or destruction of identity documents and official records and damage to properties owned by collaborators (Laplasse and Steen 2005). Assassinations and homicide attempts occurred with increasing frequency. In Belgium, we can observe 109 homicides in 1941, 216 in 1942, more than 700 in 1943 and 1,852 the next year. Hainaut can clearly be described as a hot spot in terms of such crimes (Vrints 2005; Vrints et al. 2008; Thiry 2016).[8] The rise of violence gained momentum in 1943 and climaxed in 1944. By that year the situation was out of control by Justice,[9] police or gendarmerie. The lack of official control over the situation was unprecedented in the contemporary history of France and Belgium. Within an increasingly repressive regulatory framework, the gendarmerie reports reflect a period of unrest, marked by a collective, limitless, omnipresent, unexpected, broadly political and ideological violence. This violence was exerted within both the private and public spheres and involved the population as a whole; it was not confined to only its usual targets (fringe groups, foreigners etc.).

The gendarmeries' activity reports and their tone prove the gradual loss of control by the gendarmes—and the state's structures—in carrying out their mission. Risk and uncertainty became the norm. While in the years 1940–1941 the reports still mentioned mere 'marauding' as a factor of unsafety, later reports described 'assaults',

---

[5]Paris, National Archives [hereafter NA], Secrétariat général du gouvernement et services du Premier ministre, F60 501, lettre de l'Amiral Darland au général Huntziger, n° 3994/SCa, 13 September 1941.

[6]SHD-DGN, 1A 237–275.

[7]The long-term impact of the miners's strike in Nord-Pas-de-Calais in May–June 1941 must be considered (Dejonghe and Le Maner 1999).

[8]For the case in France, similar in many ways, see Chesnais (1976), Capdevila (1999: 124–137) and Berlière and Liaigre (2012).

[9]See Jan Julia Zurné's contribution in this volume.

led by 'armed terrorist groups', which had to be countered by setting up several 'interventions plans'[10] and a will to 'regain control of the units'.[11]

Available data show the seasonal and progressive nature of security challenges and attest to growing insecurity. The Belgian example is revealing in this regard. In March 1943, the gendarmerie district of La Louvière reported the following judicial police data:

> two assaults against properties, 1 murder, 1 armed robbery attempt, 2 arsons, 1 armed extortion, 1 assault and battery, 3 armed assaults, 3 fake milk frauds, 3 lethal accidents in a coalmine, 1 fake stamp traffic, 2 deadly railway accidents, 1 breach of trust, 1 armed assault.[12]

This was still a hybrid situation, between 'regular' and 'wartime' duties. By contrast, in September of the same year, seven armed assaults against individuals took place in the district, as well as 18 crop arsons.[13] In the following months, cattle thefts increased. The April 1944 report noted nine armed assaults, seven armed attacks and 13 cattle thefts.[14] In July, 26 assaults and 23 armed robberies were committed in the district.[15] If impressive, these figures do not take into account the sabotage actions perpetrated in the region: one in April 1943 (on a railway), three in October (not including crop arsons), 14 in April 1944, 21 in July. Thus, gendarmes were increasingly called up for surveillance duties of infrastructure, factories, mines and electric lines but were also mobilised to protect public officials.[16] The number of special duties carried out by the gendarmes in order to guarantee the security of various infrastructures followed this progression to reach several hundred extra duties a month.[17]

---

[10]Like the plan 'maintien de l'ordre', in the French gendarmerie, which was activated after the Normandy landing, in order to protect gendarmes or their families from resistance attacks. It was also activated in order to group the units in some cities to avoid desertions in favour of the French resistance (SHD-DGN, 1A 482, note faisant ressortir la situation d'ensemble de la gendarmerie de la zone sud à la date du 10 juin à 18 heures, 10 June 1944). In Belgium it is also possible to observe traces of such plan during the first half of the year (Van Geet 1992, 185–188).

[11]SHD-DGN, 1A 482, note aux commandants de légion [06/1944].

[12]AEMons, Parquet du Procureur du Roi, compagnie La Louvière, 726, rapport n° 604 du commandant de compagnie au Procureur du Roi, 8 April 1943.

[13]AEMons, Parquet du Procureur du Roi, compagnie La Louvière, 726, rapport n° 1944 du commandant de compagnie au Procureur du Roi, 7 Octber 1943.

[14]AEMons, Parquet du Procureur du Roi, compagnie La Louvière, 726, rapport n° 854 du commandant de compagnie au Procureur du Roi, 8 May 1944.

[15]AEMons, Parquet du Procureur du Roi, compagnie La Louvière, 726, rapport n° 1593 du commandant de compagnie au Procureur du Roi, 7 August 1944.

[16]E.g., Police Museum, dossier individuel maréchal des logis L., rapport du SE, 26 October 1945.

[17]The same can be seen in France. See, e.g., SHD-DGN, 1A 34.

2 The Consequences of the New Security Challenges for the Gendarmeries

The discourses that were held at the *meso*-level by the gendarmerie hierarchies also provided clear evidence of this new (uncontrolled) security situation. The policing strategies to deal with these new and multiplied risks were plural, blurring old and never-seen elements. Even more than in normal times, there was a call for effectiveness and firmness. The message was clear: the security mission was absolute, and gendarmes were not supposed to question the difference between patriotic acts and common-law crimes. 'This is not a time to wrestle with one's conscience' said the Head of the French gendarmerie in June 1943.[18] After being appointed in February 1943, Colonel Van Coppenolle, the new chief of the Belgian gendarmerie and a partisan of the New Order, carried out a tour of the units where he developed these arguments.[19]

The security situation and these strong hierarchical directives, which were both repressive and ideological in nature, resulted in a transformation of professional doctrines. And so the gendarmerie's practices changed during the course of the occupation: in France, the gendarmes' education and formation was adapted, as is shown in the presentation of the gendarmes' training curriculum in France (Spring 1944): the agents' training had to emphasise the military nature of administrative police,[20] and the emphasis was more on (para)military tactics than on judicial inquiries, police matters and development of strong and fruitful relationships with citizens:

> An in-depth basic military education will be provided in order to instil discipline and military ethos in the students, as is necessary for any gendarme when assigned to a brigade, as well as training for the use of weapons on duty in the gendarmerie. Professional instruction will only be aimed at teaching students the foundational principles of gendarmerie duty. The study of offences, in particular, will be limited to those most commonly observed.[21]

Further, it was recommended to increase the unit's staffing and to carry out operations involving a high number of gendarmes, policies that no longer fit with the model of a gendarmerie that had close contact with the populations. Indeed, the population as a whole was presumed to be dangerous.[22] It is a consequence of the increase of violence in public space. It is also a consequence of war regulation on the one hand (more people are now 'outlawed') and of new profiles and practices of gendarmeries on the other. It is still linked with the growth of threats and attacks against gendarmes

---

[18]Paris, NA, GPRF, Quatrième et Cinquième République. De Gaulle avant 1959, sous-série 3 AG, n° 346, document 'la gendarmerie ne doit pas scruter sa conscience'. Copie d'un ordre du 9 Juin 1943, 27 July 1943.

[19]Police Museum, Fonds Tervueren, boîte n° 2, compte-rendu de la visite du colonel Van Coppenolle à Arlon, 4 March 1943. This idea was developped after the war by Van Coppenolle in several texts he wrote (Van Coppenolle 1953, s.d.).

[20]SHD-DGN, 1A 482, Général Martin aux unités, 12 June 1944.

[21]SHD-DGN, 1A 482, Général Martin au général commandant la gendarmerie de l'Ile de France, 22 June 1944.

[22]SHD-DGN, 1A 482, note aux commandants de légion, 11 June 1944.

and their barracks.[23] Gendarmes tried to manage the risks they lived with by being careful when dealing with (unknown) citizens.

Although these methods of 'force concentration' and 'territorial occupation' were not entirely new for the gendarmerie—such methods had been partially employed in response to the inter-war period's social movements in France and Belgium (Campion 2015a, b)—they nonetheless marked a clear shift in policy as they tended to become the norm, everywhere in the countries. This led to a paradoxal situation, where some areas were overstaffed and others understaffed. Gendarmeries concentrated units in some strategic areas, where it was possible to ensure the safety of the gendarmes or where it was necessary and/or possible to protect some infrastructure. At the same time, this made it easier for the Germans to watch the gendarmeries and intervene against them if necessary. So control by the gendarmerie was not more effective.

Then, the right to use weapons was made more flexible in France and in Belgium.[24] In France, the self-defence definition was changed. Gendarmes were now authorised to use their firearms faster in order to arrest offenders more easily but also to defend themselves. This new context led to a redefinition of the conditions of legitimate state violence, whose legacies would be discussed after the war (Lagrou 2011). From late 1943 to early 1944, this new policy resulted in the multiplication of specific plans supposed to enable the gendarmes to regain the upper hand in the best-case scenario, or to defend themselves in the worst-case scenario.[25]

The joint analysis of the increased unrest in the occupied territories and the institutional transformations within the *corps* testify to the unprecedented nature of the war for Belgian and French gendarmeries. Most of all, it reveals the blatant incapacity of the order-keeping institutions to carry out their missions and to live up to expectations. This situation, which was the same on both sides of the border, is typical of the combination of foreign military occupation, a weak state, an internal crisis of legitimacy and a socio-economic context of industrial areas, such as in the Hainaut or in the Nord department. The majority of gendarmes—often those already working before the war—suffered from this difficult situation.[26]

During the war, the gendarmes' missions grew. They had more and more to do, as a result of the increased regulation of the period. Their actions became more visible and were always more closely allied with German interests. They were thus more exposed (both symbolically and physically) to criticism, claims and retaliation. The gendarmeries were weakened and disorganised, as they were daily controlled, threatened and supervised by the Germans. Arrest and retaliation measures against gendarmes on the part of the occupying authorities multiplied. Threats and violence

---

[23] SHD-DGN, 1A 482 and 483.

[24] Brussels, Palace of Justice, Archives de l'Auditorat militaire, dossier colonel Van Coppenolle, boîte n° 5, note n° 2405 du commandant de corps de la gendarmerie, 6 August 1943.

[25] Cfr. supra concerning the French 'plan du maintien de l'ordre', or specific instructions for Belgian gendarmes of Charleroi and Mons areas (AEMons, Parquet du Procureur du Roi, n° 725–727).

[26] SHD-DGN, 1D1 23, R/4 légion de Lille, rapport n° 1/4 du colonel Demougin sur l'état d'esprit du personnel, 6 October 1944.

also came from resistance groups[27] or from collaborationist networks or institutions, like the French Milice. More than usual, policing became an individual and collective risk. Consequently, the gendarmes hesitated to undertake action in the legal and legitimacy crisis in which they lived, even if tactics and methods were reformed. As it marked a fundamental break with the previous policy that consisted in protecting the major part of the population and in restricting repression to deviant groups, gendarmes did not know how to work during the war. The political character that underpinned their actions (even more so within the French State than in Belgium), but also the direct consequences of their practices for the national citizens (arrests, deportations, hostage-takings by the Germans or simply huge everyday difficulties etc.) explain these difficulties.

3 Facing the Population: To Protect and/or to Punish?

Gradually, the conjunction of pressures that emerged from this increasing violence in a period of uncertainty and new institutional instructions directly impacted the gendarmes. As they lived with their family within the brigades' barracks, the various facets of their private (accommodation, the place of relatives, food supplies, means of subsistence) and professional lives were directly affected by the crisis context. The gendarmerie was on the frontline, assuming the role of and actor in the conflict; scapegoat and symbolic target both for the Germans, the resistance, collaborationists or the population. The gendarmes were exposed, as they were visible, easy to identify and locate. During the war, the profession of gendarme took an unprecedented turn in France and Belgium.

At the heart of the equation was the issue of defining the behaviours to adopt regarding assigned missions. Toward this end, the gendarmes working on the roads or in the villages needed to take a stance on the following aspects: obedience, effectiveness, zeal, professional achievements and relations with colleagues (Campion 2011, 2012). They had to assess the difficult balance between individual, collective groups' or social interests. A typical case for these conflicts of interest: how should a gendarme protecting ration stamps react when attacked? Should he protect supplies for the many to the detriment of the few (people defying the authority, resistants)? This was a real dilemma for gendarmes, as state servants, citizens and men, which was made even more complex by the collective nature of the assigned policing duties as well by as the difficult distinction between acts of resistance and the lure of profit for ordinary criminals. There was no certainty about motivations for offences: were they political, and so legitimate in a post-war perspective; or were they only common law crimes? The situation of gendarme M. in Lille is relevant. In 1944 he was escorting ration stamps with some colleagues when an attack occurred against them. Using his weapon, M. killed one attacker, who was in reality a true resistant. Gendarme M. had

[27] In France, it is possible to estimate that 50 gendarmes were executed by the resistance before the liberation (Cazals 2001, 171).

not been informed by his colleagues that such an attack was going to occur; there was not enough confidence between them. When other gendarmes only simulated a defence, gendarme M. was alone to react in order to actually defend the stamps, his life and the gendarmes' security.[28]

Food supply is also a relevant example. In a world where shortages were commonplace, one of the main missions of the gendarmes was to fight food-supply fraud and black-market operations. In Belgium, for example, special squads dedicated to the repression of fraud were organised in the gendarmerie in 1941 at a provincial level. These units concentrated new gendarmes, seen as more politicised and trustworthy by the collaborationist authorities. During the occupation in France and in Belgium, trafficking of all scales was repressed by special squads and ordinary gendarmes, leading to a growth of claims and resentment against them, now seen as problems by the population (Numa-Stevelberg 2007). Local compromises were sometimes seen, depending on circumstances and persons. Due to these missions, their legitimacy decreases even if gendarmes were only involved in applying new regulations and defending the law.

In France and Belgium, it is difficult to describe the behaviour of gendarmes as a whole. A minority of them had extreme behaviours, either 'true' collaboration or 'true' resistance (defined as an organised, convinced, active and early engagement). The large majority of gendarmes resided in a grey and shaded area without having very decided, constant or active attitudes. Their attitudes depend on many factors such as previous career, date of entrance into the gendarmerie (during or before the war); political motivations, familial situation and local circumstances. The personality of the gendarmerie intermediate hierarchy is also an important variable to understand the gendarmes' behaviour. In France, around Lens, the character of Lieutenant Fleurose is relevant. From 1940 to 1942—thus early during the occupation—he was a true leader for his men, giving a decisive impulse to fight the Communist party.[29] With his section, he was responsible for more than 200 arrests. He received commendations from Vichy for having disorganised the Communist party in the region. His action clearly influenced his subordinates' behaviour.

In Belgium, Capitaine-Commandant L. (Charleroi) is also representative of the hierarchy's impact on gendarmes' practices. He is also representative of the complexity of policing in wartimes. In 1942 he accepted a promotion to the rank of major—it was natural in his career path, following his views. He was later arrested by the Germans. Before these events, between 1940 and 1942, he gave an order asking to his subordinates to be efficient when they were working, even if it meant they must cooperate with Germans. He was involved in arresting communists and in investigating people who attacked members of the German Army. He asked gendarmes to transmit information on public order and on troubles to the German authorities.

[28]SHD-DGN, 1D1 12, R/2 légion de Lille, note n° 739/2, 28 February 1945.

[29]SHD-DGN, 1A 181, note n° 78/4, rapport du sous-lieutenant Millischer sur l'exécution du lieutenant Fleurose, 19 May 1945 and 1A 224, n° 43, rapport n° 76/4 du sous-lieutenant Garçon, commandant la section de Béthune, 19 April 1945.

Within his command, he focused on the importance of maintaining law, on the necessity of protecting Belgian interests, on the need for full obedience. But it was not entirely new: already in 1939, some claims from subordinates described him as a too strict, too disciplined officer. During the occupation first and then later, after the liberation, strong criticism emerged against him and his subordinates. Arrested by the resistance in September 1944, he committed suicide after a few days.[30]

The diversity of gendarmes' behaviours outlined a new type of relationship between the civilian populations and the gendarmes while they carried out their duties. New rationales for repression and protection in comparison with the pre-war period were established. In order to decide how to exercise police functions and in contrast with the instructions they were given (firmness and effectiveness), the gendarmes needed to take into account the geography, the temporality and the target groups of the missions with which they were entrusted. During the occupation at first, and later on during the liberation, the gendarmes had to face many criticisms. They became targets, more and more subjected to threats, which increased their risks. The criticisms undermined their authority and social integration. These criticisms came from different and sometimes opposed structured groups (resistance and collaboration movements) and also from ordinary citizens. On the one hand, the latter realised that policing could affect them directly by making it more difficult for them to get supplies, by hindering their movements, complicating their everyday life and jeopardising their own security (risk of deportation, arrest, compulsory work). On the other hand, the population realised that—in the context of exacerbated violence and unrest (presence of the Germans, rising criminality, violence perpetrated by the resistance and the collaborators, individuals defying the authority, fugitive Russian prisoners, etc.)—police officers and gendarmes (as well as the state they represented) were unable to ensure their protection and that of their properties for humanitarian, material, ideological and/or moral reasons. The risk—seen as a lack of safety and security—that had been an abstract notion for most people until then became concrete, ever-present and took many shapes.

Reports written by high-ranking officers regarding the situation of the gendarmerie *corps* underlined these criticisms, sometimes in veiled terms, as well as the distress they caused to the gendarmes.[31] Since they enabled people to speak 'freely'[32] again and questioned the actions taken during the war, purge proceedings carried out within the gendarmeries in the immediate post-war period provide extensive documentation about changes in the relationship between the gendarmes and civilians. Through these cases, the disclaimers—resistants or not—questioned the very existence of the institution and forced its members to take a stance on their behaviour.

---

[30] Jambes, Collection privée du colonel Claessens, doc 468.

[31] SHD-DGN, 1D1 16, note°3591, rapport du colonel Pellegrin sur les résultats des travaux de la CE de la 1ère légion de gendarmerie, 17 August 1945.

[32] A freedom of speech that must be critically interpreted by the researcher. Ideological, political or personal motivations can indeed strongly influence the argumentation.

The resistance fighters, whether they were structured in networks or not, or people who had been sued for 'patriotic' motives[33] led this undertaking. They put forward the fact that they had been victims of the gendarmes' actions. By doing so, they indirectly referred to the daily nature of the gendarmerie police force. They questioned its *habitus* between violent or authoritarian behaviours, its methods of social interactions, but also its main missions such as judicial investigations (judiciary police) and maintaining and re-establishing order (administrative police). In 1945, a gendarme of the Lille legion was denounced by the local resistance and charged with violence when he arrested two communists. The purge proceeding questions both the legitimacy of the arrest and the legitimacy of the violence against the arrestees. Finally, the purge commission did not ask to sanction the gendarme; it understood that it can be normal for a gendarme to use violence in some circumstances.[34] But within the claims, the resistance fighters also emphasised the role of randomness, which placed the gendarme in the wrong place at the wrong time so that he was forced to take action and had no possibility of avoiding it. In addition to complaints from members of resistance networks, there were also acerbic comments from 'ordinary people' who had been confronted with the gendarmes' firmness as they tried to survive during German military occupation. These complaints were related to the fact that the gendarmes had served the enemy's policy, or that of the collaborators. The 'proximity' between gendarmes and Germans is here an evidence of guilt. But mostly, the complaints were related to the direct consequences of gendarmes' actions on civilians, even if the actions were not directly involving Germans. The examples for this are varied: women who demonstrated for better supplies and were beaten by a group of gendarmes in Pas-de-Calais (1941)[35]; people arrested as they were transporting food supplies for their family whereas it was supposedly easy for the gendarmes to traffic food and participate in the black market[36]; and people arrested by gendarmes for thefts that were to the detriment of the Germans.[37] These complaints and their consequences reveal the importance of chronological variation in understanding the relationships between gendarmes and populations. Purges a posteriori shed light on these changes: at the end of the occupation, they illustrate how it seems obvious for citizens that gendarmeries are guilty. There is no understanding and no tolerance for their policing: in fact, purges confronted the various (perceptions of) personal, collective and institutional conflict temporalities. After the war, it took time to restore the understanding and the acceptation of gendarmerie policing within the population.[38]

---

[33] A notion that must be discussed in each case.

[34] SHD-DGN, 1D1 11, R/2 légion Lille, note n° 158/2, 12 January 1945.

[35] SHD-DGN, 62E 123, R/2 section Saint-Pol-sur-Ternoise, note n° 215/2, 6 March 1945.

[36] SHD-DGN, 62E 123, R/2 section Saint-Pol, note n° 147/2, 4 November 1944.

[37] Police Museum, dossier individuel gendarme D., lettre du général Leroy au commandant du groupe territorial de Mons, 1 July 1947.

[38] The *rapports sur d'état d'esprit du personnel* of the Lille gendarmerie *légion* testify to the progressive normalization of confidence between gendarmes and citizens (see SHD-DGN, 1D1 23, R/4 légion de Lille).

The purges, both judicial and internal measures, enable us to observe the difficult relationship between gendarmes and populations. These exceptional procedures, beginning at the end of 1944, had never before confronted the gendarmes. For the first time, each gendarme in Belgium and in France was under suspicion. The purge procedures must be defined as a political and exceptional justice. They testify first to the growing distance between citizens and gendarmes. They testify secondly to the legitimisation crisis lived by the gendarmes during and after the occupation. And finally, they show the support of the hierarchy and the authorities for the gendarmes. The hierarchy let time take its course in order to restore confidence between gendarmes and the population. During the purges, the gendarmerie hierarchies rendered decisions only against the most obvious 'collaborationist' or 'problematic' cases. If we look at the statistical data for the purges, the difficulties facing the gendarmeries are obvious: in the 1st *légion* of gendarmerie (Nord-Pas-de-Calais), 100% of the officers and around 12% of the subordinates were submitted to an inquiry by the purge commission. At the national level, the figures are similar: it is possible to estimate that around 10% of gendarmes and between 20 and 30% of the officers endured an internal inquiry in relationship with presumed collaboration. Claims are numerous, but the situation is nuanced by the effective rates of sanctions. More than 50% of the procedures were ended without any disciplinary measure. In Belgium, the assessment of purges is globally the same (Campion 2011).

4 Conclusions

The impact of the German occupation on security policies as well as on relations between the occupied populations and the order-keeping agents have to be analysed at several levels. War transforms the order-keeping conditions, the security definition and the ways of carrying it out. The three key elements of this new insecurity are the multiplication of acts of violence towards properties and people; the massive amount of repression exerted by both nationals and the Germans and, lastly, the competition regarding state-related functions. The conflict caused a shift related to the gendarmeries' place and the gendarmes' role at the national, local and individual levels in destructured societies. An approach focusing on the situations in Belgium and northern France enabled us to point out a few key elements in the disruption of police practices.

Firstly, it is obvious that, despite a national political frontier whose status changed due to the presence of the German occupier, (in)security conditions were largely comparable on both sides of the border. To a great extent, they were influenced by the fact that these regions were mainly industrial and densely populated and by the new stakes the conflict had brought about. In view of its purely political nature, the separation defined by the border did not alter the similarities between the social and economic contexts of both countries. The definition of the unrest; the feeling of unsafety lived by the civilians and the corresponding response from the state during the war were as much influenced by these contextual factors as by the established political regime. Vichy's political logic, imbued with a racist, anti-Semitic and repressive policy, was a multiplying factor for these general conditions.

The similarities observed on both sides of the border provide an opportunity to reconsider the chronology of the gendarmeries' policing on the one hand and the relationship between the gendarmes and the populations on the other hand. Even if the war created new ordinary (e.g., food supplies) or extraordinary tensions (e.g., acts of resistance), the tensions cannot be completely separated from the conditions that preceded the conflict. The regions of Hainaut and Nord-Pas-de-Calais were industrial areas, whose populations mostly were workers, who had long been structured around political organisations (trade unions, Communist party). During the 1930s, social movements in these regions multiplied and created resentments between the populations and the gendarmerie in some groups. The war reopened and amplified some of these sleeping conflicts in a new context. The gendarmes took advantage of their experience and their knowledge of the populations and social movements to 'behead' them when they were ordered to do so. The populations knew the reputation and the effectiveness of the gendarmes with whom they rubbed shoulders. The post-war period further strengthened the phenomenon. Indeed, the complaints voiced during the purge sometimes dated back to a time long before the conflict.

Therefore these conditions gave rise to a deep atmosphere of defiance in the execution of public functions between the gendarmes and the authorities, but also and mostly between the gendarmes and the populations. The main stake of the post-war period was twofold in this respect: on the one hand, restore the conditions for the re-establishment of order. Society needed to be disarmed and pacified in order to reassert the monopoly of the state. The gendarmerie as an institution and the gendarmes as individuals needed to regain the population's trust. Turning these goals into realities was the priority of the liberation. For the gendarmes, this required a convergence of political, material and human measures that needed to be fruitful at national, regional and local levels. Regarding the populations, it was necessary to rebuild a gradation of risks in terms of social groups considered as deviant. The chronology of these measures needs to be defined more accurately. When did the normalisation of the trust relationship between the gendarmes and the populations actually occur? More importantly, what was the exact scope of this normalisation in comparison with the pre-war period in a society where democratisation strongly accelerated? This also provides an opportunity to reconsider in the medium-term, beyond world wars, the evolution of the order-keeping practices and logics in which police institutions intervened.

References

Berlière J-M, Liaigre F (2012) Ainsi finissent les salauds. Séquestrations et exécutions clandestines dans Paris libéré. R. Laffont, Paris

Campion J (2011) Les gendarmes belges, français et néerlandais à la sortie de la Seconde Guerre mondiale. André Versaille, Brussels

Campion J (2012) Pratiques policières en temps de guerre: les gendarmes belges, français et néerlandais au prisme de l'épuration (1940–1948). Crimes, histoire & sociétés/Crimes, History & Societies 16(2):79–97
Campion J (2015a) Maintaining law and order in a democratic and Pilarised country: the Belgian Gendarmerie between 1918 and 1957. J Eur Hist Law 6(1):68–76
Campion J (2015b) Gendarmes facing political violence (Belgium, 1918–1940). In: Millington C, Passmore K (eds) Political violence and democracy in Western Europe, 1918–1940. Palgrave Macmillan, Basingstoke, pp 160–173
Capdevila L (1999) Les Bretons au lendemain de l'Occupation. Imaginaire et comportement en période d'une sortie de guerre 1944–1945. Presses universitaires de Rennes, Rennes
Cazals C (1994) La gendarmerie sous l'Occupation. La Musse, Paris
Cazals C (2001) La gendarmerie et la Libération. Résistance. Combats libérateurs. Réorganisation. Épuration. La Musse, Paris
Chesnais J-C (1976) Les morts violentes en France depuis 1926. Institut national des études démographiques/Presses universitaires de France, Paris
Dejonghe E, Le Maner Y (1999) Le Nord-Pas-de-Calais dans la main allemande, 1940–1944. La Voix du Nord, Lille
Durand Y (1988) Les pouvoirs indigènes en France et en Belgique. In: Dejonghe A (ed) L'Occupation en France et en Belgique. Revue du Nord HS 2:41–47
Emsley C (1999) Gendarmes and the state in nineteenth-century Europe. University Press, Oxford
Emsley C (2014) Gendarmerie policing. In: Bruinsma G, Weisburg D (eds) Encyclopaedia of criminology and criminal justice. Springer, New York and Heidelberg, pp 1869–1897
Fransen C (2001) Politiewerk in bezettingstijd. Emiel Van Coppenolle—korpscommandant van de Rijkswacht tijdens de Tweede Wereldoorlog. M.A. dissertation, Ghent University, Ghent
Lagrou P (2011) Regaining the monopoly of force: agents of the state shooting fugitives in and around Belgium, 1940–1950. Past and Present Supp 6:177–195
Laplasse J, Steen K (2005) Het verzet gewogen. Een kwantitatieve analyse van politieke aanslagen en sabotages in België, 1940–1944. Cahiers d'histoire du temps présent/Bijdragen voor de eigentijdse geschiedenis 15:227–260
Luc J-N (ed) (2010) Soldats de la loi, la gendarmerie au 20e siècle. PUPS, Paris
Luc J-N, Houte A-D (eds) (2016) Les gendarmeries dans le monde, de la Révolution française à nos jours. PUPS, Paris
Maes P (1993) Brigade A, bande Duquesne: 15 mois de terreur policière sur le centre. Centre de recherches et de documentation régionale, Houdeng Aimeries
Numa-Stevelberg R (2007) Les gendarmes et la population des Alpes-Maritimes face au ravitaillement et au marché noir. Force publique. Revue de la société nationale histoire et patrimoine de la gendarmerie 2:93–106
Raskin E (1995) Gerard Romsée: een ongewoon man, een ongewoon leven. Hadewijch, Antwerpen
Smeets J, Van Es T, Meershoek G (2014) In de frontlinie. Tien politiemannen en de duitse bezetting. Boom, Amsterdam
Thiry A (2016) Le tribut des temps troubles: la justice face aux homicides attribués à la résistance dans l'arrondissement judiciaire de Mons (avril 1944–septembre 1944). Presses universitaires de Louvain, Louvain-la-Neuve
Van Coppenolle E (1953) Wat ik nog te zeggen heb. Boekengilde Brederode, Sint Job-in-'t-Goor
Van Coppenolle E (s.d.) Souvenirs du chef national de la gendarmerie sous l'Occupation, 1940–1944. Mémoires 1910–1960. Unpublished
Van Den Wijngaert M (1975) Het beleid van het comité van de Secretarissen generaal in België tijdens de Duitse Bezetting. Palais des Académies, Brussels
Van Geet W (1992) La gendarmerie sous l'Occupation. J-M. Collet, Braine
Vrints A (2005) Patronen van polarisatie. Homicide in Belgïe tijdens de tweede wereldoorlog. Cahiers d'histoire du temps présent/Bijdragen voor de eigentijdse geschiedenis 15:177–204

Vrints A, Rousseaux X, Vesentini F (2008) Violence and war: measuring homicides in Belgium (1900–1950). In: Body-Gendrot S, Spierenburg P (eds) Violence in Europe: historical and contemporary perspectives. Springer, Berlin, pp 177–205

Wieviorka O (2001) Les Orphelins de la République. Destinées des députés et sénateurs français 1940–1945. Le Seuil, Paris

Wouters N (2005) Davantage la France que la Belgique. L'unicité du Nord-Pas-de-Calais 1940–1944. Cahiers d'histoire du temps présent/Bijdrage voor de eigentijdse geschiedenis 15:205–223

Wouters N (2006) Localisation in the age of centralisation: local government in Belgium and Nord-Pas-de-Calais. In: De Wever B, Van Goethem H, Wouters N (eds) Local government in occupied Europe (1939–1945). Academia Press, Ghent, pp 83–107

Zurné JJ (2017) 'Een buitengewoon verontrustend gewetensprobleem': De Belgische magistratuur en door verzetsgroepen gepleegd geweld tegen collaborateurs 1940–1950. Dissertation, Ghent University, Ghent

Maintaining Order in Occupied Belgium? The Brussels Public Prosecutor's Office and Wartime Political Violence 1940–1950

Jan Julia Zurné

Abstract During the German occupation of Belgium in 1940–1944, the Belgian judiciary struggled with its attitude towards the occupier. This essay examines the issue of political attacks on collaborators carried out by resistance groups and, more particularly, how the Brussels public prosecutor's office dealt with this. Although the German authorities demanded that the judiciary investigate these crimes, magistrates were hesitant to do so out of fear of exposing citizens to German prosecution—and rightly so, as it later turned out. After being confronted with the execution of several members of resistance groups who were shot by the occupier after having first been arrested by the Belgian police, the magistrates decided to sabotage the investigation of such crimes. This decision can be traced back not only to the magistrates' confronting experiences but also to their sense of national identity, pragmatism and the influence of certain individuals within the judiciary.

1 Introduction

If a country is invaded and occupied, the position and tasks of local judicial actors inevitably change. Will the existing judicial powers remain functional, and, if so, how will authority be shared with the occupier? Will the judiciary become an instrument of the occupier, or will it try to determine its own direction? If the latter, will it risk sanctions or even forced removal? In these circumstances, local magistrates have to determine the (often fluctuating) room for manoeuvre that has been given to them and decide how to use it.

The Belgian judiciary is a particularly interesting case in this respect. Earlier research on the attitude of local magistrates towards violence committed by resistance groups during and after the occupation has shown their hesitance to prosecute the perpetrators, particularly in the last phases of the occupation (Thiry 2015; Welter 2007). Moreover, crime statistics show how during the war period the murder

J. J. Zurné (✉)
History Department, Radboud University, Nijmegen, The Netherlands
e-mail: j.zurne@let.ru.nl

M. Bost and A. Vrints (eds.), *Doing Justice In Wartime*,
Studies in the History of Law and Justice 19,
https://doi.org/10.1007/978-3-030-72050-6_7

rates exploded, while the prosecution rates dropped (Rousseaux et al. 2008). This contrast suggests a grave infraction of the state monopoly on violence, especially if the violence went unpunished. To understand how the judiciary reacted when confronted with political violence and what consequences this had, we need to look at the Brussels public prosecutor's office, who acted as *primus inter pares*, and to focus on the entire occupation period. When confronted with political violence in wartime, whose interests did the judiciary protect, and what consequences did this have?

This essay will discuss the way in which magistrates and the officers of the judicial police (*police judiciaire/gerechtelijke politie*) working for the Brussels public prosecutor's office dealt with these issues during the German occupation of Belgium 1940–1944. Earlier research has shown how Belgian magistrates, like other elites throughout Western Europe, were initially quite willing to apply a 'policy of the lesser evil' in order to protect local interest, contain the influence of collaborationist parties and protect their own power position (Gotovitch 1972; Louveaux 1981; Van Doorslaer and Verhoeyen 1986). As the occupation situation and war prospects changed, so did the attitude of the judiciary. Several issues, very often involving judicial independence, led to confrontations with the occupier (Michielsen 2004; Peters et al. 2015). This essay will focus on one of these issues: political violence or, to be more precise: violent attacks against collaborators perpetrated by resistance movements.

The first part of the essay will outline the context of this issue and consider the division of tasks between the German and Belgian judicial actors in the occupied country—in other words: who was to prosecute which types of crime? This division of tasks proved to be increasingly problematic, especially when, from the end of 1942 onwards, violence against collaborators became an almost daily occurrence in Brussels. As a result of this increase in violence, the question of what role the local judiciary had to play in the repression of these politically motivated attacks—and specifically how the independence of the judicial procedure would be protected—was a constant source of conflict between the occupier and the Belgian magistrates.

This issue became particularly urgent when several Belgian resistance fighters who had attacked collaborators were executed by the occupying forces after having been arrested by the Belgian police. The second part of this essay will look into this matter more closely. These cases, in which local magistrates and police officers were indirectly responsible for the deaths of their compatriots, led to protests in Brussels's judiciary circles and, later, to a widespread consensus amongst the capital's magistrates that these types of incidents should be carefully avoided by 'sabotaging' the judicial procedures.

The third and final part of this essay will investigate the 'judicial sabotage' more closely. Subsequently, it aims to offer an explanation for this remarkable strategy. In the end, when it came to political violence, the Brussels judiciary mostly stayed loyal to the idea of the Belgian State and tried to obey its laws and rules, even if the reality was one of a German occupied state with different rules.

2 Dividing Competences: A Constant Source of Conflict

After the German invasion and establishment of a military government, the Belgian judiciary remained in office, following the pre-war guidelines of the Belgian government. These guidelines stated that civil servants were allowed and even encouraged to remain in function under an enemy occupation, as long as they respected their 'duties and loyalty to the Fatherland'. In case of any doubts about whether or not to obey certain orders given by the occupier, the civil servant in question should ask his or her superior for instructions.[1] The 1907 Hague Convention provided further guidelines for the attitude to be adopted towards the occupier, although it offered mostly very general conclusions on the rules of war and occupation. Because the minister of Justice, along with the rest of the Belgian government, had fled to London in 1940, it was up to the secretary-general (the highest civil servant in the department) to ensure the administration's continuation. In doing so, he was also the person to mediate between the occupying forces on the one hand and the judiciary on the other.

Immediately after the defeat of the Belgian Army on 28 June 1940, Belgian magistrates, along with the secretaries-general and other elites, adopted a 'policy of the lesser evil' aimed at the preservation of existing legal institutions and resulting in compromises with the occupier. Responsibilities for maintaining public order were divided between the local and occupation judiciary and police forces. In general, all crimes involving or aimed at German citizens or military personnel were to be prosecuted by the occupation forces, whereas general offenses were to be prosecuted by the Belgian judiciary system.

During the first two years of the occupation, the division of tasks resulted in problems mostly when German authorities ordered Belgians to arrest people on their behalf (Wouters 2006; Van Goethem 2006). As a result of the limited size of the German military occupation apparatus, the occupying regime aimed to instrumentalise the existing Belgian police and judicial institutions in order to maintain public order. Requests or orders to arrest or 'collect' people are to be seen in this light. Although the Belgian authorities stated in February 1942 that they would not execute arrests that solely served German interests, this question remained problematic, for instance when the German authorities asked local police officers for addresses or directions in order to arrest someone for breaking German regulations.

Another factor that complicated the exact meaning of the division of tasks was the exchange of information obtained in criminal investigations. In 1941, in an effort coming from both the central occupation government and local German police departments, all public prosecutors were asked to communicate criminal reports to the local German police forces. This applied particularly, although not exclusively, to crimes aimed against the occupation forces and all cases of illegal possession of arms. During the occupation of Belgium in 1914–1918, the German authorities had also asked for the communication of judicial information. Along with German orders for arrests, this had led to conflicts between the judiciary and the occupier (Bost 2013). Despite this conflict-filled experience 30 years earlier, the judiciary in 1941 agreed to

[1] *Staatsblad/Moniteur belge*, law of 5 March 1935 concerning the duties of civil servants in wartime.

transfer potentially interesting files to the German authorities. Through this measure, the occupation regime created a situation in which German police forces had access to information from Belgian investigations. This turned out to be very convenient when political violence later increased.

However, this was problematic for the Belgian police and judiciary because the results of their work was potentially used by German police forces to track down Belgian citizens. The issue of the communication of this information points out that pre-war Belgian law was not always useable or applicable during the occupation. Obviously, the duty of professional confidentiality did not allow magistrates and police officers to communicate information from criminal proceedings. However, how was this to be interpreted in the case of an occupying power that was, according to the Hague Convention, responsible for maintaining public order? This dilemma was perceived differently in 1941 than it was in 1943.

The examples above show that the division of responsibilities that at first sight seemed so straightforward was in reality quite problematic. This became even more apparent when, from 1942 onwards, politically inspired violence in Brussels rapidly increased. During the first two years of the occupation, resistance-related activities had mostly been limited to acts of sabotage, clandestine press and intelligence with allied forces. Although the first two types of activity were in theory liable to punishment on the basis of Belgian law, the secret and hidden character of these activities meant that the perpetrators were practically never found.[2] Moreover, as they hardly endangered the public order, these cases were not a priority for the public prosecutor's office.

This changed when, from 1942 onwards, Belgian resistance groups (specifically the communist ones), started to attack collaborators on a large scale. In Brussels alone, the judicial authorities counted 255 attacks on collaborators, 34 attacks on Germans and 275 bomb attacks on buildings (often occupied by collaborators or collaborationist organisations) between 1940 and 1944. The attacks on collaborators started in October 1941, with one or two incidents in the following months, peaking spectacularly in March 1943 with almost 30 attacks in that month alone (Laplasse and Steen 2005). Considering the dark number of unreported attacks, the actual number must have been even higher.

These attacks put the Belgian judiciary in a difficult position. The German authorities expected them to investigate the attacks because they were aimed at Belgian citizens and, presumably, also committed by Belgian citizens. As no Germans were involved, the crimes lay in the sphere of responsibility of the Belgian judiciary, according to the official division of tasks. Of course, the attacks were a direct consequence of the occupation, as the Brussels public prosecutor frequently pointed out.

[2]Observations of acts of sabotage were usually communicated to the German authorities, as these acts often were directly aimed at the occupying forces and thus were to be prosecuted by them. Publishing clandestine newspapers was, in theory, punishable because Belgian law obliged publishers and authors to mention their names and addresses on their work. In practice, the people behind clandestine anti-German publications were never prosecuted by the Belgian authorities, although there were certain initiatives to investigate clandestine communist publications in 1941.

However, the German authorities refused to take sole responsibility for the prosecution of the perpetrators. This can be explained by the fact that the occupying regime lacked manpower and thus desperately needed all the help it could get in maintaining public order (Roden 2015). At the same time, however, the German authorities deeply distrusted the Belgian police and judiciary, since they were supposedly 'heirs' of the pre-war elite and not at all prone to national socialism or loyally working together with the occupier in an ideological sense. Since attempts to integrate collaborators into the judiciary and police forces failed, these presumptions were, at least in Brussels, quite correct (Bost and Peters 2016). The judiciary and police indeed remained populated by employees who had been in place before the war and were, in general, loyal to the pre-war Belgian State.[3] Further on in this chapter we will discuss the consequences of this.

While the German authorities wanted the Belgian judiciary to investigate crimes committed *against* collaborators, the occupier increasingly also withdrew crimes *perpetrated* by those who supported the New Order from the local judicial procedure. This led to a sense of impunity on behalf of the collaborators. These developments seriously jeopardised the state monopoly on violence and thus confronted the Belgian judiciary with a dilemma.

If the judiciary wanted to restore public order, they could investigate the attacks on collaborators and thereby potentially expose those who had committed the crimes (in other words, members of resistance groups) to the occupier's repression. They would have to accept that the investigations and punishment of violence perpetrated *by* members of collaborationist groups were in a large majority of the cases claimed by the occupier and often not punished at all.[4]

Their other option was to give up their own duties regarding maintaining public order and leave all politically motivated crimes completely to the German police forces and military tribunals. In this case, the magistrates would have to keep in mind the following circumstances. First of all, the occupying regime did not have sufficient manpower and would not actually be able to restore public order. Secondly, if the German authorities did track down the perpetrators of the violence against collaborators, the legal and extra-legal punishments would be much harsher than any punishment meted out by a Belgian court. Of course, to further complicate the position of the judiciary, it was not always possible to decide on the spot whether a crime was politically motivated or not. So even if they did choose this last option, its realization would be complicated.

---

[3]For more information on the attitude of the gendarmerie, see Jonas Campion's contribution to this volume. For more information on the attitude of the local police in Brussels, see Majerus (2007).

[4]From September 1941 onwards, all members of the *Vlaamse Wacht, Garde Wallonne, Vlaams Legioen, Légion Wallonie, Waffen SS* and *NSKK* were formally placed under German jurisdiction.

When the first attacks on collaborators took place, the judiciary did not yet have to take a decision, because the circumstances allowed them to float somewhere in between. The police forces investigated attacks on collaborators, often quite thoroughly, but did not succeed in finding a suspect.[5]

In the fall of 1942, the issue of the prosecution of perpetrators of violence against collaborators became particularly urgent. This was the result of an increase of the number of attacks but also of pressure coming from the occupying forces. According to the German authorities, the efforts of the Belgian judiciary and police to track down perpetrators of these crimes were completely insufficient. They therefore demanded a more energetic effort.

In the preceding months, the three chief prosecutors of Brussels, Ghent and Liège and the public prosecutor of Brussels had clearly stated that they would not allow the *police judiciaire*, the service that handled serious crimes and worked under direct order of the public prosecutor, to investigate crimes that would eventually be tried by German military courts. They demanded that the independence of the judicial procedure be respected, and they explicitly refused to let the police become an instrument for the German repression of the resistance.[6] If these terms were not respected, the chief prosecutors threaten to resign.

The secretary-general, who functioned as an intermediate between the magistrates and the German authorities, was determined to come to terms with the occupying forces with regard to the repression of politically inspired violence. Although he agreed with the magistrates that the independence of the judicial procedure must be guaranteed, he also put pressure on the chief prosecutors to intensify investigations.[7] Meanwhile, the secretary-general tried to convince the German authorities to formally guarantee the independence of the judicial procedure. The occupying forces would not provide such a guarantee, because they wanted to always keep the option open to interfere in the prosecution of cases that they regarded as important. Halfway through 1942, the situation was particularly difficult: on the one hand, the magistrates refused to investigate crimes if the suspects could be claimed by the German authorities. On the other hand, those authorities refused to promise to *always* let suspects who had been arrested by Belgian police forces be tried before Belgian courts.

Suddenly, in October 1942, the secretary-general sent out a circular to the chief prosecutors. He declared that the German authorities had, contrary to their former objections, promised to leave the investigation *and prosecution* of perpetrators of

---

[5]For instance: Belgian State Archives, *archief van de gerechtelijke politie bij het parket van de procureur des Konings van Brussel* 1921–1976, nr. 4981 file 17 and nr. 4981 files 28, 29, 31, 37, 39, 41, 42, 43 and 44.

[6]Belgian State Archives, location Beveren, *archief van het Parket-Generaal te Gent* 2002a, nr. 154, minutes meetings 19 and 24 March 1942.

[7]From April 1941 to September 1943, the secretary-general of the department of Justice was Gaston Schuind. Before his appointment as secretary-general, he had been a member of the *Cour de Cassation*, the highest court in Belgium. His candidacy was supposed to counter the influence of the Flemish nationalist Gérard Romsée, who was appointed secretary-general of the department of Home Affairs in April 1941 after a failed attempt to have him appointed at the department of Justice.

political violence to the Belgian judiciary.[8] Relieved that this issue finally seemed to be solved, the chief prosecutor and public prosecutor in Brussels forwarded the message to their subordinates.

3 Turning the Tide: The Cases of Eugène Predom, Paul-Eugène Hermans and Etrusco Benci

Three separate cases soon showed that the German authorities did not respect the independence of the judicial procedure, in spite of the secretary-general's claim. We will briefly discuss each of these case and then describe the reaction of the Brussels magistrates.

In October 1942, a local police officer in the Brussels commune of Anderlecht caught a 15-year-old boy while he was distributing illegal communist pamphlets. During his interrogation, the boy revealed the existence of a group of youngsters responsible for applying graffiti on the houses of collaborators and distributing communist pamphlets. The local police officer reported this to the Brussels prosecutor, who happened to be ill that day. His substitute, after having consulted a colleague, ordered a 'discrete and meticulous' investigation into the matter. This investigation was to be conducted by the *police judiciaire*, and explicitly *not* by the local police, since the local police officer was known to be a collaborator. The substitute deemed it wiser to *act as if* the matter was looked into thoroughly by the *police judiciaire*, who would make sure that nothing would come of it. This was meant to convince the German authorities that the Belgian judiciary did not neglect politically motivated crimes.

A few days later, house searches were conducted, and with the help of other members of the 'resistance group', its leader, 27-year-old Eugène Predom, was arrested, along with his girlfriend. At this point, the public prosecutor's office deliberated upon its next step. One magistrate expressed conscientious objections against issuing an arrest warrant, but the prosecutor, who had by now recovered from his illness and was back in office, decided that at this point, they had come too far not to issue an arrest warrant. During a search of Predom's house, again attended by the local police officer who had no business there, a printing press, propaganda materials and an explosive device were found. Because of the presence of the local police officer, the officer of the judicial police did not dare to omit these findings from the reports. As a result, a new arrest warrant was issued against Predom and his girlfriend, this time on suspicion of the possession of explosives. At this point—in early November 1942—the German authorities intervened.

Oberkriegsverwaltungsrat Arnold Gentzke, who monitored the Belgian judiciary for the German authorities, demanded that all reports concerning the 'Predom case' be transferred to him. It is unclear how he had been informed of the whole matter:

[8]Archives of the *auditorat général*, personal file Gaston Schuind, letter from Schuind to chief prosecutors, 8 October 1942.

the local police officer who was known for his pro-German sympathies might have had a part in it. The public prosecutor, unsure about what to do next, consulted the chief prosecutor, who decided that all reports concerning the case would indeed be transferred to the German authorities. In the meantime, the explosive found in Predom's house was examined by an expert. In his report he tried to trivialise its possible effects. During yet another house search, this time without the presence of the local police officer, incriminating documents on the organisation of communist networks were found. This was *not* mentioned in the report, and the documents were destroyed.

A few days later, both Predom and his girlfriend, who had been incarcerated in a Belgian prison, were transferred to a German-run prison by the German authorities. The chief prosecutor tried to get them back into Belgian hands, but instead Predom was transferred to a concentration camp. On 13 January 1943, he was executed as part of a retaliation action following the murder of German soldiers in Brussels. His girlfriend was kept in German custody for another eight months and was later released (Zurné 2016).

One month after the start of this Predom case, in November 1942, a similar case occurred elsewhere in Brussels. An employee of the postal services was attacked on his way home from work. The victim was not severely harmed but nonetheless failed to give a clear description of his attackers. He did, however, claim that it was a politically motivated crime, because he had sympathies for the collaborationist Flemish nationalist party *Vlaams Nationaal Verbond* (VNV). He suspected some of his colleagues, who distributed clandestine newspapers at work, were involved. When these colleagues were interrogated by the Belgian police, it turned out they all had convincing alibis.

Still, they were arrested by the Gestapo a few days later. The public prosecutor protested against their arrest and the interference of the German authorities in the investigation of a crime in which no Germans were involved. His superiors supported the protest, but to no avail. Although two of the 'suspects' were released, a third one, chief-postman Paul-Eugène Hermans, was incarcerated in the Breendonk concentration camp and shot in a retaliation action on 12 December 1943.

The third man who was shot as a result of German interference in Belgian investigations is the 37-year-old Italian communist Etrusco Benci. In December 1942, the local police in the Brussels commune of Oudergem stopped Benci and a friend because they seemed to be acting suspiciously. Not long before, several houses of local collaborators had been the target of explosions. When the policeman studied their identity cards and wanted to conduct a body search, one of the men shot him in his hand. Benci and his friend got away, but the former was arrested later when he returned to his apartment. While being interrogated by a Belgian policeman, Benci demanded to be released and said that if he were not, he would make sure his comrades would avenge him. Not long after that, Benci was indeed taken over by the German authorities. The police officer who had interrogated him was shot by members of Benci's communist guerrilla group. Benci himself was sentenced to death by a German military court and executed in June 1943.[9]

In only a few months, these three cases made clear that the German authorities did not respect the independence of the Belgian judicial proceedings. In the following spring, at least two more resistance fighters were either taken out of Belgian custody and shot by the Germans or found because of information from the Belgian investigation. One man who had attacked a denouncer was able to escape from the hospital where he was held during the criminal investigation by the Brussels public prosecutor's office, before the German police could arrest him.

These incidents showed that any cooperation between the Belgian and German police and judicial institutions was potentially lethal for the suspects, if they were members of resistance groups.[10] For the judiciary, this was not only a moral but also a legal problem. In Belgian law, exposing citizens to prosecution by the enemy ('denunciation') was considered a crime against the security of the state.[11] Moreover, an amendment in December 1942 altered this law by stating that the denunciation no longer had to include malicious intent. As a result, civil servants and magistrates who were 'just following orders' and did not mean for anyone to get arrested by the occupier now possibly became liable to (post-war) punishment.

When the full ramifications of cooperation with the occupier became clear towards the end of 1942, the Brussels public prosecutor reacted with a clandestine order to the *police judiciaire*: where political violence is concerned, they must make sure no useable evidence or information was included in the official reports. In reality, several members of the criminal police already acted that way whenever possible. Despite the public prosecutor's stance, it took approximately six months before the chief prosecutor agreed with this method and informally suspended the maintaining of public order in his jurisdiction. In the meantime, as the examples make clear, not all magistrates on the ground were aware of the fact that the German authorities did not respect the Belgian judicial independence. Through clandestine newspapers and personal letter to magistrates, resistance groups tried to inform magistrates of this reality and warned them to be extremely careful when investigating (presumed) politically motivated crimes. By the summer of 1943, regardless of the official division of authority, investigations into political violence had come to a standstill. Despite several German attempts to reverse this situation, it would not change until the liberation.

In the meantime, investigations into attacks against collaborators were seemingly conducted as usual. Through the tactics of 'judicial sabotage', police officers

[9]Belgian State Archives, *archief van de gerechtelijke politie bij het parket van de procureur des Konings van Brussel* 1921–1976, nr. 4982, files 212 en 215.

[10]We also know of some cases (outside of Brussels) where the prosecution of possession of firearms that had no (clear) connection with resistance activities was claimed by the occupier, sometimes with fatal results. These harsh measures against not-politically motivated possession of firearms was possibly meant to set an example.

[11]After the liberation, the public prosecutor's office of the military court started investigations against some Brussels magistrates under the suspicion of denunciation, but these did not lead to any trials (see Zurné 2016).

and magistrates continued to write reports, conduct house searches and question witnesses. However, they made sure not to find a suspect and, if possible, to include no information that could be useful in finding the perpetrator(s). Since judicial files were being communicated to the German authorities, they had to make sure that these files contained no elements that could lead to arrests, as had happened in the cases of Predom, Hermans and Benci.

For the German authorities, who never held much trust in the Belgian judicial system as a potential instrument for their own rule (but nonetheless tried), this was very frustrating. The collaborationist parties, who regarded the judiciary as a detestable heritage of pre-war parliamentary democracy, also grew increasingly resentful and, in the last years of the occupation even violent towards magistrates. Despite these threats, German *Berufsverboten* and other measures to intimidate magistrates—for example, hostage taking as a form of retaliation (Bost and Peters 2016)—the occupier and collaborationist parties did not get a hold on the Brussels public prosecutor's office. This indicates to what extent the judiciary had room for manoeuvre and even, to a certain extent, held a power position vis-à-vis the occupier.

4 Interpreting Attitudes: National Identity, Pragmatism and the Importance of Individuals

By describing the context surrounding the decision by the Brussels public prosecutor's office to suspend its own role in the maintaining of public order, I hope to have shown that this was by no means a rash or even a particularly radical decision. Of course this context alone does not explain why the Brussels magistrates opted for this approach. Three other factors might help explain their attitude: national identity, pragmatism and the influence of individual magistrates.

In his article 'Transitional Shortcuts to Justice and National Identity', philosopher of law Derk Venema argues that in times of political transformation (whether from democratic to authoritarian or vice versa), rule of law principles are often violated or dodged in order to restore order (Venema 2011). According to Venema, two factors are crucial in this process: national identity, because supporters of the old and new regime have opposing claims in this respect; and—in a later stage—also pragmatism because, for the sake of the protection of the state, rule of law principles are simplified or ignored. These two factors also help to understand the attitude of the magistrates in the Brussels public prosecutor's office when it came to political violence during the occupation.

As far as national identity is concerned, the magistrates, who predominantly had a liberal or conservative Belgicist profile, clearly identified with the pre-war conservative establishment of which they had been part.[12] The collaborationist Belgian National Socialist parties contested the position of the pre-war elite, including the

[12]Because of the social background of most law students, the Belgian judiciary was comprised of conservatives and liberals from the upper class or upper middle class (Schandevyl 2008).

judiciary. From the beginning of the occupation (and in fact even preceding it), an increasing distrust and polarisation existed between the two groups, expressed in collaborationist publications such as *Pays Réel* and *Volk en Staat* and even more so in the attempted (and some successful) assaults on magistrates in 1944. It is important to note that, in spite of some attempts by the occupation regime, the collaborationist parties were supported by very few already appointed magistrates and did not succeed in infiltrating the judiciary during the occupation (Peters 2009). From the perspective of national identity, it is not surprising that the magistrates indirectly sided with the perpetrators of the violence against collaborators, especially because to *not* do so (i.e., to prosecute the perpetrators) would directly endanger resistance groups.

While the attitude of the judiciary is not particularly surprising when keeping in mind their troubled relationship with the collaborationist victims of the attacks, it is all the more so when looking at the perpetrators. In Brussels, the violent attacks were mostly (though not exclusively) the work of communist groups like the *Gewapende Partizanen/Partisans armés*, the armed forces of the communist-linked resistance group *Onafhankelijkheidsfront/Front de l'Indépendence* (Gotovitch 1992). During the interwar period, the Belgian judiciary had fought the communists like they had other 'subversive' groups (some of which during the occupation became collaborationists). The judicial fear of communism was intense and already dated back to the 19th-century fear of socialism (Keunings 1996; Gotovitch 1996; Diagre and D'Hoore 1996). From this perspective, it is all the more surprising that the magistrates, some of whom were outright anti-communists, still chose to protect members of communist resistance groups who might fall in the hands of the Germans. Apparently, the idea of protecting citizens who resisted the occupier overruled political antitheses. The experience of the first German occupation in 1914–1918 had been formative for this patriotic view, since it had boosted patriotism and had created a strong anti-German sentiment among the Belgian elite.

Clearly, the judiciary and police, despite their own claims of independence, are not neutral forces in a political sense. By politically and symbolically submitting themselves to the law, the judiciary seeks a position of immovability and innocence. In other words: by maintaining public order, the judiciary (like the police) acknowledges and supports the ruling political order and often fights opposition (Bancaud 2002; Fijnaut 1979). In Belgium, the politicisation of members of the public prosecutor's office already started during their appointment by the minister of Justice. In the Brussels public prosecutor's office, politicisation was so evident that even a guarantee of political balance between liberals and Catholics was built into the system: when a Catholic was appointed chief prosecutor, the public prosecutor had to be a liberal (or vice-versa) (Schandevyl 2011).

Interestingly, in the Belgian case during the Second World War, the judiciary did not serve the politics of the actual ruler (i.e., the occupier) but instead remained loyal to the pre-war Belgian state. This is not very surprising, since the magistrates were, generally speaking, part of the liberal and Catholic elites that had ruled the country in the interwar period. Still, it means that, although clearly politicised, the judiciary did not necessarily serve *every* regime.

This might be an obvious statement, but it is nonetheless an important one. The Brussels case points out that magistrates can be open to follow a policy of the lesser evil vis-à-vis an occupier but, under the right circumstances, might later refuse to accommodate to that foreign regime if they risk exposing citizens to harsh punishment by the occupier. In this light, pre-war conflicts between the political establishment and 'subversive' groups can either be intensified (judiciary vs. collaborationist groups) or temporarily shelved (judiciary vs. communists).

It is important to note that, in relation to their independence, this politicisation is a potential risk, because it may harm the legitimacy of the judiciary (Guarnieri 2007). In this particular case, the judiciary lost all legitimacy in the eyes of the collaborators, which established an increasing state of impunity (at least from the side of the Belgian judiciary) with regard to crimes committed against members of New Order parties.

The issue of having to choose what groups of citizens to protect not only has the political connotation of national identity but also is linked to the second factor of pragmatism. The magistrates were faced with a dilemma: they either would have to prosecute the perpetrators of the attacks on collaborators (and thereby, in practice, they would be exposing Belgian citizens to prosecution by the occupier) or neglect certain tasks in the maintaining of public order and thereby not respect the 'victim's rights' of the collaborators. From a pragmatic[13] point of view, postponing tasks in the maintaining of public order was 'only' a breach of 'normal' criminal proceedings, whereas exposing citizens to prosecution by the occupier was included in Belgian law as a crime against the safety of the state, and thus much more liable to post-war punishment.

Not only was the option chosen by the Brussels public prosecutor's office more pragmatic during the occupation itself but also it was a safer bet in protecting the magistracy against post-war criminal proceedings, which would severely harm the image and power position of the entire judiciary. In the light of military proceedings from 1942/1943 onwards, this was, of course, an important consideration for the future protection of the judicial professional group. Previous research has shown that protection of their own independence was a very important element in the attitude of the Belgian magistrates during the First World War (Bost 2013). Looking out for their own professional group can thus be seen as a recurrent motive for the Belgian magistracy during the twentieth century, specifically during times of crisis.

In this sense, the pragmatism of the judiciary turned out quite well: the post-war judiciary as a whole focused on its 'resistant' stance during the last years of the occupation and managed—at least to a certain degree—to contain the discussion on the communication of reports and other forms of accommodation preceding their more firm stand.[14] This happened in spite of developments that would suggest the opposite: some of the cases that had 'gone wrong', notably the Predom case, were

[13]"Pragmatic" means here 'the most efficient course of action to attain goals at the lowest possible costs' (Venema 2011).

[14]The communist press and party were nonetheless particularly critical of the policy of the lesser evil and continued to voice their criticism during the post-war years.

investigated after the liberation (and dismissed), and the three chief prosecutors were purged (but their hierarchal subordinates usually were not). Despite these post-war investigations and demands from the population that the judiciary be purged more extensively, the post-war governments held enough confidence in the magistrates to entrust the legal reckoning with collaborators to them.[15] Through this mutual consent and support, the government and judiciary helped to legitimise each other in the tumultuous post-war period. This allowed the judiciary to play a large role in the re-establishment of the pre-war political order (Huyse and Sabbe 1995).

Whereas pragmatism is always a factor in the practice of justice, magistrates during the occupation were *more* pragmatic than they had been in peacetime. In fact, they were forced to be, because the law and their usual practices did not offer straightforward answers to the dilemmas they faced during the occupation. The law was less easily applicable in this period of crisis. To find a way of dealing with their dilemma's, magistrates were to an increasing degree led by pragmatism and notions of national identity. Since their national identity was to a large extent determined by traditional Belgian patriotism, that is what they turned to.

The third and last explanatory factor in the attitude of the magistrates is the influence of certain individuals on their colleagues. In the case of Brussels, it is important to note that it was not necessarily the highest magistrate in the hierarchy who had the largest moral authority. From 1940 on, *premier avocat général* Charles Collard temporarily replaced his superior, chief prosecutor Camille Pholien, who had been forbidden to return to office after he had fled the country following the German invasion.

However, not Collard but his subordinate Lucien Van Beirs, the Brussels public prosecutor, had more moral authority.[16] Although Van Beirs respected the hierarchal customs within the judiciary, he never tired of promoting his own views, which were particularly principled and keen on protecting the independence of the judiciary. Chief prosecutor Collard usually defended Van Beirs's arguments but had a different personal view and style on how the judiciary should be led vis-à-vis the occupier. His was more of a formalist attitude, whereas Van Beirs's main concerns were primarily patriot-inspired and principled.

Several examples show that Collard, despite his rank, had relatively little moral authority over his colleagues. When public prosecutor Van Beirs was prohibited from pursuing his profession in February 1943 because of his particularly principled stance on the question of the prosecution of perpetrators of political violence, judicial protocol demanded that he inform his superior first. As Van Beirs was at that moment detained as a hostage, together with several other magistrates, he did not approach Collard but instead ran to Camille Pholien, whom Collard had replaced and who was also held hostage. Although this was partially a result of the circumstances, as

[15]The post-war trials against collaborators were carried out by the military courts and not the ordinary judicial system. However, many magistrates held a function in the expanded system of military justice (Luyten and Magits 1998).

[16]Raoul Hayoit de Termicourt, who from 1942 onwards led the public prosecutor's office of the *Cour de Cassation* and was thus the highest magistrate, also had plenty of moral authority amongst his colleagues.

Van Beirs had access to Pholien and not to Collard, it also implies that the public prosecutor still regarded the former as his legitimate superior.[17]

Another sign of Collard's weak position amongst his colleagues occurred at approximately the same time, when his subordinate *avocats généraux* and substitute addressed a letter to him about the recent death of Eugène Predom. In this 'cri d'alarme' the magistrates pointed out that under these circumstances, the chief prosecutors should end all communication of legal information to the occupier, including the practice of handing over judicial reports. If the prosecution of these types of crimes continued, and more citizens risked being handed over to the occupant, the magistrates threatened to 'only listen to their conscience'—and not to their boss—in deciding whether or not they chose to work on certain cases.[18] In the particularly hierarchal environment of the judiciary, such an outright threat of mutiny is very revealing.

By contrast, Van Beirs seemed to have had more moral authority. He was arrested and detained as a hostage by the German authorities several times, although the occupier claimed this had nothing to do with his firm stance and anti-German reputation. After the German authorities granted him a *Berufsverbot*, Van Beirs's replacement continued his policy. Outside of his own office, Van Beirs's moral authority was particularly important to the members of the *police judiciaire*, whom he—directly following the arrest of Eugène Predom by the Germans—ordered not to find any evidence or suspects in politically motivated crimes.

Although it is difficult to tell whether Van Beirs personally held a unique position amongst his colleagues or whether his ideas were supported and also propagated by other influential magistrates—in other words, whether he was a figurehead or part of a larger movement—it is clear that he had an important influence on the development of the attitude of the Brussels judiciary. The fact that his successor held on to his policy is also telling, especially since Van Beirs had been discarded for precisely this reason and his substitute therefore took a real risk in continuing this line. This shows how a strong individual can have an important influence on an entire professional group.

5 Concluding Remarks

National identity, pragmatism and the influence of certain individuals on the corps of magistrates help to explain why the Brussels public prosecutor's office decided to informally end its own role in the prosecution of perpetrators of violence directed at collaborators. Of course, the former experiences in the Predom, Hermans and Benci cases are another crucial part of the explanation. These cases 'gone wrong', along

---

[17]Despite of his *Berufsverbot*, Pholien stayed in close contact with his colleagues during the entire occupation.

[18]Archives of the *auditorat général*, personal file of Charles Collard, letter of the *avocats généraux* and substitutes to the chief prosecutor, 2 February 1943.

with the lack of clarity and conflicts about the divisions of tasks, are specific to the Belgian case and created a particularly hazy situation, which helps explain why it was possible for the magistrates to act the way they did.

Nevertheless, it is important to note how the attitude of the Belgian judiciary, at least from 1942 onwards, differed from that of many of their Dutch and French counterparts. The circumstances of the occupation in Belgium (German military regime with limited manpower, need for a large role for local police and judiciary in maintaining public order, limited influence of the occupying regime on these local institutions) allowed the judiciary relatively large room for manoeuvre. Moreover, the Belgian judiciary had a homogeneous liberal-conservative profile, it identified with the pre-war Belgian establishment and it was not very susceptible to New Order influence or influx.

The Belgian magistrates seem to have acted differently than their counterparts in neighbouring countries. In the Netherlands, the influx of collaborationist magistrates was bigger and the creation of special 'peace courts' provided a new stage for trials for (minor) political offenses (Venema 2007). In France, many magistrates agreed with the political repression carried out by the Vichy regime: they sentenced resistance fighters to severe punishments and never publicly protested (Bancaud 1995; Sansico 2015). Although 'judicial sabotage' on a local level was possible in France and indeed did exist (Israël 2005), it seems these practices were far from equalling the Brussels example.

How to explain these differences, aside from the different circumstances of occupation? The experience of the first German occupation in 1914–1918 was very important for the Belgian magistrates. From this experience they had learned that compromises were inevitable. More importantly, the strike of 1918 (Bost and François 2009) had taught them that even after having made certain compromises, it was possible to draw the line and take a more principled stand when absolutely necessary. Clearly, this drawing the line took on a very different form in 1943 than it had in 1918—instead of a publicly exposed strike, the 'judicial sabotage' was a secretive matter.

This partly explains why, after the liberation of Belgium in 1944, the judiciary had an ambiguous image, whereas in 1918 they were regarded as forerunners of the resistance. Because the government decided it needed the judiciary for the legal reckoning with collaborators and to help legitimise its own rule, the magistracy was able to profit from this aura of respectability, despite the fact that particularly in the left- and right-wing press their position was undermined. This allowed the judiciary to gradually restore it pre-war position of power.

References

Bancaud A (1995) Les magistrats face à la lutte armée. Paper presented at the international conference La Résistance et les Français: lutte armée et maquis, Bensançon, 15–17 June 1995

Bancaud A (2002) Une exception ordinaire. La magistrature en France 1930–1950. Gallimard, Paris

Bost M (2013). Traverser l'occupation 1914–1918. Du modus vivendi à la grève, la magistrature belge face aux occupants allemands. Unpublished PhD thesis, Université catholique de Louvain, Louvain
Bost M, François A (2009). La grève de la magistrature belge (février à novembre 1918). Un haut fait de la résistance nationale à l'épreuve des archives judiciaires. In: Heirbaut D, Rousseaux X, Wijffels A (eds) Histoire du droit et de la justice: une nouvelle génération de recherches/Justitie- en rechtsgeschiedenis: een nieuwe onderzoeksgeneratie. Presses universitaires de Louvain, Louvain-la-Neuve, pp 19–44
Bost M, Peters K (2016) Belgian magistrates and German occupiers: a diachronic comparison (1914–1918/1940–1944). In: Hondeghem A, Rousseaux X, Schoenaers F (eds) Modernisation of the criminal justice chain. Springer, Cham, pp 233–260
Diagre D, D'Hoore M (1996) Les libéraux belges et la peur du rouge. Regards sur l'anticommunisme libéral 1919–1939. In: Delwit P, Gotovitch J (eds) La peur du rouge. Éditions de l'Université de Bruxelles, Brussels, pp 100–117
Fijnaut C (1979) Opdat de macht een toevlucht zij? Een historische studie van het politie-apparaat als een politieke instelling. Kluwer, Antwerp
Gotovitch J (1972) Note relative à la magistrature sous l'occupation. CREHSGM Notes de travail 5:1–20
Gotovitch J (1992) Du rouge au tricolore. Les Communists belges de 1939 à 1944. Editions Labor, Brussels
Gotovitch J (1996) La peur du rouge dans les dossiers de la justice belge: la signification du procès de 1923. In: Delwit P, Gotovitch J (eds) La peur du rouge. Editions de l'Université de Bruxelles, Brussels, pp 87–97
Guarnieri C (2007) Judicial politicization. In: Clark DS (eds) Encyclopedia of law and society: American and global perspectives. Sage Publications, Los Angeles, pp 855–856
Huyse L, Sabbe H (1995) De magistratuur na de oorlog. In: Huyse L, Hoflack K (eds) De democratie heruitgevonden. Oud en nieuw in politiek België 1944–1950. Van Halewyck, Leuven, pp 131–149
Israël L (2005) Robes noires, années sombres. Avocats et magistrats en résistance pendant la Seconde Guerre mondiale. Fayard, Paris
Keunings L (1996) La peur du rouge et les forces de l'ordre à la fin du XIXe siècle: le cas de la police de Bruxelles. In: Delwit P, Gotovitch J (eds) La peur du rouge. Editions de l'Université de Bruxelles, Brussels, pp 37–52
Laplasse J, Steen K (2005) Het verzet gewogen. Een kwantitatieve analyse van politieke aanslagen en sabotages in België 1940–1944. Bijdragen tot de Eigentijdse Geschiedenis 15:227–260
Louveaux CL (1981) La magistrature dans la tourmente des années 1940–1944. Revue de Droit pénal et de Criminologie 7:619–664
Luyten D, Magits M (1998) Aspecten van de werking van de krijgsauditoraten en de rekrutering van militaire parketmagistraten na de Tweede Wereldoorlog. Belgisch Tijdschrift voor Nieuwste Geschiedenis 1(2):205–225
Majerus B (2007) Occupations et logiques policières: la police bruxelloise en 1914–1918 et 1940–1944. Académie Royale de Belgique, Classe des Lettres, Brussels
Michielsen J (2004) The 'Nazification' and 'Denazification' of the courts in Belgium, Luxembourg and the Netherlands: the Belgian, Luxembourg and Netherlands courts and their reactions to occupation measures and measures from their governments returning from exile. Universitaire Pers Maastricht, Maastricht
Peters K (2009) L'influence de l'administration militaire allemande sur les changements de personnel au sein de la magistrature belge (1940–1944). In: Heirbaut D, Rousseaux X, Wijffels A (eds) Histoire du droit et de la justice: une nouvelle génération de recherches. Presses universitaires de Louvain, Louvain-la-Neuve, pp 61–76
Peters K, Roden D, Van Haecke L (2015) De Tweede Wereldoorlog en de naoorlogse repressie. In: De Koster M, Heirbaut D, Rousseaux X (eds) Tweehonderd jaar justitie. Historische encyclopedie van de Belgische justitie. Bruges: Die Keure, pp 539–561

Roden D (2015) In naam van het Duitse volk! Het Duitse krijgsgerecht en de openbare orde in bezet België (1940–1944). Unpublished PhD thesis, Ghent University, Ghent

Rousseaux X, Vesentini F and Vrints A (2008) Violence and war: measuring homicide in Belgium (1900–1950). In: Body-Gendrot S, Spierenburg P (eds) Violence in Europe: historical and contemporary perspectives. Springer, New York, pp 177–204

Sansico V (2015) La Justice déshonorée 1940–1944. Tallandier, Paris

Schandevyl E (2008) Changements ou continuité? Rapports de force linguistiques et (im)mobilité sociale dans la magistrature bruxelloise après la Deuxième Guerre mondiale. In: Bernaudeau V, Nandrin J-P, Rochet B (eds) Les praticiens du droit du Moyen Age à l'époque contemporaine. Presses Universitaires de Rennes, Rennes, pp 255–270

Schandevyl E (2011) Walter Ganshof van der Meersch, een topmagistraat in zijn professionele en maatschappelijke context. Een kijk op het Belgische gerecht in de twintigste eeuw. Bijdragen tot de Eigentijdse Geschiedenis 24 pp 97–133

Thiry A (2015) Le tribut des temps troubles. La justice face aux homicides attribués à la 'résistance' dans l'arrondissement judiciaire de Mons (avril 1943–novembre 1944). Presses universitaires de Louvain, Louvain-la-Neuve

Van Doorslaer R, Verhoeyen E (1986) L'Allemagne nazie, la police belge et l'anticommunisme en Belgique (1936–1944): un aspect des relations belgo-allemandes. Belgisch Tijdschrift voor Nieuwste Geschiedenis 1(2) pp 61–125

Van Goethem H (2006) La convention de La Haye, la collaboration administrative en Belgique et la persécution des Juifs à Anvers 1940–1942. Bijdragen tot de Eigentijdse Geschiedenis 17 pp 117–197

Venema D (2007) Rechters in oorlogstijd. De confrontatie van de Nederlandse rechterlijke macht met nationaal-socialisme en bezetting. Boom Juridische uitgevers, The Hague

Venema D (2011) Transitional shortcuts to justice and national identity. Ratio Juris 1 pp 88–108

Welter F (2007) Criminalité populaire, brutalité structurelle et clémence judiciaire? Les morts violentes dans l'arrondissement judiciaire de Namur de la fin de l'Occupation à la Libération (1944–1945). Unpublished Master's thesis, Université Catholique de Louvain, Louvain

Wouters N (2006) De Führerstaat. Overheid en collaboratie in België (1940–1944). Lannoo, Tielt

Zurné, JJ (2016) Een 'bedrijfsongeval' met verregaande gevolgen. Het parket van Brussel en de zaak Predom (1942–1947). Journal of Belgian History 46 (34) pp 12–45

‘Ich habe noch nie sterben gesehen, wie man in Belgien stirbt’: Military Chaplain Otto Gramann and the Execution of Hostages and Convicts in German-Occupied Belgium and Northern France (1940–1944)

Dimitri Roden

Abstract Between May 1940 and August 1944, at least 900 prisoners were executed in German-occupied Belgium and northern France following a death sentence; 420 others were shot as hostages in reprisal for unsolved acts of violence against members of the *Wehrmacht* or their local collaborators. According to German military law, all convicts and hostages facing execution could ask for the assistance of a clergyman. In occupied Belgium and northern France, it was Monsignor Otto Gramann, head chaplain to the German military administration, who assisted most of these inmates during their last hours. Gramann kept detailed records of his encounters with the executed, documents which have never been studied before. They do not only give an insight into the study of execution of the death penalty in occupied Belgium and northern France from a grass-roots perspective. The case of Otto Gramann also provides the opportunity to research the complex relationship between the military chaplaincy and the Nazi regime in general.

‘To the Chaplain of the prison of Saint-Gilles, who assisted me during my last hours and who gave me the courage and strength to die as a real Christian and a patriot. May God bless your soul’. On the night of 9–10 February 1944, shortly before his execution at the shooting range of Schaarbeek-Brussels, Belgian resistance fighter Eugène Haesaerts expressed on a small prayer card his gratitude towards Otto Gramann, head chaplain of the German armed forces in occupied Belgium and northern France.[1] Between 1940 and 1944, the Austrian-born priest assisted hundreds of Belgian and French prisoners facing execution in the German-occupied territory. Most of these civilians were condemned to death by a German military court for acts of resistance

[1] Prayer cards of the executed (Breendonk Memorial, n° 378).

D. Roden (✉)
Royal Military Academy, Brussels, Belgium
e-mail: dimitri.roden@warheritage.be

Breendonk Memorial, Willebroek, Belgium

M. Bost and A. Vrints (eds.), *Doing Justice In Wartime*,
Studies in the History of Law and Justice 19,
https://doi.org/10.1007/978-3-030-72050-6_8

such as espionage, sabotage or illegal possession of firearms; others were destined to be executed as hostages in reprisal for unsolved acts of violence against the occupier or his local collaborators.

Haesaerts's prayer card is just one of dozens given to Gramann by the prisoners as a token of appreciation for his assistance. These poignant and historical documents, preserved at the archives of the Breendonk Memorial in Willebroek, were long believed to be some of few personal documents of Gramann relating to executions in German-occupied Belgium and northern France, as most of his papers were lost in an allied air raid on Münster in September 1944. Around 2008, however, a Belgian collector presented himself at the Breendonk Memorial with a pile of disorganised documents originating from the personal archives of Gramann's former Belgian secretary, Madame Annie Poelmans.

Classification of the records revealed a wealth of information, complementing the scarce personal belongings, documents and pictures of Gramann that were already in the possession of the Breendonk Memorial created in 1947 (Roden 2009).[2] The content of the archives varies from Gramann's family archive to post-war correspondence with family members of executed or deported prisoners, newspaper clippings on the priest's wartime activities and even the transcript of a couple of last letters of the executed. By far the most important documents are a diary and notebook in which he reveals details about his encounters with the prisoners he assisted as well as on their execution.

Gramann's records not only enable the historian to study the execution of the death penalty in occupied Belgium by using a grass-roots perspective but also allow him to research in detail the role of the military chaplain in the execution process. What do the documents reveal about Gramann's aid to the executed? Was he just doing his job or did he do more than the occupier allowed him to do? How can it be explained that he was considered a friend by most of the former prisoners and their families although he wore the uniform of the *Wehrmacht*? And what does Gramann's case teach us about the complex relationship between the military chaplaincy and the Nazi regime in general?

1 An Austrian Priest Serving in the German *Wehrmacht*

Born on 18 October 1885 in Meidling-Vienna, Otto Gramann was the youngest son in a family of eleven. His father worked as a self-employed carpenter, his mother was a former housemaid.[3] After graduation from the local gymnasium, Gramann joined the Austro-Hungarian military. He volunteered for the cavalry, serving with

[2]Records on Mgr. Gramann, 1945–1965 (Breendonk Memorial, n° 372); prayer cards and drawings, given to Mgr. Gramann (Breendonk Memorial, n° 377, 378 and 379); missal (Breendonk Memorial, n° 780 and 841). For more details on the content of the archive, see the unpublished inventory preserved at the Breendonk Memorial (www.breendonk.be).

[3]Collection of newspaper clippings on Otto Gramann's mother Rosalia (Gramann-Groven collection, n° 4).

the *Husarenregiment 'Arthur Herzog von Connaught und Strathearn' Nr. 4*. After his one year of service, Gramann remained in the military. He was transferred to the Uhlans and promoted to *Rittmeister der Reserve* (Captain in the reserve). Shortly before the outbreak of the Great War, the young cavalry officer experienced a vocation to religious life. On 25 July 1914, three days before the Austrian declaration of war on Serbia, Gramann was ordained a priest. From September 1914 onwards, he successively worked as a chaplain in Retz and Wiener Neustadt before being called up for military service at the end of 1915. As a military chaplain, he served at both the Russian and Italian fronts (Broneder 1963, 7–8; Loidl, s.d., 3; Nefors 2004, 164–165).

During the interwar period, Gramann practised different religious professions: padre of the War Hospital n° 2 in Vienna (1919), religion teacher at the Sancta Christiana boarding school in Rodaun (1920–1924), subsequently lawyer and judge at the *Erzbischöfliches Metropolitan-und Diözesangericht* of Vienna (1930–1935) and finally *Kirchendirektor* at the Salesianerinnen Abbey in Vienna (1935). In November 1935 Gramann was appointed honorary papal chamberlain, a position that gave him the right to be addressed as Monsignor. From 1936 onwards, he combined his position as priest with a job as military chaplain (*Militärkaplan*) in the Austrian *Bundesheer*. Following the 1938 *Anschluss* of Austria to Nazi Germany and the incorporation of the Austrian Army into the German *Wehrmacht*, he remained active as chaplain to the armed forces. He was appointed *Wehrmachtoberpfarrer* in 1939, which equals a commissioned officer with the rank of Lieutenant-Colonel (Broneder 1963, 7–8; Loidl, s.d., 3; Nefors 2004, 164–165).

In the summer of 1940, Gramann was attached as head chaplain to the newly installed military administration in Belgium and northern France. Led by General Alexander *Freiherr* von Falkenhausen, the main objective of this *Militärverwaltung* was to restore and assure public order in the occupied territory in order to increase the contribution of the local economy to the German war effort. From June 1940 onwards, von Falkenhausen acted as military governor to Belgium and the two French departments Nord and Pas-de-Calais, making him the highest legislative, executive and judicial authority in this territory (De Jonghe 1974, 9–81, 1982, 13–77; Roden 2015).

In exercising the extensive powers of a *Militärbefehlshaber*, von Falkenhausen had two general staffs at his disposal: the *Kommandostab* assisted him in all military and security matters; while the *Verwaltungsstab* helped the General to govern the occupied territory. Furthermore, the *Militärbefehlshaber* had several police forces at his disposal. Military police units such as the *Geheime Feldpolizei* (GFP) and the *Feldgendarmerie* (FG) had to track down and arrest all civilians suspected of violating the law and decrees of the occupier. At the end of the investigation, prisoners were either released or handed over to the German military justice to be judged on basis of German law (Roden 2015, 45–60; Gérard-Libois and Gotovitch 1971, 133–135; Van den Wijngaert 2004, 49–50; Weber 1978, 19–47).

However, from the beginning of the occupation, the military police forces were in competition with the *Sicherheitspolizei-Sicherheitsdienst* (Sipo-SD), the civilian police of the SS. Due to a lack of manpower of the military police units, *Militärbefehlshaber* von Falkenhausen and his collaborators were forced to accept the assistance of the SS in maintaining public order in the occupied territory. Although the Sipo-SD was officially placed under the control of the military administration, it took its real orders directly from the *Reichssicherheitshauptamt* (Reich Main Security Office) in Berlin. The SS saw the Sipo-SD as an instrument to undermine the authority of the military administration from within and to extend its own powers over the occupied territory. Its ultimate goal was the installation of a Higher SS and Police Chief (*Höherer SS- und Polizeiführer*, HSSPF) responsible for all security matters in Belgium and northern France (Roden 2015, 60–66; Van den Wijngaert 2004, 153–163; Verhoeyen 1993, 393–412; Weber 1978, 19–47).

During the four years of German occupation, the Sipo-SD succeeded in extending the powers of the SS over the occupied territory. At first the SS police acted as a subordinate to the GFP without any autonomous executive police powers. In February 1941, however, the military administrations allowed the Sipo-SD to arrest suspects on its own, resulting in the extra-judicial deportation of prisoners to the concentration camps in the Reich. The Sipo-SD became the most important police force in occupied Belgium and northern France, pushing aside and restricting police forces such as the GFP and the FG to the narrow military sphere. Until the summer of 1944, however, the military administration successfully fought off every attempt of the SS to install a HSSPF in its territory, making Belgium and northern France an exceptions in German-occupied Europe. The SS succeeded in getting SS-General Richard Jungclaus appointed to HSSPF only in the summer of 1944—just a couple of weeks before the liberation of the territory by the Allies—when Hitler decided to replace von Falkenhausen's military administration with a civilian one (De Jonghe 1974, 9–81, 1982, 13–77).

The struggle for power in occupied Belgium led to a competition between different German law enforcers at the expense of its prisoners. As a military chaplain working in various prisons in occupied Belgium, Gramann was a firsthand witness to the complexity of the German system. Although his records clearly focus on convicts awaiting execution in occupied Belgium, the chaplain ministered to nearly all types of prisoners: civilians under interrogation by military and civilian police forces, resistance fighters awaiting trial before a German military court, political prisoners facing an extrajudicial punishment in a concentration camp, hostages arrested in reprisal for unsolved acts of resistance, common-law offenders, convicts awaiting deportation to a prison in the German Reich etc.

2 Chaplain of the Executed

Upon arrival in Belgium, Gramann settled his office in Brussels, in the former Ministry of Colonies, Rue royale n° 7. The priest's daily job was to provide pastoral, spiritual and emotional support to all military and civilian personnel, both active and reserve, attached to the military administration in Belgium and northern France.

He soon combined this job with a position as chaplain to the military prison of Saint-Gilles, Brussels. From May 1940 onwards, the German military administration installed separate sections in many of the existing Belgian prisons destined for the imprisonment of civilians who had violated the laws and decrees of the occupier. The prison of Saint-Gilles has an exceptional status, however. In contrast to most other Belgian prisons, the occupier requisitioned it in its entirety. Between 1940 and 1944, the *Wehrmachtuntersuchungsgefängnis* Saint-Gilles became by far the most important prison in occupied Belgium. It was not only used as a jail for suspects arrested by the German police or as a prison for convicted civilians serving their punishment; Saint-Gilles also functioned as a transit camp for prisoners awaiting deportation to a prison or concentration camp in the Reich. The last major difference with other prisons in German-occupied Belgium is the fact that Saint-Gilles had a separate section for the detention of suspected or convicted military personnel subject to the jurisdiction of the German armed forces, including local collaborators serving within the ranks of a German military formation or police unit (Roden 2015).

Following his appointment as prison chaplain, Gramann opened an office in the *Wehrmachtuntersuchungsgefängnis*. Daily he received prisoners seeking spiritual or emotional support. On Sundays he organised Masses in the prison chapel. One week the Mass could be attended by the inmates of sections A and B, the following week by those of sections C and D. As stated in his own records, Gramann distributed the Holy Communion to about 50–80 inmates each week. In addition to organising Masses, the priest also offered the prisoners the possibility to confess their sins.[4]

Around 1941, the occupier asked Gramann for the first time if he was willing to provide moral and spiritual assistance to prisoners facing execution, both condemned resistance fighters and common-law convicts. The priest accepted this task, although he was certainly not the only one to assist convicts in their last hours. Abbé Mathieu Voncken, the Belgian chaplain of the Saint-Léonard prison in Liège, was present at the execution of 34 civilians that took place at the local *citadelle* between May 1941 and January 1943. However, from 1943 onwards, the occupier seemed to prefer the assistance of a German chaplain over that of a Belgian priest, a choice possibly motivated out of safety concerns. The presence of a Belgian chaplain at the execution place meant a potential risk that details might be leaked to the family, information that could have fed the resistance in the occupied country. In order to avoid this kind of leaks, Voncken was replaced by various German chaplains, including Monsignor Gramann (Voncken 1945, 1953, 1963).

The presence of a chaplain at the place of execution was stipulated in article 103 of the Wartime Judicial Proceedings Code (*Kriegsstrafverfahrensordnung*), published in August 1939 in the German *Reichsgesetzblatt*. The officer in command of the firing squad had to ensure that the convict was given a last chance to confess. Although the German legislation enabled the commanding officer to proceed with an execution without the intervention of a chaplain, Gramann's archives seem to suggest that this procedure was rarely put into practice in German-occupied Belgium and northern

[4]Door signs on Gramann's office in the *Wehrmachtuntersuchungsgefängnis* Saint-Gilles (Breendonk Memorial, n° 375); diary for the year 1942 (Gramann-Groven collection, n° 23).

France.[5] Moreover, the same procedures were also used when executing hostages as a warning for future acts of resistance.

Gramann's records not only give insight into the way executions were carried out in the occupied territory but also reveal information about the last moments of the prisoners. The priest accurately described each meeting in his notebook, using a form of shorthand. He sometimes even drew sketches of the execution poles accompanied by the names of the executed, thus revealing the order in which the prisoners were tied to the poles. Although the description of each meeting must have been written shortly after the execution, it is clear that his notebook is in fact a transcript of older reports, as the executions are treated in a non-chronological order. Moreover, his archives also contain loose pages covering the description of an execution, most of which content is copied literally in his notebook. Nevertheless, his notebook, which covers for the most part the year 1943 and the beginning of 1944, clearly reveals Gramann's modus operandi.

The evening before an execution, the priest would be informed of the upcoming event. In military prisons such as Saint-Gilles, the chaplain was granted one night to assist one or a group of prisoners awaiting execution, on the condition that these inmates had explicitly asked for his assistance. In other locations, such as in the SS transit camp of Breendonk, his time with the convicts was limited to a couple of hours (Nefors 2004, 163).

In the course of the evening and night, Gramann would visit the prisoners in their cells. Most of the time, he was also present when a judicial official informed the convict of the fact that the death penalty has been confirmed by the military authorities and that the sentence would be executed in the morning. According to Gramann, the majority of the prisoners remained calm when they were informed of their upcoming execution. Some of them started to cry in the presence of the chaplain, but most of them regained the strength to keep their head up high. It seems that most of them had already accepted their fate.[6]

During his visits, Gramann quickly gained the confidence of most of the inmates. The priest, who spoke fluent French, offered the prisoners cocoa, cheese, bread and brandy. He helped them write their last letters and heard their confession. In the Saint-Gilles prison, the chaplain also organised nightly Masses for the death-row inmates, during which he distributed the Holy Communion. Most of the convicted resistance fighters had no regrets about the acts they had committed. In their last hours, they no longer seemed to fear their execution. Some were concerned about the future of their loved ones. In November 1943, a condemned resistance fighter spent his last night looking at his wedding picture. As reported by Gramann, the prisoner constantly worried about the fate of his wife. 'He fears that she might commit suicide. He asks me [Gramann] to support her. She must remain courageous in order to get to heaven'. Another resistance fighter urged the priest to watch over his younger brother so that

[5]Reichsgesetzblatt, Teil I, *Kriegsstrafverfahrensordnung*, 26 August 1939.

[6]Notebook (Gramann-Groven collection, n° 26).

he would not follow in his footsteps, as his parents would not be able to overcome the loss of a second son.[7]

Most inmates did not seem to fear death but were already thinking about the afterlife. In order to keep his memory alive, one prisoner wanted his loved ones to make an *in memoriam* card, embellished with his picture and fragments of his letters. Another convict hoped to be buried with his cufflinks on, as it might facilitate the identification of his remains once the war is over.[8] For most of the prisoners, even for some of the non-religious, gaining access to heaven was a major concern. In the face of death, some atheists expressed the desire to be converted to Christianity. In his archives, Gramann conscientiously registered the baptisms he performed in prison, even when some prisoners explicitly asked him to keep their conversion a secret from their loved ones. A former member of the resistance movement *Front de l'Indépendance* was baptised in his cell shortly before being executed as a hostage on 26 January 1944. As his father was a socialist and probably would not understand his son's last minute conversion, Gramann wrote in his notebook: 'Do not tell the father of the baptism'.[9]

Granting the last wishes of the prisoners is something Gramann took very seriously. In his notebook, he underlined the phrases covering these wishes in red pencil. They vary from making the prisoner's will or delivering his personal belongings to his relatives to baptising family members of the executed. According to post-war testimonies, it seems an established fact that the chaplain made contact with the families of the prisoners. Professor Franz Loidl states in his post-war biography on Gramann that the chaplain smuggled written messages out of prison by hiding them under his clothes or in his chalice, messages that he afterwards delivered to the relatives (Loidl, s.d., 5).

In the early morning, the prisoners were transferred by car or truck to the execution place, which was often located on the grounds of a former Belgian military post. Most of the prisoners of Saint-Gilles were brought to the shooting range of Schaarbeek, *Avenue Auguste Reyers*. In the provinces of Oost- and West-Vlaanderen, the executions took place in Oostakker and Rieme, in Limburg on the military post of Hechtel, in Liège on the grounds of the local *citadelle* and in Luxembourg in the courtyard of the Arlon prison. Other prisoners were executed in 'hangar 9A' on the Antwerp docks, the shooting range of Marcinelle near Charleroi, the military post of Maria-ter-Heide or the SS transit camp of Breendonk (Nefors 2004; De Craene 2009; Roden 2015).[10] As stated in Gramann's diary and notebook, it is certain that

[7]Ibid.

[8]Ibid.

[9]Gramann's notebook offers an interesting insight into the religious, civil and familial views of the inmates. See also the analysis by Emmanuel Debruyne and Laurence Van Ypersele of about 100 last letters of civilians facing execution in occupied Belgium during World War I (Debruyne and Van Ypersele 2011).

[10]List of the executed buried at Maria ter Heide (War Victims Brussels, Rap. 599 Tr. 33.403); Gräbnisliste für Begräbnisplatz II Tir National in Brüssel, Bd. Auguste Reyers (War Victims Brussels, Rap. 497 Tr. 137.889); Report on the exhumation of the executed at the prison of Arlon, 28 November 1945 (War Victims Brussels, Rap. 148 Tr. 39.358); List of the executed buried at

he witnessed executions that took place in Schaarbeek, Charleroi, Liège, Mons and Breendonk.

Gramann's records clearly show him accompanying the prisoners to their final destination. During the drive to the execution place, the priest would sit in between the inmates. He accurately described in his notebook the prisoners' last moments. Some of them would grab the chaplain by his arm whilst praying; others would sing the national anthem *Brabançonne* or try to keep up the morale of their fellow compatriots.[11]

The execution of convicts and hostages itself is strictly bound to the rules of the Wartime Judicial Proceedings Code, yet Gramann reported in his notebook various abuses that occurred at the execution place. Prisoners trying to convince the judge of their innocence were ignored. On 10 February 1944, the execution of a group of condemned partisans on the shooting range of Schaarbeek was delayed for more than 20 min because the lead judge could not make it on time. Gramann even reports about an execution that never took place. In January 1942, on the same shooting range, the priest was assisting a former communist. After a judge had read the verdict for the last time, the inmate was bound to the execution pole. Just before the execution squad opened fire, the inmate's lawyer intervened on the shooting range with the decision of the military authorities to review the case. The German judicial official was furious: '... entweder ist er geistig gesund, dann muß er sterben, oder er ist geisteskrank, dann bekommt er die Spritze' (if he is mentally fit, then he must die. Or in case he is mentally ill, then he should be given an injection). In the end, the prisoner was unbound and brought back to prison.[12]

The most severe violations occurred in the SS camp of Breendonk. On 10 May 1943, Gramann was present at the execution of three convicted partisans. Arnaud Fraiteur, Maurice Raskin and André Bertulot were found guilty of the murder of Paul Colin, the editor of the Rexist journal *Cassandre*. For the first time in German-occupied Belgium and northern France, General Alexander von Falkenhausen commanded that the death penalty be executed by hanging instead of by firing squad (Nefors 2004, 174).[13] Questioned in 1946 by a Belgian military court on the hangings in Breendonk, Gramann stated that he was only allowed to accompany Raskin, Fraiteur and Bertulot up to the fence that separates the execution place from the rest of the fortress. However, in February 1944, the chaplain was present at the execution place when the SS hung 12 resistance fighters sentenced to the death penalty for their involvement in the murder of three soldiers of the German air force (*Luftwaffe*). Gramann later declared that the resistance fighters were hung in groups of three, while the others had to watch the execution. According to the chaplain, the

Hechtel (War Victims Brussels); List of the executed buried at the Citadelle of Liège (War Victims Brussels); *Duitsche Gruwelen in het Vlaamsche Land. Oorden van Verschrikking en Beproeving: Vinkt-bij-Deinze, Oostakker, Antwerpen, Maria-ter-Heide, Zwijndrecht, Oud-Turnhout, Beverloo, Merksem*, Bevrijding nr. 5, Antwerpen: Uitgeverij 'Ontwikkeling' [1945].

[11] Notebook (Gramann-Groven collection, n° 26).

[12] Ibid.

[13] Minutes of the hearing of Mgr. Gramann, 25 March 1946 (Breendonk Memorial, transcripts of the trial against the former camp personnel of Breendonk).

first group of prisoners was still alive when they were placed in a coffin and had to be given a *coup de grace*. Therefore the SS extended the duration of hanging from 10 to 20 min.[14]

The mistreatment of hostages and convicts in Breendonk was not limited only to those who were to be hanged but occurred also with those facing the firing squad. On 14 July 1944, ten hostages were shot that day in reprisal for a number of unsolved acts of violence against Belgian collaborators. In his notebook, the priest made a detailed report on the way the execution is carried out:

> They bring in some cheese bread and coffee. I give them cigarettes. They have to be ready in 1 hour—we leave around 5 AM—6.30 AM all are ready—1 fell [...] and nobody helped him to get up. The lieutenant pushed him with his foot. All are very skinny and starving. [...] Then they must take off their clothes except for their pants and shoes. They have to be completely silent on their way to the poles. They are quickly tied to the poles. No sentence is read. 2 start to sing the Internationale—[...]—A lot of them are badly hit. All of them need a coup de grace, some of them even 2 or 3. [...] They are thrown into coffins—[...]—there's brandy before and after the execution for the officers and men—Schmidt [Philipp Schmitt, the SS major commanding the Auffanglager Breendonk] has not shown up. He said that they all had to be hanged and burned.[15]

Gramann's account on the executions seems to be strictly administrative and does not explicitly reveal what he thought about the death penalty. However, it is clear that his job weighed heavy on his mind. In letters and postcards sent to his relatives or the nuns of the Salesianerinnen Abbey in Vienna, he secretly described the executions he witnessed. He used to express the executions in transportation terms, in order to be sure that his messages would pass the German censor. In Gramann's words, executions were called *Abreisen* (departures) while the execution place is defined as a *Bahnhof*' (train station). On 8 February 1942, he wrote: 'Today's night will be heavy as will be tomorrow morning, two 'departures''. A couple of months later, on 2 April, he addresses a card from Lille in northern France: 'My dearest Sister! I just got back from this city after a train journey of 4 h. Last week, the 'departure' from this city of 35—in 2 days ...' (Loidl, s.d., 6; Nefors 2004, 165; Broneder 1963, 5).[16]

Between May 1940 and August 1944, at least 900 prisoners were executed in occupied Belgium and northern France following a death sentence. The majority of the executed were civilians condemned by a German military court for acts of resistance such as espionage, sabotage, communist activities or illegal possession of firearms. Others were civilians convicted for severe common-law offences such as armed robbery or were German soldiers found guilty of military crimes such as desertion or 'undermining the military strength' of the *Wehrmacht*. Furthermore, 420 civilians were shot as hostages in reprisal for unsolved acts of violence against members of the German *Wehrmacht* or their local collaborators: 305 from Belgium,

---

[14]Hearing of Otto Gramann, 1946 (Breendonk Memorial Willebroek, digital copy of the judicial files on the Breendonk-trial of 1946).

[15]Notebook (Gramann-Groven collection, n° 26).

[16]Fragments published in Volksblatt, 1 June 1963. The original documents, however, are missing. The correspondence was borrowed by Dr. Franz Loidl from the Vienna Salesianerinnen Abbey but never brought back.

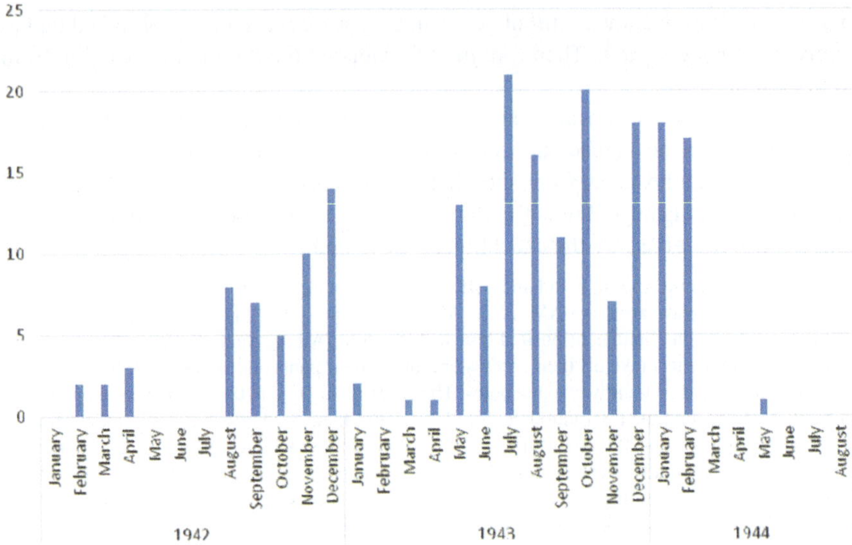

Fig. 1 Number of executed convicts and hostages per month (based on the Gramann-Groven collection)

115 from the French departments Nord and Pas-de-Calais (Roden 2015; De Jonghe 1984, 176–177; Konings 1982; Thierry 2013; Verhoeyen 1993, 415–422).[17]

Gramann's diary and notebook cover respectively the year 1942 and the period from 1943 to the beginning of 1944, yet it is an established fact that he assisted more prisoners than those cited in his documents. In total, they reveal the fate of some 160 convicts and hostages. The majority of the prisoners mentioned in the diary seem to be inmates of the Saint-Gilles prison executed on the shooting range of Schaarbeek. The only exception are the eight hostages shot at the *Auffanglager* Breendonk on 27 November 1942.[18] The notebook, in contrast, mentions the names of about 120 prisoners, mostly executed between 1943 and the beginning of 1944. Unlike the diary, the notebook contains a detailed description of Gramann's encounters with death-row prisoners and hostages.[19] Nevertheless, both documents are of great historical value, as they contain not only the names of the executed but also the date and place of the execution. The diary and notebook complement the existing official German documentation on the execution of convicts and hostages, as they allow the historian to check details that are, for the most, not mentioned in other German sources, out of security reasons (Fig. 1).

[17]Liste über Bestätigung und Aufhebung von Urteilen XI–XIII (War Victims Brussels, archives of the Oberstkriegsgerichtsrat beim Militärbefehlshabers in Belgien und Nordfrankreich); documents on the execution of hostages in occupied Belgium (War Victims Brussels, Rap. 497 Tr. 22.397).

[18]Diary for the year 1942 (Gramann-Groven collection, n° 23).

[19]Notebook (Gramann-Groven collection, n° 26).

3 The Ambiguous Legacy of Gramann

Gramann remained active as head chaplain to the German armed forces in occupied Belgium and northern France until the summer of 1944. He was severly wounded in mid-September 1944 during an air raid on Münster. After recovering in hospital, he returned to Vienna, where he resumed his pre-war job as *Kirchendirektor* at the Salesianerinnen Abbey.

By the beginning of 1945, Belgian war correspondent Paul Lévy learned of Gramann's story. Lévy, a former prisoner of the SS transit camp of Breendonk himself, was especially interested in the fate of the Belgian deportees. As a journalist, he followed the trail of the allied armies on their way through Nazi Germany, thus participating in the liberation of various concentration camps and prisons. With the help of a Belgian officer, Lisfranc, he succeeded in making contact with Gramann. Lévy, who already dreamed of transforming the former camp of Breendonk into a memorial, wanted to hear Gramann's story about the executions he witnessed. The war correspondent successfully convinced Gramann to return to Belgium once more. In order to facilitate such a return, military prosecutor Wilfried Hallemans invited Gramann to be heard as a key witness on the execution of political prisoners in the upcoming Breendonk trial, as the other parties involved were either dead, missing or sitting on the bench of the accused. On 10 March 1946, Lévy left Brussels in the company of Captain Maurice Panquin, a former political prisoner who had met Gramann during his time in prison. Three days later, the duo arrived in Vienna where they arranged a meeting with the priest.[20]

On 19 March 1946, Gramann returned to Brussels, where he received a warm welcome. The Belgian press portrayed the Austrian priest as a true hero, willing to meet up with the families of political prisoners who are still missing or who were executed during the war. In February 1946, the newspaper *La Libre Belgique* had already described him as a man 'dressed up in the uniform of the enemy' who should nevertheless be considered as 'one of us' because he shared the feelings and convictions of the Belgian people. 'All who received help from him, loved him'.[21]

During his stay in Belgium, Gramann testified in the Breendonk trial on the execution of political prisoners in the former SS camp. He also celebrated a Mass in the *Notre-Dame au Sablon* church of Brussels in honour of all victims of the Nazi regime. On 8 April 1946, Lévy brought Gramann to Breendonk for an interview. They were joined by Marcel Roothoofd, a cineaste who was preparing a documentary on the history of the SS camp. Gramann was interviewed about the former execution site within the fortress. With the interview finished, the priest wished to return as quickly as possible to Brussels where he wanted to try on a new cassock. Captain Philippe Quersin, a fellow war correspondent of Lévy who had joined the group in Breendonk, offered to bring Gramann, Lévy and Panquin back to the capital. Near the village of Merchtem, Quersin's vehicle was involved in a car accident, flipping over a couple of times. Gramann was catapulted out of the car and suffered head wounds.

---

[20]Correspondence of Paul Lévy regarding Mgr. Gramann (Breendonk Memorial, n° 372).

[21]*La Libre Belgique*, 7 February 1946.

British medics working at the Brugmann hospital in Jette gave the priest first aid, followed in the afternoon by a surgery at the Saint-Pierre hospital in Brussels.[22]

After recovering from his head wounds, the Austrian priest returned to Vienna. In July 1946, he wrote to Lévy that he was experiencing pain in the neck, which according to his doctor still might be the result of the car crash. However, it soon became clear that Gramann was suffering from cancer. On 10 November 1947, the 62-year-old priest died in Vienna. Five days later, his remains were put to rest in the family grave on the Meidling-Vienna cemetery. His coffin was covered with the Belgian national flag. Present at the ceremony was the former Belgian minister, Charles Gobert Comte d'Aspremont Lynden, who paid his last respects in the name of the whole nation. Belgium's gratitude towards the Austrian priest was also expressed by the fact that the tombstone of Gramann's family grave, which had been severely damaged during the war, was restored with the help of Belgian funds. The inscriptions on the headstone read: 'A la mémoire vénérée de Monsigneur Otto Gramann. Aumônier des prisonniers belges 1940–1944. La Belgique reconnaissante' (In respectful memory of Monsignor Otto Gramann, Chaplain to the Belgian prisoners 1940–1944. Grateful Belgium).[23]

The historical value of Gramann's archive is undisputed, as it is probably the most comprehensive document on the execution of hostages and convicts in occupied Belgium. However, the image of a hero, almost a friend of the Belgian resistance, could be at least submitted to a form of criticism. Although it cannot be denied that Gramann showed a lot of friendliness and humanity in his encounters with Belgian political prisoners, one may ask whether his motives were as sincere as the majority of the Belgians believed them to be. Was Gramann's behaviour simply a result of his religious beliefs? Or was his conduct influenced by a certain pragmatism? Was it, for instance, a way to protect himself against possible prosecution for war crimes in case Germany should lose the war? Or should his humanity be considered as a way to resist Nazism and an expression of his sympathy for the Belgian cause?

Definitive answers to these questions are hard to formulate. Although it is an established fact that Gramann provided assistance to the executed and their families, one can sense that his motives were more than just religiously inspired. The Breendonk Memorial holds dozens of praying cards of prisoners expressing their gratitude towards Monsignor Gramann. Such a high number cannot be a result of chance. It is hard to conceive that he would have asked them explicitly to do so in order to avoid a possible prosecution for war crimes in case of an allied victory over Nazi Germany.

Like most of his colleagues, Gramann must have been faced with a moral dilemma. On one hand he was assisting death-row convicts and hostages awaiting execution; on the other hand he was ministering to wounded German soldiers or organising Masses for fallen Belgian collaborators. The personal archives of the Austrian chaplain not only contain various articles published in collaborationist newspapers such as *Le*

---

[22]Collection of newspap*er clippings (Gramann-Groven collection, n° 13).*

[23]La Nouvelle Gazette, 15 and 18 November 1947; In memoriam card of Mgr. Gramann (Breendonk Memorial, n° 645); funeral oration pronounced by Comte d'Aspremont Lynden (Breendonk Memorial, n° 693).

Pays Réel on the funeral services he led in honour of fallen Belgian collaborators but also hold remembrance cards of soldiers who fell on the Eastern Front while serving in Rex leader Léon Degrelle's Walloon Legion.[24] His archive even contains a post-war letter from a Belgian collaborator, asking the Austrian priest if he could testify in his favour.[25] In 1964, the Belgian satirical magazine *Pan* openly dared to question Gramann's legacy. The article entitled 'De mortuis ... nisi bene' (Of the dead, nothing unless good), portrayed the priest as the chaplain of the 'Belgian collaborators':

> The veterans of the Walloon Legion and their "non" entitled parties still remember with great emotion the sermon he pronounced at the barracks of the Grenadiers during a commemoration of the legionaries who fell on the Eastern Front.[26]

Furthermore, according to *Pan*, Gramann was confronted one day with a Belgian priest who refused to organise a Mass in honour of a fallen Belgian volunteer in the German armed forces. This refusal was in all probability dictated by the stance of Cardinal Jozef Van Roey, Archbishop of Mechelen, who by 1941 had openly condemned any assistance for Catholics who had assisted implementation of a national-socialist order in Belgium. The Belgian collaborationist movements stated that they were recruiting volunteers for the *Waffen-SS* or the *Wehrmacht* to fight the anti-clerical communists on the Eastern Front, but the Belgian Church never supported the collaboration (Van de Vijver et al. 1988, 8–9; Dantoing 1991; Boudens 1997). *Pan* stated that Gramann tried to convince the priest not to oppose organisation of the Mass, thus asking the clergyman to act against the directives of the cardinal. Was Gramann just doing his job or did he also feel a connection with the goals of the collaborators? It is a question that remains unanswered, due to the lack of relevant sources.[27]

At the same time, there are also sources that seem to confirm Gramann's status as a 'friend of the Belgian resistance'. In a post-war article, fellow clergyman and former resistance member Henri Neybergh (known as Dom Cyprien) states that the priest was even interrogated by the *Sicherheitspolizei-Sicherheitsdienst*, a statement that cannot be checked, however, due to a lack of sources.[28] Monsignor Honoré Van Waeyenbergh, rector of the Catholic University of Leuven who was arrested as he refused to communicate the addresses of his students to the occupier, met Gramann during his imprisonment in Saint-Gilles. 'He wore the uniform of the enemy during the distinguished exercise of an assignment of pure charity, but in his soul, feelings and convictions, he was one of ours', Van Waeyenbergh declared after the war (Nefors 2004, 164). Herbert Prack, a member of von Falkenhausen's military administration and a fellow Austrian, confirms the idea of Gramann's activities being known by at

[24] In memoriam cards of fallen Belgian collaborators (Gramann-Groven collection, n° 57); *Le Pays Réel*, 22 May 1942.

[25] Letter addressed to Mgr. Gramann, 1946 (Gramann-Groven collection, n° 35).

[26] *Pan*, 23 September 1964.

[27] *Pan*, 23 September 1964.

[28] Newspaper clipping of an article by Cyprien Neybergh (Breendonk Memorial, n° 380).

least a small group of German officials. In his personal account (dated 1944) on his four-year stay in German-occupied Belgium, Prack even dedicated a few lines on Gramann's activities as 'chaplain of the executed':

> Last but not least will I mention the name of Monsignor Otto Gramann, who has acquired a good reputation in Belgium and is almost considered a Saint. As the catholic chaplain assigned to the Oberbefehlshaber [von Falkenhausen], he assisted the victims of the German regime in Belgium on their last journey. I got to know him by chance and we immediately discovered that we as good Austrians shared the same political views. More than 400 Belgians were accompanied by Gramann on their way to the execution place after spending the last night together. It was commonly known that he has alleviated the last walk of these poor people by his gentle, solely religiously inspired approach. Just even try to imagine. Gramann proved himself to be incredibly kind. I can hardly understand how he bore this psychological burden. 'I have to do this', he often said to me. 'It is my duty, I have to persist'. And he persisted until the end. He secretly kept a list with the location of the graves of these Belgian victims, which he wanted to hand over to Belgium after the war. This list was unfortunately lost as a result of a bombing raid on Münster, in which Gramann himself was severely injured and all of his belongings were destroyed. [...] Let us hope that Monsignor Gramann survives the war so that he can at least inform Belgium by heart of the grave sites of its victims. (Prack 1944, 40)

Gramann was certainly not the only *Wehrmacht* chaplain in German-occupied Western Europe to provide assistance to non-German civilians facing execution. In occupied France, a territory administered by a military administration like in Belgium and northern France, the rector of the German Catholic mission in Paris, Franz Stock, assisted the convicts and hostages. From September 1941 onwards, the priest acted as head for pastoral care to the military prison of Fresnes. Instead of wearing a military uniform, Stock always dressed up in his vestment. Between December 1941 and August 1944, he witnessed the execution of around 700 hostages and condemned resistance fighters. A further 162 others were assisted by two other *Militärpfarrer*, Theodor Loevenich and Paul Steinert. In fact, these two chaplains took more chances than Stock: beyond organising Masses for the prisoners and helping them to write their last letters, they also transgressed the German interdiction to contact the relatives of the inmates. By early 1942, Loevenich and Steinert were transferred to the front. In the case of Loevenich, his transfer was explicit punishment for writing to the family members of prisoners. Following the transfer of his two aides, Stock was left alone to minister to the inmates of the Fresnes prison (Albert 1960; Bücker 1964; Kock 1962; May 1978, 195; Rossi 2015, 139–140; Stolberg-Wernigerode 2013, 366–367).

While assisting death-row convicts and hostages in German-occupied Europe, chaplains like Stock and Gramann were forced into an uncomfortable position that was the result of the difficult relationship between the Church and the Nazi regime. In Germany, clergyman were not only loyal to God, the pope and the bishops. Because of their status of quasi-civil-servant, the clergymen were also bound to the rules of the state, even if the regime itself was not in favour of religion. This is one reason why the Church authorities never openly opposed the Nazi regime but instead chose to accommodate. As stated by Professor Kevin Spicer, some clergyman, for example, saw the mandatory Nazi salute for priests not as a sign of sympathy for the regime but more of an expression of national unity or just a way to avoid problems. The only times the Church authorities opposed the regime was when Nazi officials questioned the moral authority of the clergy or formulated regulations that were contradictory to canon law (Spicer 2011, 66–95).

Moreover, in their daily work, military chaplains were constantly faced with moral dilemmas and contradictions. First, they had to deal with the morality of war. Second, the pastor had to serve a regime whose ideology was radical and in fact completely opposed to any practical or institutional form of religion. Although some of the chaplains might have disagreed with the ideological program of the Nazi regime, just by serving in the ranks of the *Wehrmacht* they all aimed in one way or another to assure the final victory of Germany over the Allies (Lewins 2004). In Gramann's case, it should be noted that he wrote a message to the nuns of the Salesianerinnen abbey of Vienna on 10 July 1941, just a couple of weeks after the German invasion of the Soviet Union, in which he expressed the wish that 'this triumphant war' will soon be over (Nefors 2004, 166; Loidl, s.d., 6).

In order to describe the attitude of military chaplains towards the Nazi regime, German historian Martin Broszat distinguishes between *Widerstand* and *Resistenz*. While *Widerstand* is applicable for the minority of Catholics who actively resisted because of political motives such as discontentedness with the regime's racial policy or anti-clericalism, *Resistenz* is defined as a more indirect way to oppose the Nazi policies (Broszat 1987, 691–709). In Gramann's case, assisting death-row convicts and hostages can be seen as performing his duty as a chaplain. However, by smuggling the last letters out of prison and contacting the relatives of the executed, he knowingly violated the rules established by the German occupier. It is certain that his assistance made a difference to the executed and their relatives, yet it remains unclear whether the chaplain acted out of plain compassion for the executed or out of discord with the Nazi regime. As long as there is no proof of a political motivation, Gramann's actions are—in accordance with Broszat's theory—to be described as a form of *Resistenz* rather than an act of *Widerstand*.

References

Albert A (1960) Das war Abbé Stock. Ein Leben zwischen den Fronten. Verlag Herder, Freiburg, Basel and Vienna

Boudens R (1997) Kardinaal Van Roey en de Tweede Wereldoorlog. Altiora, Averbode

Broneder H (1963) Otto Gramann, deutscher General und Priester. Ein Hörbild von Herta Broneder

Broszat M (1987) Resistenz und Widerstand. Eine Zwischenbilanz der Forschungsprojekts. In: Broszat M, Fröhlich E (eds) Alltag und Widerstand—Bayern im Nationalsozialismus 4. Oldenbourg, Munich, pp 691–709

Bücker H (1964) Abbé Stock. Ein Wegbereiter der Versöhnung zwischen Deutschland und Frankreich. Herder, Freiburg, Basel and Vienna

Dantoing A (1991) La 'collaboration' du Cardinal. L'Eglise de Belgique dans la Guerre 40. De Boeck, Brussels

Debruyne E, Van Ypersele L (2011) Je serai fusillé demain. Les dernières lettres des patriotes belges et français fusillés par l'occupant, 1914–1918. Editions Racine, Brussels

De Craene T (2009) Terechtgesteld. Duitse executies in Oost-en West-Vlaanderen 1941–1944. Flying Pencil, Erembodegem
De Jonghe A (1974) De strijd Himmler-Reeder om de benoeming van een HSSPF te Brussel (1942–1944). Eerste deel: De Sicherheitspolizei in België. Bijdragen tot de Geschiedenis van de Tweede Wereldoorlog 3:9–81
De Jonghe A (1982) Hitler en het politieke lot van België (1940–1944). De vestiging van een Zivilverwaltung in België en Noord-Frankrijk. Koningskwestie en bezettingsregime van de kapitulatie tot Berchtesgaden (28 mei–19 november 1940). De Nederlandsche Boekhandel, Kapellen
De Jonghe A (1984) De strijd Himmler-Reeder om de benoeming van een HSSPF te Brussel (1942–1944). Vijfde deel: Salzburg voor en na. Politionele ontwikkeling van september 1943 tot het einde van de bezetting. Bijdragen tot de Geschiedenis van de Tweede Wereldoorlog 8:6–234
Gérard-Libois J, Gotovitch J (1971) L'an '40. La Belgique occupée. CRISP, Brussels
Kock E (1962) Franz stock. Priester zwischen den Fronten, Heimatschriften für die Arbeit in den Jugendgruppen. Gruppe 5: Berühmte Westfalen, Heft 9. Münster, Westfalen, Bielefeld and Bethel
Konings J (1982) De terechtstelling van gijzelaars tijdens de Duitse besetting. Master's thesis, Catholic University of Leuven
Lewins A (2004) Sheep Among Wolves or Part of the Pack? Men of God in Hitler's Armies. Research paper for USCB History 133P proseminar, UC Santa Barbara
Loidl F (s.d.) Mons. Otto Gramann (Gest. 1947)
May G (1978) Interkonfessionalismus in der deutschen Militärseelsorge von 1933 bis 1945. John Benjamins Publishing, Amsterdam
Nefors P (2004) Breendonk 1940–1945. De geschiedenis. Standaard Uitgeverij, Antwerp
Prack H (1944) Vier Jahre Besatzungszeit in Belgien. Persönliche Erinnerungen, Vienna
Roden D (2009) Inventaris van het archief van Wehrmachtoberpfarrer Otto Gramann (1885–1947). Willebroek
Roden D (2015) 'In naam van het Duitse volk!' Het Duitse krijgsgerecht en de openbare orde in bezet België (1940–1944). PhD thesis, Ghent University, Ghent
Rossi LF (2015) Wehrmacht Priests: Catholicism and the Nazi War of Annihilation. Harvard University Press, Cambridge, MA and London
Spicer KP (2011) 'Tu ich unrecht, ... ein guter Priester und ein guter Nationalsozialist zu sein?' Zum Verhältnis zwischen Katholizismus und Nationalsozialismus. In: Gailus M, Nolzen A (eds) Zerstrittene 'Volksgemeinschaft'. Glaube, Konfession und Religion im Nationalsozialismus. Vandenhoek & Ruprecht, Göttingen, pp 66–95
Stolberg-Wernigerode O (2013) Stock, Franz. Neue deutsche Biographie 25:366–367
Thierry L (2013) La répression allemande dans le Nord de la France 1940–1944. Presses Universitaires du Septentrion, Villeneuve d'Ascq
Van de Vijver H, Van Doorslaer R, Verhoeyen E (1988) Het verzet deel 2, België in de Tweede Wereldoorlog VI. Pelckmans, Kapellen
Van den Wijngaert M (ed) (2004) België tijdens de Tweede Wereldoorlog. Standaard Uitgeverij, Antwerpen
Verhoeyen E (1993) België bezet 1940–1944. Een synthese. BRTN-Instructieve Omroep, Brussels
Voncken M (1945) Nos fusillés nous parlent! Mes quatorze stations à la citadelle de Liège. Lettres des fusillés (du 21 mai 1941 au 29 janvier 1943). Soledi, Liège
Voncken M (1953) Le jociste Jean Clokers de Vivegnis, fusillé à la citadelle de Liège le 10 avril 1942. Esgy, Liège
Voncken M (1963) L'eucharistie et nos fusillés. Marie-Médiatrice, Genval
Weber W (1978) Die innere Sicherheit im besetzten Belgien und Nordfrankreich 1940–1944. Ein Beitrag zur Geschichte der Besatzungsverwaltungen. Droste Verlag, Düsseldorf

Foreigners, Penal Justice and *Eigensinn* in Berlin During the Second World War

Julia Albert, Herbert Reinke, and Michael Wildt

Abstract Keeping the German war economy successfully going in order to keep the war successfully going was one of the prime objectives of Nazi Germany. As German men were at war, the workforce for the Nazi war economy was therefore recruited from the countries and territories occupied by Nazi Germany. Most of the women and men who were recruited were forced to work in Germany, some volunteered, and the borderline between 'forced' and 'voluntary' not always clear and was constantly shifting. Although foreign workers were urgently needed for the smooth running of the Nazi wartime economy, they were nevertheless seen as a threat in many respects. Foreigners not only posed a threat because of their sheer numbers but they also constituted a threat to the pure and homogeneous German(ic) society, the so-called *Volksgemeinschaft* (see Bajohr and Wildt in Volksgemeinschaft. Neue Forschungen zur Geschichte des Nationalsozialismus. Fischer Taschenbuch Verlag, Frankfurt am Main, 2009; Wildt in Visions of community in Nazi Germany: social engineering and private lives. Oxford University Press, Oxford, 2014), which was, from the point of view of Nazi ideology, the essence of the German people. Berlin-based industries held a key position in the war economy (electrotechnical industries, armaments etc.); the work force had grown accordingly: by the end of the war, the population of Berlin counted approximately 370,000 foreigners, i.e., one seventh of the city's population by that time. The Berlin police and the Berlin judiciary tried to maintain efficient and tight control strategies in order to cope with the enormous number of foreigners in the city, but they had increasingly difficulty maintaining control and experienced erosion of control as the war went on. The control issues became more urgent as more members of the foreign work force in the city displayed *Eigensinn*; in particular foreigners from Western Europe were free to move in the

J. Albert
German Resistance Memorial (Gedenkstätte Deutscher Widerstand), Berlin, Germany
e-mail: albert_julia@gmx.de

H. Reinke (✉) · M. Wildt
Institute for Historical Sciences, Humboldt University, Berlin, Germany
e-mail: herbert.reinke@gmail.com

M. Wildt
e-mail: michael.wildt@geschichte.hu-berlin.de

M. Bost and A. Vrints (eds.), *Doing Justice In Wartime*,
Studies in the History of Law and Justice 19,
https://doi.org/10.1007/978-3-030-72050-6_9

city, displaying a wide spectrum of individual patterns when organising their lives in the city individually, which quite often escaped the attention of the police and other authorities in Nazi Berlin.

1 'Doing Justice' in Nazi Germany: Research Lines and *Lacunae*

Research on the history of justice in Nazi Germany, on the law codes under Nazi rule, on particular Nazi components of the justice system during that period, on penal strategies after the Nazi seizure of power and on the institutions and the personnel of justice began intensively in Germany during the 1970s and since that time has given deep insights into the structures and the functioning of justice during the 'Third Reich'. The research questions, which have been dealt with, changed during the 1970s; some gained considerable interest, while others rather on the margins of the attention of historical research. A recent account of the evolution of research on justice under Nazi rule points to a number of phases of historiographic interest in Nazi justice (Schoenmakers 2015). According to this account, historical research during the 1970s focused primarily on the ideological loading of justice under Nazi rule. From the beginning of the 1980s onwards, the interest of research shifted to the institutions and the personnel of justice in Nazi Germany, among them a number of research enterprises, which resulted in reference publications for the understanding of justice in Nazi Germany (Gruchmann 1988), in particular for understanding the cleavages within the system, i.e., the conflicts between penal justice as such on the one side (the courts, the prisons, judges, public prosecutors) and the police on the other side as actors and institutions of penal justice (Werle 1989). Later studies added significantly to this picture by analysing the role of the police (Wagner 1996; Reinke and Roth 2014) and the prisons as part of the justice system in Germany (Wachsmann 2004).

An analysis of 'doing justice' in Nazi Germany, in particular, an analysis of the practice of penal justice as 'doing justice', must recognise that the efforts to control, prevent and sanction different forms of crime and deviance merged increasingly with overall societal and political control strategies. These not only aimed at everyday-life crime and deviance and at political opponents but also were designed to enhance a societal model, based on racial categories, which was to divide Nazi Germany into those who were included into the German people proper and who were excluded (Jews, foreigners, asocials etc.). Those included were seen as members of the so-called *Volksgemeinschaft* (national community); penal justice was seen as an institution for protecting the *Volksgemeinschaft* and for sanctioning violations of this community (Stolleis 1972; Schoenmakers 2015).

The Nazi party did not have a detailed and coherent penal policy and strategy when it gained power in 1933, but it soon adopted very repressive penal policy programs and strategies that had been on the agenda already in previous years. These programs differed from the rehabilitative penal policy goals and strategies that had been at the core of the Weimar Republic's democratic parties of the political system. One penal policy that the Nazis adopted had already developed around the turn of the nineteenth to the twentieth century; it focused on the perpetrator and the damage done by the criminal act rather than on earlier 19th-century penal policy philosophies that had emphasised guilt and deterrence. Nazi penal policy not only adopted perpetrator-orientated penal strategies but borrowed significantly from criminal biology as well, transforming these approaches selectively and radicalising them not only as a penal policy strategy but also as a *Weltanschauung*, legitimising genocidal ends.

Research during the 1990s emphasised institutional settings and the earlier research on the ideological loadings of justice polices, to be followed after 2000 by a 'boom' (Schoenmakers 2015) of research on the so-called special courts (*Sondergerichte*) within the justice system of Nazi Germany.[1] Research on the *Sondergerichte* has pointed out that these special courts became a major institution of penal justice in Nazi Germany, in particular during the Second World War. This 'boom' reflects the significant position that the special courts held within the Nazi system of power and also draws attention to the basic fact that many of the files of the special courts' penal proceedings have been preserved in German archives.

Research on these courts has emphasised their role in enforcing overall strategies of the Nazi regime during the war years. A key element of these strategies consisted of not allowing a rise of those factors considered to have been decisive for Germany's defeat during the previous war. These factors were manifold; in reviewing them, the Nazis and many members of traditional administrative and judicial elites who supported the war efforts raised the spectre of different forms of crime and deviance in general (juvenile crime, female delinquency) as threatening the home front and thus threatening (again) the victory of (Nazi) Germany. To these already well-known threats, the regime and its supporters added another threat during the war: the enormous number of foreigners who were forced to work for the German war industry in Germany. The special courts responded to these threats with harsh sanctions, in particular, by issuing massive numbers of death penalties (Angermund 1990; Evans 1996). Research on the special courts has quantified the perceptions of these courts about the threats deriving from the foreigners within Germany, as well as the racial implications of its penal strategies in relation to foreigners: foreigners suffered comparatively harsher punishments than Germans tried before these courts, including the application of the death penalty.

Up to now, research on the history of justice during the Nazi period has focused very much on institutional top-to-bottom perspectives. Approaches for adding bottom-to-top perspectives are rarely introduced when analysing Nazi Germany. Applying substantial bottom-to-top perspectives when analysing the practices of the special courts is difficult; the procedural regulations for these courts allowed for drastic abbreviations of the penal procedures, which hardly gave the people before the bars of these courts any opportunity to express themselves. The files from common

[1] See Schoenmakers (2015) for a comprehensive bibliography of studies on special courts in Nazi Germany.

penal law court proceedings from the Nazi period are, from a more general point of view, much more open for the application of bottom-to-top perspectives,[2] but very few of these files have been preserved in German archives. Berlin is an exception in that respect; its state archive (*Landesarchiv*) preserves files from common-law court proceedings in very large numbers.

2 Berlin: Foreigners, Control Issues and *Eigensinn* During the War

In order to keep the war going successfully, it was essential for Nazi Germany to keep the German economy going successfully. Doing so required a quantitatively and also, in some sectors, a qualitatively significant labour force. Because most German men were away at war, labour was recruited from the countries and territories that Nazi Germany occupied. Some of these women and men volunteered, most were forced to work in Germany, and the distinction between 'forced' and 'voluntary' was not always clear or stable.

The enormous number of foreigners transferred into Germany resulted in a complex set of—sometimes conflicting—control issues and ambivalences, which grew as the war went on. The literature on foreign forced labour in the economy of wartime Nazi Germany has depicted three main lines:

1. A basic ambivalence derived from the fact that the foreign labour force, due to its quantitative dimension, turned into a threat as such, while at the same time it was urgently needed for the continuation, efficiency and output of the German war industry.
2. German big business, medium-sized companies, even small family businesses such as bakeries and the German authorities themselves had to balance between providing incentives to encourage good and efficient work and the introduction and enforcement of structures and measures of control and sanctioning in the case of non-compliant workers or deviance from expected behaviour in a more general sense.
3. Control and sanctioning of the large number of foreigners living in Nazi Germany during the war pertained not only to their work performance but also included ideological and racial aspects as well: foreigners were seen as a danger to the purity of the German people and the Germanic race respectively and, as such, were not welcome.

These issues became particularly pronounced in Berlin, where, in comparison to other German cities and regions, a very high number of foreigners, mostly forced labourers, were working in the war industry. Many of them, when not at their work places or in the camps, occupied literally the public space of the city, as they were more or

[2]For a pioneering approach in German historiography, attempting to combine bottom-to-top perspectives and an analysis of 'doing justice', see Habermas (2008).

less allowed to move there freely. Personal memories of wartime Berlin reflect this situation: during the second half of the war, Ursula von Kardorff, a Berlin journalist, wrote a diary summarising her war experiences while in the city. Being a professional journalist and someone between non-Nazi and anti-Nazi, her observations on wartime Berlin are extremely significant. On 30 November 1944 she wrote in her diary:

> *Friedrichstrasse* train station with its wide escalators leading into some sort of underworld, is supposed to be a safe place in regard to aerial attacks. Down there it is like my imagination of Shanghai. Colourful people in rags and padded jackets and the typical face of the Slav people, very blond Danes and Norwegians, coquettish made up French women, Polish men with hate in their face, pale, freezing Italians, altogether a mix of people, which has never been seen in a German city. With almost only foreigners down there, the German language is almost absent. Most of these people had been forced to work in the war industry. But they are not in a depressed mood. Many are loud and gay, they laugh, they sing, they trade things and they follow their own rules … In the big beer halls around *Friedrichstrasse* train station, you see very few Germans. … Everyone who does not belong there is looked upon with suspicion. … They know each other very well. Girls walk from table to table, young men in flashy scarves are lingering around … in between isolated figures, which are shunned, probably informers or members of the *Kriminalpolizei*. … It is said that the foreigners are extremely well organised. (von Kardorff 1992)

This diary entry from the end of November 1944, as well as the diary altogether, says as much about the author as it says about the situation in Berlin during the last full year of the war (see Wildt and Kreutzmüller 2013 for a comprehensive account). The very high number of foreigners in wartime Berlin, which excited many Berliners such as Ursula von Kardorff, was very much due to the specific position of the Berlin economy within the war economy. Berlin was both the capital of Nazi Germany and also one of its economic and industrial powerhouses. Berlin was one of the major sites of the German armament industries, and its electro-technical industries (AEG, Siemens) had a world-wide reputation. At the end of the war, approximately 370,000 foreigners lived in the city, i.e., one-seventh of the city's total population. At more than 3000 addresses within the city limits, accommodation (camps and smaller lodgings) for these foreigners had been made available. Due to the bias of the Berlin industrial structure towards manufacturing industries and towards services, comparatively more workers from Western Europe engaged in the Berlin war industry than in the entirety of Nazi Germany (Pagenstecher and Buggeln 2013; Pagenstecher et al. 2008).

Nazi Germany categorised the foreign labour force according to racial hierarchies: people from occupied countries whose population was supposed to be Germanic or close to that category ranked high in this hierarchy, while female and male workers labelled as Slav were ranked at the bottom. French workers and French-speaking Belgians were located somewhere in the middle.[3] Italians, after Italy had changed sides during the war, were seen as traitors and were placed at the bottom of the hierarchy as well. In order to control foreigners, Nazi Germany had manifold institutional arrangements and actors at its disposal, among them the different police and security

---

[3]In her book on Belgian labour in Nazi Germany, Harrison (2011) argues that the German side (companies, the police, the public in general) made no distinction between Dutch- and French-speaking Belgians.

forces, which held a core position in this regard. The Gestapo maintained its own labour camp system in Nazi Germany (more than 200 camps with approximately 40,000 inmates), which did not have the quantitative size and genocidal character of the Lager system run by the SS, but the system nevertheless became an instrument for controlling and terrorising both Germans and members of the foreign workforce (Lotfi 2000). One Gestapo labour camp for female foreign workers was located near Berlin (Geschichtswerkstatt 2004). Another Gestapo labour camp within the city limits of Berlin (*Wulheide*) was seen by officials of the Nazi security forces authorities as a model for these types of camps (Pagenstecher and Buggeln 2013). But despite these efforts, the security forces experienced growing deficiencies when trying control foreigners in the city. In 1943, Berlin saw a fear-of-crime wave, which the detective branch perceived as originating primarily from an increase in crime committed by foreigners. The police and the judiciary tried to crack down on these patterns, the Berlin special court issuing in 1943 an extremely high number of death penalties against foreigners, but the results of this hardening remained insignificant. The police finally had to concede that crimes committed by foreigners were only one side of a coin; perhaps even more concerning was the rise in numbers of deviant or criminal patterns in which ordinary Berliners increasingly engaged.

2.1 Eigensinn

The emphasis that much research has put on the special courts and, although to a lesser extent, on the camps run by the Gestapo has enhanced a narrative that gives the impression of tight and efficient controls and rigid top-to-bottom hierarchies. But the results of recent research (Harrison 2011; Fauroux 2020) allows for interpretations that may elaborate and modify this narrative of tight and efficient control. In pursuit of alternative interpretations, this contribution borrows heavily from a concept that has become very popular among German scholars: *Eigensinn*. There are different origins of this concept, which is nowadays widely used by scholars in Germany and elsewhere.[4] It is an open concept, focusing very much on the making of meaning in relation to a situation or a context by oneself—and acting accordingly, differently or in contrast to the meaning given to it by someone else. Originally used in only a very few research fields, such as the history of workers on the factory level, it has now been integrated into a wide variety of research approaches.

Making sense of a situation, a context etc. by oneself should not necessarily be connected with resistance: even acting 'criminally' might be some sort of *Eigensinn*, not as resistance but, rather, as sort of 'despite the norms imposed from above'. Using the city and its possibilities, as did many foreign workers in Berlin, being forced to live and work there could be seen as an expression of *Eigensinn*, but so

[4]The concept has been introduced into German historiography and else where by Lüdtke (1993, 1996) and has been used widely since then (Davis et al. 2008). Fauroux (2020) translates the concept as 'popular individualism'.

could participation in wartime local economies such as black markets (Zierenberg 2015; Mörchen 2001) or handling of conflicts at the workplace. The following three cases help to indicate *Eigensinn*, expressed by foreigners in wartime Berlin, as well as the problems the police and other security forces had when trying to control foreigners.

3 The Cases[5]

3.1 Walter F., the Victim-Police Officer and René P., the French Baker[6]

On 13 September 1944, Walter Fink, a Berliner in his mid-fifties, issued a complaint at a small police station in a southern, supposedly quiet middle-class suburb of Berlin, where he had a house and where he lived. He indicated that he had become the victim of a burglary the previous night. Walter F. some time ago had dug an extensive hole in his garden, had reinforced the walls of the hole, had covered it solidly and equipped it with a trapdoor, trying to use it as an air-raid shelter. The investigating police officers called it an *Erdbunker*. The air-raid shelter in the garden of the house had been used by the victim and by neighbours as a sort of shelter not for persons but for household and family goods and valuables against damages and eventual loss caused by the frequent allied air-raids touching Berlin in 1944. Because the part of Berlin where the victim and his neighbours had their homes had been a relatively wealthy suburban part of Berlin, the personal belongings of Walter F. and his neighbours, mostly clothing, were of considerable value.

Interestingly, Walter F., the victim, was by that time a member of the Berlin *Kriminalpolizei*, the detective branch of the Berlin police. One of the neighbours, whose personal belongings of some value were also kept in the *Erdbunker*, was also a member of the *Kriminalpolizei*. Maybe because of colleagues being affected by a crime, the Berlin *Kriminalpolizei* started an extensive investigation to detect and arrest the perpetrators. The *Kriminalpolizei* started the investigation with a tracking dog, which tried to follow tracks of the perpetrators—but without success. Likewise a search operation in a nearby camp that housed foreigners brought no results.

Not surprisingly, Walter F. intervened into the investigations of his colleagues by sending them some of his own observations and investigation results. Due to this rather unofficial investigation, a young Frenchman, René P., who worked in a small nearby bakery, came under suspicion. The team at the bakery where René P. worked

---

[5]The following cases are drawn from the files of the Berlin common penal law justice 1933–1945, preserved in large numbers at the Berlin State Archive (Landesarchiv Berlin/LAB). For a more detailed account of French and Belgians before the bars of Berlin penal justice during the Second World War see Albert (2013a, b).

[6]LAB (Landesarchiv Berlin), A Rep 358–02, Nr. 14223.

consisted of the wife of the baker (the baker himself was a member of the *Wehrmacht* on the Eastern front), the wife's brother, René P. and a Dutch-speaking Belgian.

Walter F. was not only a member of the Berlin *Kriminalpolizei* but also the neighbourhood's air shelter guard (*Luftschutzwart*). On the night of the burglary, he had met René P. while on patrol because of an air-raid around midnight. When interrogated about his whereabouts during that night, René P. indicated that he had spent the night in a bar on *Kurfürstendamm* in downtown Berlin and that he had to hide in a shelter on his way home because of an air-raid. Walter F. also collected additional information—or, rather, rumours running around in the neighbourhood—about René P. And there were quite a lot running around: one neighbour indicated that René P. was quite often out at night, usually coming home very late. Other neighbours indicated that on many evenings a group of Frenchmen came onto the street where René P. lived, indicating their presence by whistling signals and leaving later together with him. According to information collected by Walter F., a woman from the neighbourhood had indicated that on one of these nights, while she was escorting her visiting sister to a nearby train station late at night, a group of Frenchmen was lingering around on both sides of the street. They had frightened the two women so much that they had not gone on to the station but had returned home. The wife of a former employer of René P. added to this—again according to the report of Walter F.—that René P. quite often had been out at night, insinuating that he very probably spent nights in the apartments of German women.

In order to make a stance at this point of the investigation, the *Kriminalpolizei* deployed at night a group of officers behind bushes and trees of the gardens of the neighbourhood, in order to observe and to detect what had been described as a group of whistling Frenchmen. All they could see was René P. coming home late again, but no French whistling gang came under the observant eyes of the *Kriminalpolizei* officers. At this point, The *Kriminalpolizei* decided to search René P.'s room, but after finding no incriminating evidence they took him in for questioning. When questioned, René P. admitted to being out quite often in and around the bars on the *Kurfürstendamm*, explaining to the *Kriminalpolizei* that—as the Berlin suburb where he lived and worked was boring to him—he simply had been taking the opportunity to go out there as often as possible. And when by bad chance an air-raid occurred while he was out in *Kurfürstendamm* bars, he was forced, as he explained, to walk home a long way, because trams did not run during air-raids and thereafter. Yet René P.'s current employer confirmed that he was always on duty very early in the morning, when the bakery's stove was to be lit for the early morning customers and deliveries. Moreover, further questioning of the neighbours by police officers revealed that the evidence that their victim-colleague had collected about whistling French gangs was very much based on rumours, hearsay etc. That already did not make the case against René P. look good, but the final blow came when the police questioned the Belgian who worked with René P. in the bakery. This Belgian shared a room with René P. but nevertheless had little personal contact with him, for René P. spoke French and he only spoke Dutch. The Belgian confirmed that René P. often came home quite late but emphasised that he always had been on time for the start of the work. And he confirmed the information on the whistling—but in a completely different direction.

According to the Belgian colleague of René P., there had not been any whistling French, but only the brother of the baker's wife, giving signals from down on the street to their room, in order assure their waking and getting got up for their early morning shifts in order to bake the breads for the good *Berliner Hausfrauen.* With that, the police and the public prosecutor closed the file, stating that no evidence could be established against René P. René P. very probably continued to work in the bakery after the investigations, but the file does not say anything about that. Nor does it say whether or not Walter F., the victim-police officer had continued his private investigation and had been able to regain his and his neighbour's belongings of some value.

3.2 André F., the Migrant Belgian Worker[7]

In an interrogation by the Berlin police, André F. reported on his life before he had arrived in Germany. He had been born in Nimy near Mons in 1922 and had worked as a baker's assistant in different parts of Belgium. After the beginning of the war in Belgium, he had fled to France in May 1940 and had been interned in Toulouse for about two weeks. From there, he returned to Belgium for a month before he was placed in Germany as a labourer, apparently voluntarily. The Brussels labour office initially sent him to the Leuna works in Merseburg near Leipzig, which produced synthetic fuel. After three months he left the Leuna works without permission; in his interrogation he stated that he didn't like it there any more. He went to the Lauta works of the Vereinigte Aluminium-Werke AG near Cottbus. There he was granted leave in December 1940 and went home to Belgium. He did not return to the Lauta works either, because he earned too little there and wanted to work in his usual profession, as he states in his interrogation.

After this leave, he came in January 1941 to Berlin, to work for the baker Paul Stange, who had a bakery close to the centre of Berlin. André F. worked there as a baker and confectioner for 35 Reichsmark a week, with free food and lodging. In July 1941, Paul Stange sold his bakery to the master baker Heinz Korth, who took over also the employees. Shortly thereafter, Heinz Korth reported him to the Gestapo for theft. He claimed that André F. had stolen margarine, sugar, cream powder and jam from the bakery on repeated occasions, by mixing fewer ingredients into the dough for the baked goods and taking the remaining ingredients for himself. In the course of the Berlin Gestapo's investigations, further offences allegedly committed by André F. were added to the file: a further theft from his time at the Lauta works (stealing clothing and a watch from three Belgian colleagues); and two cases of fraud. He had allegedly borrowed money from an apprentice at Korth's bakery and not paid it back, but instead had been renting a room for his French girlfriend, Yvette G. But he had not paid any rent for that, only the deposit.

---

[7]LAB A Rep 358–02, Nr. 122113, 67538.

André F. admitted the thefts in his first interrogation, stating he had given the food to his girlfriend Yvette G. They both then were charged with theft, fraud and receiving stolen goods, as the indictment states. In the trial on 26 March 1942, André F. was sentenced to one year and four months in prison, and his girlfriend Yvette G. to three weeks in prison. André F. served his sentence in Tegel prison, from which he was released in July 1943. But he still kept the Berlin police and penal justice busy: he was sentenced to several months of imprisonment because of theft on two subsequent occasions. In one case he had stolen flour from the bakery *Buttler* in Lichtenberg, a district in the northeast of Berlin, where he had worked after his release from prison in 1943. He did not have to serve this sentence because he had been held in detention on remand for some time. In March 1945, very close to the end of the war, he was sentenced to five months in prison because he had (again) stolen ten loaves of bread from his new employer, the *Liebing* bakery. When interrogated by the police about it, André F. admitted the theft by saying: 'I had enough bread to eat and did not live in want. I took the loaves of bread only to trade them, because I did not get along with the ration of fat and other groceries. When being asked who else but me steals bread at the bakery, I have to respond: everybody does'. André F. was taken to Spandau prison, in the west of Berlin. The last information in the file is a letter from Spandau prison: André F. had escaped in April 1945 another workplace in Berlin.

3.3 Robert V., the Belgian Souteneur[8]

Robert V., born in Kapellen near Antwerp in 1920, had been a member of a gang of *souteneurs* (pimps) consisting of French and Belgian workers. Robert V. had come to Berlin at the beginning of September 1940 at the age of twenty. He had been a soldier for a few months and had ended up in a German prisoner-of-war camp, from which he had managed to escape. The Antwerp labour office had sent him to Germany. The police investigation files indicate that Robert V. had been employed as an interpreter by the *Teves* Company in Berlin-Wittenau in the spring of 1943 but had been off sick for several months due to a sexually transmitted disease. He did not live in a camp but as a sub-tenant in a private lodging in the *Rosenthaler Strasse*, close to the centre of Berlin. It was while he was off work that he came into contact with the 'Henry Gang', a label attached by the detective branch of the Berlin police after the name of the supposed gang leader of a group of men who procured women. The group consisted of about ten French and Belgian men between their mid-twenties and mid-thirties who forced at least as many French women, probably working voluntarily in Berlin, into prostitution. Most of the men did not have previous convictions for procuring, either in Germany or their respective home countries. These men had no permanent employment—and thus no regular income—and usually lived in hotels or as sub-tenants in private apartments. They extorted the money necessary to survive from the women they had forced into prostitution. They all spent their free time in

[8] LAB A Rep 358-02, Nr. 123628, 123629.

the bars and cafés close to the Alexanderplatz in the centre of Berlin, from where they had organised and supervised the prostitution of the women.

The women solicited customers in the bars and *Kneipen*, where other workers usually went with them to nearby hotels and boarding houses. All the women working as prostitutes for the gang were French and very young, between 18 and 24. They all had regular employment and only participated in prostitution during their free time. Many of these groups of *souteneurs* had operated for several months before the police had been able to arrest most of them and before the public prosecutor could charge them with the procurement of women.

In one of the bars near the *Alexanderplatz* named *Brennpunkt*, Robert V. met Marguerite C., whom he forced into working for him as a prostitute as well. She carried out prostitution in this bar, earning an average of around 80 Reichsmarks per day, a significant earning compared to the 35 Reichsmarks that André F. earned a week in the bakery (see above). She had to give 50 Reichsmarks of her takings to Robert V. She also had to pay the bill when the two of them went out. This relationship lasted for about four weeks, until Robert V. was admitted on 19 April 1943 to the municipal Rudolf Virchow Hospital for a sexually transmitted disease. For Marguerite C., however, the exploitative situation by no means ended when her *souteneur* was admitted to this hospital, for just a short time later, the gang members made her choose between selecting another man as a *souteneur* or being banned from the *Brennpunkt* bar. She decided to work for one of the Frenchmen. For the women, the bars and cafés were not only sites of prostitution but also social places, as they were for many other foreigners; places of contact with their compatriots. They spent their free time there and exchanged news. The bars and cafés were also trading places for the black market, upon which many of the forced labourers relied, for example to obtain additional food or clothing. Thus for many forced labourers, these bars and cafés were the centre of their social lives, offering distraction from their working days and also helping them to maintain links to their home countries, friends and acquaintances. Being excluded from this community would have meant losing all these social contacts.

When Robert V. was discharged from hospital in mid-May 1943, not as cured but as 'capable of working', the Berlin criminal investigation department was in the midst of investigations into the 'Henry Gang'. As one result of these investigations, Robert V. was arrested on 1 June 1943. During the interrogations by officers from the detective branch of the Berlin police, Robert V. denied all allegations. But Marguerite C. was perceived as a reliable witness, and Robert V. therefore was charged with the procurement of women in the case of Marguerite C. and sentenced to 15 months of penal servitude by a Berlin penal court on 6 September 1943. He presumably served the entire sentence prison, but there are no records on his time in prison. He returned to Belgium at the end of June 1945.

Almost all of the other members of this gang were sentenced to penal servitude or prison sentences, with the exception of three men: René C. was shot dead by a police officer in May 1943 in broad daylight on a Berlin street while he tried to escape arrest. The two main people of the group (Henry L. and Marceau V.) were sentenced to death in August 1943 by one of the Berlin special courts for robbery and violation of the so-called *Gewaltverbrecherverordnung* (regulation against violent criminals). They had robbed a Frenchman by threatening him with a gun and a knife and had stolen money and clothing. Both men were executed at one of the central execution sites within Nazi Germany, in the Berlin-Plötzensee prison on 8 September 1943.

4 Epilogue

When trying to summarise the cases presented above, one point has to be made first: on the basis of the knowledge currently available, it cannot be determined, at least not on the level of reliable statistical reasoning, whether the cases can be considered as representative, but there are probably very many similar cases to be found. Each of these foreigners—a French baker who seeks entertainment in the bars on the *Kurfürstendamm* and must be released when accused of burglary by the police and the public prosecutor; the young Belgian who migrates within Nazi Germany, gets involved in black-market activities and serves prison sentences but always returns to workplaces; and finally another Belgian who manages to be absent from work for a considerable time while at the same time procuring women—was able—despite the control apparatus that tried to fence them in—to exert different variations of popular individualism. (Fauroux 2020).

Reasons for the failure of attempts to punish these offenders might be found in an exchange between two high-ranking officials of the Berlin judiciary and the Berlin police, which took place in April 1943, the year of the fear-of-crime wave in the city. Wilhelm Kelsch, the official solicitor of Berlin (*Oberamtsanwalt*), complained to Wolf-Heinrich Graf von Helldorff, the Nazi head of the Berlin police, that Berlin courts had increasingly to cope with organisational difficulties resulting from the growing numbers of foreign delinquents: '… sittings [of the court had to be] fixed for foreign accused and witnesses only, making the most of the few interpreters: on specific days Frenchmen and Wallonian Belgians, on other days Czechs, Serbians, Ukrainians etcetera'. The head of the police lamented in his reply that '… some of those already sentenced are back in the dock again …', which he put down to the fact that expulsion regulations were not applied to foreigners (*Ausländerpolizeiverordnung*). He thought the expulsions would be a warning and a relief for the police and the justice system, who 'have more important tasks to do than to be occupied again and again with the same foreigners unwilling to work'. From his point of view, as a member of penal justice court confronted with the large number of 'criminal' foreign workers, this might have been a coherent suggestion. But from the perspective of the Nazi war industry and its constant shortage of workforce, this was not viable, as von Helldorff responded: 'We have to take into account the war industries constant need of workforce, which cannot be satisfied'.

References

Albert J (2013a) Ausländische Straftäter als Teil der Kriegskriminalität am Beispiel belgischer Zwangsarbeiter. In: Dobler J (ed) Großstadtkriminalität. Berliner Kriminalpolizei und Verbrechensbekämpfung 1930 bis 1950, Metropol, Berlin, pp 169–186

Albert J (2013b) Von "arbeitsunwilligen Ausländern." Französische Zwangsarbeiter vor Berliner Gerichten in der Kriegszeit. In: Dobler J (ed) Großstadtkriminalität. Berliner Kriminalpolizei und Verbrechensbekämpfung 1930 bis 1950. Metropol, Berlin, pp 187–246

Angermund R (1990) Deutsche Richterschaft. 1919–1945. Krisenerfahrung, Illusion, Rechtsprechung. Fischer Taschenbuch Verlag, Frankfurt am Main

Bajohr F, Wildt M (eds) (2009) Volksgemeinschaft. Neue Forschungen zur Geschichte des Nationalsozialismus. Fischer Taschenbuch Verlag, Frankfurt am Main

Berliner Geschichtswerkstatt (ed) (2004) Arbeitserziehungslager Fehrbellin. Zwansgarbeiterinnen im Straflager der Gestapo. Brandenburgische Landeszentrale für politische Bildung, Potsdam

Davis B, Lindenberger T, Wildt M (eds) (2008) Alltag—Erfahrung—Eigensinn. Historisch-anthropologische Erkundungen. Campus, Frankfurt am Main and New York

Evans RJ (1996) Rituals of retribution: capital punishment in Germany 1600–1987. Oxford University Press, Oxford

Fauroux C (2020) Produire la guerre, produire le genre. Des Françaises au travail dans l'Allemagne national-socialiste (1940–1945). Editions EHESS, Paris

Gruchmann L (1988) Justiz im Dritten Reich 1933–1940. Anpassung und Unterwerfung in der Ära Grüttner. R. Oldenbourg, Munich

Habermas R (2008) Diebe vor Gericht. Die Entstehung der modernen Rechtsordnung im 19. Jahrhundert. Campus, Frankfurt am Main

Harrison SM (2011) Belgian labour in Nazi Germany: a social history. PhD dissertation, University of Edinburgh, Edinburgh

Lotfi G (2000) KZ der Gestapo. Arbeitserziehungslager im Dritten Reich. Deutsche Verlagsanstalt, Munich

Lüdtke A (1993) Eigen-Sinn, Fabrikalltag, Arbeitererfahrungen und Politik vom Kaiserreich bis in den Faschismus. Ergebnisse, Hamburg

Lüdtke A (1996) Ouvriers, Eigensinn et politique dans l'Allemagne du XXème siècle. Actes de la recherche en sciences sociales 113(1):91–101

Mörchen S (2001) Schwarzer Markt. Krimnalität, Ordnung und Moral in Bremen 1939–1949. Campus, Frankfurt am Main

Pagenstecher C, Buggeln M (2013) Zwangsarbeit. In: Wildt M, Kreutzmüller C (eds) Berlin 1933–1945. Siedler, Munich, pp 127–142

Pagenstecher C, Bremberger B, Wenzel G (2008) Zwangsarbeit in Berlin. Archivrecherchen, Nachweissuche und Entschädigung. Metropol, Berlin

Reinke H, Roth T (2014) Police in Nazi Germany. In: Bruinsma G, Weisburd D (eds) Encyclopedia of criminology and criminal justice. Springer, New York, pp 2296–2309

Schoenmakers C (2015) 'Die Belange der Volksgemeinschaft erfordern ...' Rechtspraxis und Selbstverständnis von Bremer Juristen im 'Dritten Reich'. Ferdinand Schöningh, Paderborn

Stolleis M (1972) Gemeinschaft und Volksgemeinschaft. Zur juristischen Terminologie im Nationalsozialismus. Vierteljahreshefte für Zeitgeschichte 20(1):16–38

von Kardorff U (1992) Berliner Aufzeichnungen 1942–1945. Unter Verwendung von Original-Tagebüchern neu herausgegeben und kommentiert von Pater Hartl. Beck, Munich

Wachsmann N (2004) Hitler's prisons: legal terror in Nazi Germany. Yale University Press, New Haven

Wagner P (1996) Volksgemeinschaft ohne Verbrecher. Konzeptionen und Praxis der Kriminalpolizei in der Zeit des Nationalsozialismus. Christians, Hamburg

Werle G (1989) Justiz-Strafrecht und polizeiliche Verbrechensbekämpfung im Dritten Reich. Walter de Gruyter, Berlin

Wildt M (2014) Volksgemeinschaft: a modern perspective on National Socialist Society. In: Steber M, Gotto B (eds) Visions of community in Nazi Germany: social engineering and private lives. Oxford University Press, Oxford, pp 43–59

Wildt M, Kreutzmüller C (eds) (2013) Berlin 1933–1945. Siedler, Munich

Zierenberg M (2015) Berlin's black market. Palgrave Macmillan, Basinstoke

Belgian Judicial Actors and the Establishment of the Punishment of Collaboration with the Enemy in the East Cantons

Christoph Brüll and Lawrence Van Haecke

Abstract Belgian historical research concerning the repression of collaboration after the Second World War, has mostly overlooked the East Cantons. This mostly German-speaking region only became a part of Belgium in 1920, as a consequence of the treaty of Versailles. The integration of these populations turned out to be a very complicated process. In 1940, Nazi-Germany did not only occupy the East Cantons like the rest of Belgium, but annexed them back into the Third Reich. One of the main conclusions of the regional historiography is to view the repression of the collaboration as another step in the general misunderstanding between the local inhabitants and Belgian State authorities. This is evidenced by the high conviction rate (2.41% of the local population) and by assimilationist discourses which accompanied the workings of the Belgian military courts. In this contribution, we study the role of judicial actors in the actual establishment of the repression of collaboration and the civic purge in a top-down and a bottom-up approach. We analyse the special prosecution policy developed by the military prosecution office during the post-war period for with the enemy. We also show how political and administrative actors reinforced the living sentiments of injustice among the local population.

1 'To Think Belgian, to Feel Belgian'

> The area Eupen-Malmedy presents many problems. The inhabitants of this area have changed their nationality about three times in the last thirty odd years, according to the changing fortunes of war and the claimants of the respective Belgian and German Authorities. It

---

C. Brüll (✉)
Centre for Contemporary and Digital History,
University of Luxembourg, Esch-sur-Alzette, Luxembourg
e-mail: Christoph.Brull@uni.lu

L. Van Haecke
NMBS, Brussels, Belgium

M. Bost and A. Vrints (eds.), *Doing Justice In Wartime*,
Studies in the History of Law and Justice 19,
https://doi.org/10.1007/978-3-030-72050-6_10

> remains that the population of Eupen and Malmedy have alternated between being good Belgians and good Germans. At the moment, these people are good Belgians ...[1]

These words used in a report in March 1947 by R. Staneley, director of the pass permit service in the British Occupation administration in Germany, describe rather accurately the perception of the situation in the little border region in Belgium's East with regard to the population's national loyalty difficulties during the first half of the twentieth century.

The two *Kreise* Eupen and Malmedy had been ceded in 1920 to Belgium by Germany as a consequence of the Treaty of Versailles. Article 34 of the Treaty accorded to the population the possibility to reject this change of sovereignty. This 'public expression of opinion' was organised by Belgian authorities, and the Belgian government was in charge of communicating the results to the League of Nations. Only 271 of 33,726 potential voters said 'no' to the cession. Rumours of pressure and some resignation seem to have been the main reasons for this, but in the end, the so-called 'referendum' reflected the negotiations at Versailles. On the one hand, the 'martyr nation' of Belgium obtained territorial reparations; on the other, a semblance of the right to self-determination was preserved.

The annexation and the conduct of the 'referendum' remained controversial throughout the interwar period. Public life was characterised by a polarisation between supporters of the 'old' German fatherland and those who supported integration into the Belgian State. The Belgian Worker's Party (POB) reclaimed a new free and secret referendum until the beginning of the Nazi regime and the interdiction of the Social Democratic Party (SPD) in 1933. The 'pro-German' camp was financed and guided by Germany (since before 1933, but German influence grew much stronger after 1933) and consisted of political parties, cultural and sporting associations and paramilitary organisations resembling the model of the *Sturmabteilung* (SA). The Belgian parliamentary elections in April 1939 marked the nadir of the confrontation between the *Heimattreue Front* (HF), the political party of the 'pro-Germans', and the pro-Belgian Catholic Union (which was backed by the Bishop of Liège), when the HF obtained 45.2% of the vote in the three cantons of Eupen, Malmedy and Sankt Vith.

During the 'drôle de guerre' from September 1939 to May 1940, more than 100 young men of the region who had been mobilised deserted from the Belgian Army (Brüll 2011). Even if the German authorities did not unanimously welcome these desertions, we think that ±10% of the region's soldiers deserted and crossed the Belgian-German border. After the German invasion on 10 May 1940 and during the 'campaign of 18 days', desertions were much less frequent. By a *Führer* decree, the region was reannexed by Germany on 18 May 1940 (Schärer 1978). On 29 May 1940, the *Reich* annexed also ten municipalities in the northeast of the province of Liège and in the province of Luxembourg that had never been German before (Radermacher

[1]National Archives (Kew/GB), FO 1049/933, R. Staneley to 'Political Division' in Berlin, 5 March 1947.

2015).[2] Another very important decree, of 23 September 1941, finally fixed the German nationality of the population, leading—among other consequences—to the enrolment of 8700 young men into the *Wehrmacht* (Quadflieg 2008; Brüll 2011).

In the immediate aftermath of World War II, the question of the fate of the inhabitants was not a strictly judicial one. Undoubtedly Belgian authorities considered Eupen-Malmedy, whose official name had become the 'East Cantons',[3] as a 'failed region' (Cremer 2001; Lejeune 2005, 2007; Tiedau 2006; Brüll 2009). The integration policy of the interwar period had ended in failure—proven by the quite warm welcome given to the German Army in 1940. Conceived as a relatively liberal policy—the goal had been to ensure the population's 'passive loyalty' to the new Fatherland—it had proven too weak to counter German interference and the organisation of a pro-German and pro-Nazi party, the *Heimattreue Front*, in 1936 (Pabst 1964; Mennicken 2016).

Guaranteeing the population's future loyalty to Belgium, therefore, was the most important goal of all local post-war policy that the Belgian administrative and political authorities conducted out of Brussels, through Liège and Verviers to the region. The role of the judicial actors was crucial; their cooperation with local political authorities was stronger than in other Belgian regions. Two central measures taken at this time were particularly significant: the closing of the border between Belgium and Occupied Germany, with the introduction of a very severe system of border pass permits; and the *francisation* of the secondary school system (Lejeune and Brüll 2014). This assimilation policy was conducted until the middle of the 1950s but never fully supplanted the German language.

Above all, a new way of thinking had to be diffused within the population. On 6 April 1945, the Belgian minister for War Victims, Henri Pauwels, visited the town of Eupen in the east of the country. He was welcomed by Hugo Zimmermann, in charge of the town as a special civil servant-mayor since 1927 (with an obvious interruption between 1940 and 1944), with a very emotional speech: 'All the [inhabitants] are now openly and sincerely ready to think Belgian and to feel Belgian'.[4] Two weeks before, however, the veteran's association *Ceux de 40* from Welkenraedt, a village near Eupen, had published their own point of view in a local newspaper, claiming the need for strong purges for the population of the region: 'We can affirm without exaggeration that 70 to 80 p.c. of the canton's population were or are good Nazis or, at least, good Germans'.[5] Welkenraedt had been one of the ten municipalities also annexed by Germany in 1940. The hate of all things German was here turned toward the population of the cantons Eupen, Malmedy and Saint-Vith. But this perception was in fact quite common among the French-speaking population in the province of Liège as well.

---

[2]The prosecution of collaboration in these municipalities after 1945 was clearly separated from the prosecution in the East Cantons. It always took place in Verviers. See Cremer and Mießen (1995).

[3]The term 'East Cantons' was then used for the municipalities belonging to the cantons of Eupen, Malmedy and Saint Vith.

[4]*Grenz-Echo*, 7 April 1945.

[5]*La Presse Verviétoise*, 23 March 1945.

These quotations refer to two different post-war realities. Zimmermann's speech was a clear encouragement to denounce people. The State Archives in Eupen conserve dozens of files of denounced inhabitants, accused of not having been or not being those 'good Belgians' about whom Zimmermann talked. The declaration of the Veteran's association clearly indicated the strong resentments towards the inhabitants of the East Cantons that were largely present among the population of the neighbouring regions. These feelings were expressed most violently in the weeks following the liberation in September 1944. This wild street purge conducted by the Résistance movement 'White Army', of course, did not only happen in the East Cantons, but it led to deep wounds within the local population. Beyond the violence, the wild purge in the East Cantons had two other specific and painful characteristics: a wilful ignorance of the region's recent past; and the sole use of French by the Résistants (who often did not came from the region)—which a large part of the population did not understand. Together with the widespread destruction caused by the Battle of the Bulge, the massive administrative internment in special camps during the first month of 1945 (Roberti-Lintermans 2015) and eventually also the repression and the civic purge, this wild purge formed the narrative base for the victimisation or, more precisely, the auto-victimisation of the border population (Fickers 2004).

When the repression started in the East Cantons at the beginning of 1945, the crucial judicial issue was whether special laws and rules were to be applied to the region because of the specific situation caused by the annexation into Nazi Germany. There were two possibilities: make new legislation for the region; or take its specificity into account through a different interpretation of the already existing laws. The first possibility was excluded, because Belgian authorities had never politically recognised the annexation between 1940 and 1944. As a consequence, the judicial punishment had to be grounded in the existing crimes named by the Belgian penal code.

In June 1947, the Cassation Court did give a jurisdictional appraisal of the validity of the German annexation. First Advocate-General Raoul Hayoit de Termicourt decided to reject this recognition. He based his decision on the prescripts of international law: the annexation had been pronounced before the end of military combat. Also, the Belgian constitution does not allow territorial changes without a parliamentary vote (articles 3 and 68 at the time).[6] Although it does not belong to the main subject of this paper, it is not irrelevant to mention that the Belgian government-in-exile had seemed to accept this annexation by resignation in autumn 1940. There were no official protests at all, until the weeks preceding the liberation in August 1944 (Wynants 2004; Lejeune 2005; Brüll 2009, 60–61). Nevertheless, it is important to mention that Hayoit de Termicourt did explicitly recognise the 'quasi permanent state of constraint' to which the East Cantons had been submitted through the annexation.

The regional historiography has primarily analysed the social and political consequences of the post-war repression in the region itself. In a view of 'longue durée', the post-war repression represents the nadir of the perception of Belgian justice among the German-speaking population. All military courts functioned in French.

---

[6] *Journal des Tribunaux*, 26 October 1947: 513.

In 1946, there were only three lawyers for the whole judicial arrondissement of Verviers capable of trying cases in German. Although (not necessarily professional) interpreters could be present for the court proceedings, German-speaking suspects could not avoid the suspicion that they would not be understood sufficiently by their judges (Brüll 2013). The regional historians' critical judgement is mainly grounded in the paradox between the governmental refusal to provide a specific legal base for the repression in the region, on the one hand, and the creation of the special decree-law from 20 June 1945, which permitted the loss of Belgian nationality, on the other (Lejeune 2005, 2007). In this context, the regional historiography developed the hypothesis that the post-war repression led to an 'externalization of the past' (as sociologist Lepsius 1993, pointed out for the Austrian case) by showing that the widespread sentiment of injustice caused by the repression actually provoked the refusal among the population to question its recent past and its responsibility for its attitude during the war (Reip 2014; Cremer 2008).

This intra-regional analysis presents the Belgian authorities as a monolithic block that is mainly characterised by its inability to comprehend the region's particular situation. Our aim in this essay is to bring a more nuanced view to the Belgian actors of the post-war policy by focusing on the judicial actors and, especially, on the role that they played during implementation of the post-war repression.

2 Implementation of 'the Repression'

From 1942 onwards, the Belgian government-in-exile in London prepared and drew up the necessary decree-laws for the organisation of the liberation of Belgium. An important part of these plans concerned court procedures for punishment of civilians who supported the occupying forces of Nazi Germany against the Belgian State. Because of the experiences of collaboration during the First World War, the Belgian penal code seemed already rather well adapted to this post-war task. In 1917, the Belgian government-in-exile in Le Havre (France) had already added political collaboration with the enemy and denunciation to the enemy as new crimes in the penal code.[7] This was an answer to the German *Flamenpolitik*. In order to gain the support of the Flemish movement and to weaken Belgium, the German occupier had given benefits to the Flemish and also promised an independent Flemish State. Flemish nationalists who took the bait became known as Activists. After the First World War they were punished for their collaboration with the German occupier (Rousseaux and Van Ypersele 2008; Monballyu 2011; Verfaillie in the present volume).

Partially due to the more ideological nature of the Second World War, there was far more widespread political collaboration. In contrast to the Netherlands and France,

---

[7]Alongside different forms of espionage, the chapter 'crimes and misdemeanours against the external safety of the state' of the Belgian penal code had previously contained only military and economic collaboration with the enemy as punishable behaviour. See Collin and Bekaert (1949) and Gilissen et al. (1967).

Belgium's penal code seemed well prepared. The decree-law of 17 December 1942 therefore did not add new crimes. It did, however, reinterpret certain dispositions and add clarifications to make possible a more encompassing and more severe punishment of military and political collaboration and denunciation to the enemy (Van Haecke 2014, 130–146). In 1944, moreover, the government-in-exile gave the military courts a central role. Just like after the First World War, these courts would oversee punishment of persons deemed to be 'collaborators with the enemy' (Van Haecke 2014, 167–177). In Belgium, the whole of these court procedures became known as 'the repression' (Huyse and Dhondt 1991). Henceforth, with this concept, we also refer to the condemnation of collaborators in military courts after the Second World War in Belgium.

The Belgian post-war punishment of collaboration with the enemy eventually did use a more diverse set of tools to finish this enormous task. Because of the slow progress of the military courts throughout Belgium during the first year after the liberation, the government developed new laws to speed completion of the post-war judicial procedures. Punishment by the military courts, however, did stay at the core of the repression. In November 1945, the government decreed a new 'simplified court procedure' for cases in which military prosecutors would not demand a punishment greater than five years of imprisonment. In this new procedure, the military prosecutor could conclude a deal with the suspect. In exchange for his admission of guilt, the prosecutor proposed a punishment for the suspect with the addition of a loss of civil and political rights. Afterwards, the judge of the military court only had to accept this deal for the punishment to take effect. Secondly, in December 1945, the government also allowed the formation of 'small military courts' (three judges instead of five) for cases in which the military prosecutors would not demand a greater sentence than 15 years in prison (Van Haecke 2014, 228–231, 473, 482–485).

A major shift in the punishment of collaboration with the enemy did take place with the enactment of the decree-law of the 19th September 1945, however. This decree-law established a civil purge procedure. Military prosecutors could now quickly deprive a fixed number of categories of 'small collaborators' of their civil and political rights solely by inscribing them on a purge-list. A condemnation by a military court was not necessary for this punishment to take place, but an appeal in civil courts against this inscription was allowed (Van Haecke 2014, 335–347, 398–468). Specifically for the East Cantons, there also was the aforementioned decree-law of 20 June 1945, which made it possible for local government officials to draw up lists of political collaborators who would lose their Belgian nationality after the publication of these lists in the *Moniteur belge* (Van Haecke 2014, 354–356, 555–561). This kind of punishment had been promoted by some politicians, such as socialist senator Louis Gob of Malmedy, who had fought against the pro-German movement during the 1930s.

The liberation of the majority of Belgium happened quickly (De Vos 2004). Equally rapid was the establishment of military courts and prosecution offices throughout the country, charged with investigating the numerous cases of military, economic and political collaboration with the enemy and denunciation to the enemy. In September 1944, the military court of Verviers in the province of Liège was the responsible seat for investigations concerning the East Cantons. The Battle of the Bulge (December 1944–January 1945) severely interrupted these early proceedings. Partially in order to end the growing delays of the judicial investigations, the central military prosecution office installed two special sections of the Verviers military court in the East Cantons after the end of the military operations in the area. On 1 March 1946, moreover, each section became independent. Pierre Koumoth[8] was appointed head of the military prosecution office of Eupen; Lucien Gillard[9] took up the same responsibility in Malmedy. The government also installed additional territorial sections of the Secret Service in Eupen, Malmedy and Burg-Reuland to lend assistance with the investigations of the military prosecution offices. From February 1946 onwards, the military prosecution offices could also rely on a specific Documentation Service for the East Cantons.

Already at the start of the judicial investigations in the East Cantons, Walter Ganshof van der Meersch,[10] head of the general military prosecution office, foresaw that it might not be advisable for the repression in the East Cantons to follow the penal law interpretations generally used in the rest of the Belgian territory. The annexation of the East Cantons into Nazi Germany had made German laws fully applicable in the region and could be construed as a situation of 'duress' for the local population. This viewpoint could have far-reaching implications for the possible existence of any guilt that the courts had to determine. Ganshof advocated a more lenient punishment of collaboration by the military courts for the East Cantons, based on the fact that in 1939 *only* 45% of its voters had actually supported the pro-German *Heimattreue Front*. Because a minority had then supported the plans of this eventually collaborating political party, Ganshof concluded that the people of the East Cantons should not be considered as lost for the 'Belgian idea'. This perception, since then largely deconstructed by historians, did have a great influence on the construction of historical representations in the East Cantons (Cremer 2012).

In order to have a locally successful repression of collaboration, Ganshof deemed it vital that East Canton patriots would see that Belgium did not turn a blind eye to the special circumstances of the annexation into the German Reich. Tangible proof of this concern is the important meeting in the town hall of Verviers on 2 October

[8]Pierre Koumoth (*1908) studied Law at the University of Liège and worked as a prosecutor in Verviers since 1939. By the liberation in September 1944, he became a military prosecutor, first in Verviers, then in Eupen and Malmedy (Lejeune 2007, 73).

[9]Lucien Gillard (*1910) was appointed as a judge in Verviers in October 1939 and, at the same moment, as a military prosecutor by the 3rd Belgian Army Corps. He worked as a military prosecutor in Verviers since March 1945 and in Malmedy since February 1946 until October 1946 (Lejeune 2007, 73).

[10]Walter Jean Ganshof van der Meersch (*1900) studied Law at the Free University of Brussels. He was a lifelong magistrate, occupying various important functions in Belgian and later European courts. He also had a very prolific career as a professor of Law in the Free University of Brussels. He not only led the military prosecution office in post-war Belgium But also during the liberation period led the High Commissariat for the Security of the Kingdom. This commissariat controlled and coordinated all services that occupied themselves with maintenance of law and order. He was sometimes called 'the viceroy of Belgium' because of all his power and influence (Schandevyl 2011, 97–133).

1945 between the minister of Justice, the provincial governor, the responsible district governors and mayors, and also Ganshof along with the local military prosecutors among others. This was a unique meeting in the context of the repression during the Belgian post-war period. It helped to secure the contours of the exceptional situation that the East Cantons had had to endure. The local newspaper *Le Gaulois* wrote:

> On a fait valoir les circonstances tout à fait spéciales où se sont trouvées les administrations, spécialement les fonctionnaires, lors du retour des Allemands et la pression à laquelle les habitants ont été soumis. Il semble que des critères juridiques tout particuliers devront être établis pour ces régions.[11]

Joseph Baltus gave a clear example of these special criteria in June 1946 to his colleagues in the Senate.[12] He argued that although membership in the *Nationalsozialistisches Kraftfahrkorps* (NSKK) in Brussels clearly proved an allegiance to the New Order and should be considered as a form of military collaboration, this was not the case for the same membership in the East Cantons. The already existing sport car clubs had been forced to merge into the NSKK, and leaving this Nazi organization was sure to cause loss of the driving license, which some people needed in order to perform their job. Other people, he also argued, joined the NSKK so they would avoid a forced membership into the National Socialist German Workers' Party (NSDAP). Although Baltus's colleagues disagreed with his nuanced views, the local military prosecutors did keep similar examples in their mind during their investigations and during the formation of their prosecution policy.

Having established the general frame of the repression, we can summarise the repression in the East Cantons with the following numbers: 15,623 instructions were opened by the military prosecution office—on a total population of about 60,000 people— and 3201 cases came before the military courts. Thus the prosecution was abandoned in 82.6% of the cases—a number that corresponds almost exactly to the Belgian average (83.4%). In the end, 1503 people were condemned, most of them to correctional sentences.[13] The percentage of instructions was six times higher than in the rest of Belgium, that of the condemned no less than four times (2.4–0.6%). But the fact that the sentences were generally less severe than in the rest of Belgium seems to reflect the more informed opinion of certain judges.

By comparison: in the French Department of Moselle, approximately 1% of the population (±400,000 people at the end of the war) were judged between 1944 and the amnesties of 1953. There were 3243 condemnations and 859 acquittals (Hiegel 1983).

---

[11] CegeSoma. Instructions Générales. Z/238–1. Dossier inzake de werking van de derde consultatieve commissie te Eupen, oktober–december 1945.

[12] Joseph Baltus (1903–1996) came from the village of Montzen and practised as a doctor in Eupen. From 1946 to 1947 he was a senator of the Belgian Christian-Social Party (PSC). See Cremer and Mießen (1995).

[13] A 'correctional sentence' technically means a prison sentence of at least 8 days and up to, but not including five years. A punishment of five years or higher is generally known as a 'criminal sentence'. The minimum prison sentence for military, political and economic collaboration was actually one year of imprisonment, because the maximum sentence was the death penalty. See Collin and Bekaert (1949).

2.1 Punishment for Military Collaboration

Judicial prosecution of military collaboration in the East Cantons mostly concerned four groups of suspects: members of the *Wehrmacht*, *Kriegsmarine* and *Waffen SS* and also certain members of the NSKK. For members of the German Army (*Wehrmacht* and *Kriegsmarine*), the main question was which kind of 'duress' the German conscription law had actually caused. Because desertion in Nazi Germany was punishable by death, the military prosecution office set out to differentiate its cases person by person. However, already in 1944, the military prosecutor in Verviers concluded that as much as the administrative internment of military collaborators was necessary in the East Cantons, because of the ongoing war against Germany and because of safety issues with the allied armies, there did not exist a judicial need for their condemnation by the military court.

In December 1944, Ganshof van der Meersch followed this idea in general lines, stating that members of the *Wehrmacht* and *Kriegsmarine* only deserved punishment if their membership had been voluntary, spontaneous or in pursuit of personal profit. Proving this was the case, however, was not an easy task. Some prosecutors hoped to find clear and actual proof of the duress caused by the German conscription law and also tried to differentiate the small or large amount of duress a person had felt during the war. According to military prosecutor Koumoth, however, this duress had existed implicitly for all, because of the annexation and the German citizenship of the people living in the East Cantons. His belief was at least partially based on practical considerations: if all those who had worn a military uniform if all civil servants who had sworn the oath of fealty to Adolf Hitler had to be locked up, then half of the East Cantons had to be put away. Military prosecutor Noël Dubois[14] added—as Baltus also mentioned—that membership in a paramilitary organization (i.e., NSKK) did not automatically constitute military collaboration with the enemy. Some men had only joined these groups to avoid conscription into the German Army.

On 16 January 1945, Ganshof van der Meersch ordered a temporary stop to the trials for military collaboration in the East Cantons. As was common practice in the context of the repression, a few test cases would be put to court in order to develop a specific jurisprudence and to see which kind of common ground existed between the views of the prosecution office and the military courts before the prosecutors advanced too many cases too far.

The courts ultimately accepted duress, but only under certain conditions. Due to the German laws of conscription, people in the East Cantons had faced a real dilemma. They could either disadvantage themselves or their loved ones, or break the law. This disadvantage was sure and unavoidable, but also actual, imminent and unjust. As duress was difficult to prove, the courts also took into account how the suspect had behaved before and after he had served his time in the German Army.

Practically, people who had voluntarily joined the *Wehrmacht* or who had joined the SS were prosecuted for military collaboration with the enemy. A third group

[14]Noël Dubois was a military prosecutor in Verviers in 1945. He is known for his strict but fair attitude against the populations of the East Cantons (Lejeune 2005, 136–142).

consisted of local deserters from the Belgian Army, who often had become members of the *Bau-Lehr-Bataillon z.b.V. 800 'Brandenburg'* that participated in the invasion of Belgium on 10 May 1940. Local NSKK leaders also were put on trial. In the beginning, all other NSKK members were inscribed on the purge list of the military prosecutor, but these inscriptions were eventually limited to the members who had been politically active during the war. This was strikingly milder than elsewhere in Belgium, where a regular NSKK membership could lead to a prison sentence ranging from three to six years.

Women who had become nurses for the German Red Cross under duress were also left undisturbed by the military prosecution office. The most serious Red Cross cases did have to go through the simplified procedure, which meant a maximum prison sentence of five years. The other cases were designated for the civil purge. Specifically for the East Cantons, two special groups of nurses of the German Red Cross were not put to trial: former nurses of the Belgian Red Cross or similar organisations; and women who became nurses due to forced labour laws (Van Haecke 2014, 348–350, 548–549).

In the end, 205 people were condemned for military collaboration, and some 510 people for military collaboration combined with other forms of collaboration, mostly political (in case of Belgian army deserters) (Gilissen 1951).

2.2 *Punishment for Political Collaboration*

The repression of political collaboration with the enemy in the East Cantons focused on the leaders of the NSDAP—with special attention for the pro-German *Heimattreue Front*—and the *Sturmabteilung*. Just like in the rest of Belgium, in general, the military courts were somewhat more lenient with punishment for political collaboration with the enemy than with punishment for military collaboration. Nevertheless, two kinds of political collaborators needed to be put to trial in any case:

1. Civil servants of the Belgian State who, despite their oath of fealty to the Belgian State, had joined the side of the enemy;
2. All propagandists of the East Cantons who had helped the instauration of national-socialist law and its institutions.

The grounds for punishing political collaboration with the enemy proved to be more difficult to establish than for military collaboration. A first attempt at the military court of Verviers to condemn local government officials for swearing the oath of fealty to Adolf Hitler failed. This was partially due to the lack of witnesses who were willing to testify. This distrustful attitude stemmed from fear in the general population that the condemned would not be locked up for a sufficiently long time.

All the important local leaders of the NSDAP were brought before the military courts. This group also included the most important propagandists and denouncers. Next to them, the main leaders of other politically collaborating organisations (such as the *Bauernschaft* and the *Hitlerjugend*) were also brought before court. The secondary leaders of the NSDAP and subordinate organisations were punished through the simplified procedure. Members of the NSDAP and hierarchical subordinate organisations were put on purge lists. Compared to the rest of Belgium, the main principles and procedures were used in a very similar fashion for the post-war punishment of political collaboration in the East Cantons, but the acceptance of duress by the military courts clearly softened the general prosecution policy (Van Haecke 2014, 350–351, 549–550).

Nevertheless, 2022 sentences were pronounced for political collaboration, some 800 of which were in combination with other forms of collaboration (Gilissen 1951).

The aim of the denationalization law of 20 June 1945 was clear: to punish the leaders, *Kreisleiter*, *Amtsleiter*, *Ortsgruppenleiter*, *Wirtschaftliche Leiter*, *Kreisbauernleiter*, *Leiter der Bund der Deutsche Frauen* (list A) and also other important propagandists of the NSDAP (list B). As these people had not shown the slightest amount of allegiance to Belgium during the Second World War, they would only hurt the moral reconstruction of the Belgian State and its people. Responsibility for drawing up these lists was placed into the hands of the local authorities. They had to send copies to the assistant district commissioner, the head of the regional Belgian secret service and the commander of the regional state police. Then these lists went to the civil prosecutor of Verviers, who informed the minister of Justice and sent the lists to the governor of the province of Liège. With the addition of his advice, the lists were finally considered ready for publication in the *Moniteur belge*. Publication would cause the loss of nationality to take effect for those mentioned and their family.

During the aforementioned meeting of 2 October 1945, it was agreed that the loss of nationality was meant as punishment for those collaborators who were deemed to be insensitive to the Belgian idea. Ganshof van der Meersch complained about the lack of general rules for this procedure and the noticeably divergent attitudes and viewpoints held by the different local governments. According to him, the current lists had a broader scope than originally intended. Agreeing with Ganshof, the meeting decided to change the procedure temporarily. Instead of sending the lists to the civil prosecutor, Assistant District Commissioner Hoen had to include the local military prosecution office. The lists that eventually followed this enhanced procedure were published in May 1946 and encountered no criticism. A follow-up list, drawn up without the help of the military prosecutors, did receive criticism, however, due to its vast scope.

Until now, it was largely unknown that the government had considered plans to broaden the law of 30 July 1934, through which Belgians who did not receive their nationality by birth could lose their nationality if they had severely failed to uphold their civic duties. Once again, this was a policy measure that had been asked for by certain local authorities in the East Cantons. It was mainly meant to counter the growing interference of the NSDAP in the East Cantons. The law had been applied to a case in 1935, when four leaders of the pro-German movement had lost their nationality and left Belgium for Germany.

The 1945 plan contained two reforms:

1. The law of 1934 also needed to apply to the sons of Belgians who did not get their nationality by birth;
2. The effects of this law needed to incorporate the family of the perpetrator as well.

In August 1945, the left-wing government led by socialist Achilles Van Acker had already rejected this idea, because the difference drawn between native Belgians and immigrants was deemed arbitrary and racist. After the meeting of 2 October, Koumoth still supported this plan. He considered some inhabitants of the East Cantons immune to the Belgian idea, namely, the leaders of collaborating organisations. Ganshof sent Koumoth's report to the minister of Justice. In July and August 1946, the government studied this proposal again and sent it to the parliament. The Justice Commission in the Chamber vociferously criticised this law project. While the biggest traitors, denunciators and torturers of Belgian descent could lose their nationality only after a condemnation in absentia by a military court, this loss of nationality would be made possible in the East Cantons for actions that were not even necessarily a part of the penal code. Moreover, statelessness was against the stipulations of international law. Surprisingly, however, the Commission in the end did accept the project, and the whole Chamber consequently followed suit. An astonished Justice Commission in the Senate chose to follow the objections that the Chamber commission originally had mentioned and refused support for the project. As such, the Senate Commission prevented this project from becoming law (Van Haecke 2014, 354–356, 555–561).

The law of 1 June 1949 not only ended the time of war in Belgium but also finally changed the decree-law of June 1945 to allow appeals against the loss of nationality in certain circumstances. It also ended the automatic loss of nationality for the family of the collaborator. In the beginning, more than 1335 people (and their family members) were listed. After appeals against the decisions, only 461 of them definitively lost their nationality (Aerts 2014, 367–368).

2.3 Punishment for Economic Collaboration

Post-war punishment for economic collaboration in the East Cantons is the most telling show-case for the tension that arose between the rebuilding of the Belgian nation and its economy on the one hand and the need to do a thorough research of crimes of collaboration on the other. By June 1945, industry in Eupen had come to a standstill because of all the suspicions being raised. The general criminal prosecution office demanded the necessary care and speed from the criminal prosecution office of Verviers. The fear of a slowed economic recovery was shared with the pro-Belgian groups in the East Cantons. Substitute Military Prosecutor Trousse began to look with Assistant District Commissioner Hoen and Chief Inspector Habay from the Ministry of Finance for ways to support the recovery of the local economy. A first measure was the removal of all the unwanted leaders from the big regional companies, as happened with the *Kammgarnwerke* and the *Kabelwerke*.[15] At the end of July 1945, the *Industrie-Und Handelskammer zu Eupen* sent the general military prosecution office the idea proposed by Mayor Zimmerman of Eupen to establish a special committee for revitalization of the local economy. The committee's members were honourable citizens, with the necessary authority and power, and also included representatives from the Ministry of Economic Affairs, the Ministry of Justice, the Ministry of Internal Affairs, the general military prosecution office, *l'Economie libre* and possibly also the provincial and communal governments.

The second measure was judicial policy. The general military prosecution office informed the military prosecutor in Verviers that he should not follow the regular rules and criteria:

> Il paraît (…) indiqué d'apprécier de façon particulièrement large les contraintes dont ils ont pu être l'objet et de s'attacher spécialement à la complaisance particulière qu'ils ont pu apporter dans l'exécution des fournitures et prestations qui étaient exigées d'eux.

Substitute Military Prosecutor Trousse informed his superior that he was focusing on companies that had clearly had pro-German leaders. To that end, he performed a quick and discreet investigation into not only the political behaviour of the local industrialists but also their desire to produce as much as possible and any changes they made in their production in order to accommodate the wishes of Nazi Germany. Except where it concerned weaponry, Trousse did not consider the nature of the goods produced. He also paid no attention to the relative weight of the deliveries made to the enemy in relation to total production. The magistrate deemed this research politically necessary, because the leaders of companies are at the same time the local leaders of the public opinion.

General Military Prosecutor Ganshof and Substitute Military Prosecutor Trousse agreed upon the foundations of the prosecution of economic collaboration. Two rules in particular—agreed upon during a special meeting—were deemed important:

> 1. s'attacher tout spécialement à la complaisance particulière que les industriels et négociants ont pu apporter dans l'exécution des fournitures et prestations qui étaient exigées d'eux.
> 2. Il s'indique de limiter les poursuites à des cas particulièrement caractérisés où la collaboration économique s'allie quasi nécessairement à la collaboration politique.[16]

Trousse followed these guidelines closely while working on his local policy of prosecution during the month of August and afterwards. It became apparent that—relatively speaking—the military justice system had to put more time and effort into the

---

[15]A report from the military prosecution office states: 'Nous croyons qu'il est extrêmement (!) urgent de réunir l'assemblée de chacune de ces usines et de procéder à l'élection de nouveaux conseils d'administration. Suivant l'art.8 de l'arrêté-Loi du 17 janvier 1945 et l'art.9 de l'arrêté-loi du 23 août 1944, les individus suspects seront représentés par le séquestre. Il est possible que pour certaines usines vous jugiez préférable de faire ordonner la mise sous séquestre des biens appartenant à la société suivant l'art.2 de l'arrêté-loi du 17 janvier 1945'. CegeSoma. Instructions Générales. Z/238–9-3. Letters between the General Military Prosecution office and the Military Prosecution office of Verviers, June–November 1945.

[16]CegeSoma. Instructions Générales. Z/238–9-3. Letters between the General Military Prosecution office and the Military Prosecution office of Verviers, June–August 1945.

construction of its prosecution policy for economic collaboration with the enemy than it did for military and political collaboration. It is a more difficult and complex exercise because of the ties of these companies with the economic future of the East Cantons and its possible political consequences. In a statement in 1947, Ganshof wrote that economic collaboration in the East Cantons in the end proved to be a limited problem: only a few companies from Eupen and one in Malmedy received a conviction. Apart from a broad application of 'duress', the military justice used the same prosecution criteria as was used in the rest of the country (Van Haecke 2014, 351–352, 550–554).

2.3.1 The Closure of Companies in the East Cantons

In the immediate post-war period, punishment for economic collaboration with the enemy in the East Cantons had an important special characteristic. The local governments closed a number of businesses that belonged to collaborators. In October 1945, intermediaries still held stocks of wartime goods. In order to halt the growth of any possible civilian unrest, Mayor Zimmerman from Eupen proposed various measures. One possible solution was to allow members of resistance movements and political prisoners to take over the businesses (shops and pubs) that the Mayor had closed. Substitute General Military Prosecutor Gilissen had to look for possible ways in which the local military prosecution offices could play an active role in solving this dilemma. Trousse favoured use of sequestration as an efficient instrument for the military prosecution office.

Advocate-General Constant represented the general prosecution office at a 12 December 1945 meeting with the governor of the province of Liège, the general civil prosecutor of Liège, the military prosecutor from Verviers and a representative of the Ministry of Economic Affairs. The ministry did not think that businesses should be kept closed in the context of maintaining law and order. The only acceptable reasoning behind these kinds of closures should be economic legislation or collaboration with the enemy. Ultimately, this meeting came to a double conclusion. The Mayor of Eupen would, firstly, send the civil prosecutor a list of persons who would open the closed businesses. At the same time, secondly, there would be investigations into the stocks of goods and provisioning. If secret stocks of goods were indeed found, the civil prosecutor could close down the business concerned. The military prosecutor would also study the list of persons. This way, it would be possible to command the sequestration of companies whenever it was deemed necessary. One of the downsides of this system, according to the military prosecutor from Verviers, was the slow progress made by the service of sequestration. It could take several months before the sequestration effectively happened and was enforced. The military prosecutor from Verviers promised Ganshof van der Meersch that he would write a report, so that the service could begin working faster and more efficiently.

In this context of the aforementioned closures of companies, Minister of Justice Marcel Grégoire asked General Military Prosecutor Ganshof van der Meersch about the desirability of installing a special commission for the purge of the management boards of companies in Eupen. A plan for this commission had been available in the Ministry of Economic Affairs since June 1945. Mahaux, one of Ganshof's substitutes, answered the minister of Justice in July that the military prosecutors should not be part of this commission because it is more important for the magistrates to keep their full independence. This opinion notwithstanding, Trousse did have a meeting in November 1945 with the mayor, a technical adviser from Eupen and a researcher from the Ministry of Economic Affair concerning this kind of commission. They developed the idea of installing a new committee that would be responsible for the tutelage of the companies that were subjected to judicial research in the context of collaboration with the enemy. This committee would coordinate various services. Trousse identified one downside: because the proposition would be favourable for the companies involved, it should be a functioning system for the whole of Belgium and not only for the small region of Eupen. Any activity directly linked to the purge (such as delivery of proof of civic conduct) should not be in the hands of separate commissions or committees. Ideas such as this were always opposed quite strenuously by the general military prosecutor, who wanted the military prosecution offices and courts to retain a monopoly on post-war punishment of collaboration with the enemy. He wanted to exclude as much as possible any influence from the local population upon the workings of the military justice systems (Van Haecke 2014, 351–352, 550–554).

2.3.2 The Local Policy of the Military Prosecutors

Punishment of economic collaboration in the East Cantons focused on '(les) entreprises dont les Conseils d'administration se sont montrés particulièrement complaisants vis-à-vis de l'ennemi'. This shows—again—to a certain degree that there was leeway in the interpretation of the behaviour of the company executives. This was the case for the whole of Belgium and even more so in the East Cantons.

Trousse developed a special prosecution policy for these companies that could be very influential for the political future of the region. It began with the possible assimilation of the East Cantons into Belgium. Influenced by Mayor Zimmerman, who said that the companies in Eupen had never furthered the growth of a Belgian national spirit before the war, the military prosecution office was charged with making sure that the big regional companies would no longer be centres from which all kinds of pro-German propaganda is spread. But Trousse found little support in the field. Some companies in fact postponed their reopening or reopened with less qualified personnel in order to sabotage the military prosecutor's office. Because of these tactics, the false impression grew that the repression of collaboration was hindering the region's economic revival. In truth, Trousse was looking for ways to remove these hindrances.

In order to punish those responsible for economic collaboration with the enemy, Trousse used a combination of the basic collaboration crime as written in the Belgian penal code and also the civic purge. He described his policy as follows:

> ... je considère que le dol général requis par l'article 115 résulte du comportement personnel des intéressés durant l'occupation. L'activité politique (...) constituera une présomption très nette de sa volonté de fournir ou de ne pas fournir. Je ne crois pas qu'à Eupen, un industriel qui, dans l'ambiance du moment, a travaillé directement pour l'armement doit nécessairement être poursuivi. Il a peut-être été contraint de le faire par les offices du Rüstungsministerium. Mais il sera pou(r)suivi s'il a mis tout en œuvre pour activer cette production ou s'il s'est compromis en faisant de la politique active en faveur des Nazis.[17]

This description closely aligns with the explanation given by Ganshof van der Meersch two years later in 1947. The broader use and acceptance of duress helps to take the annexation of the region into Nazi Germany into account, as well as the growing pressure that had been put on the active companies to produce in support of the war. This is why, in itself, even the production of weapons for the German Army was not sufficient grounds for conviction by a military court. It is clear that the prosecution of economic collaboration was stronger and more openly political in the East Cantons then elsewhere in Belgium.

When Trousse wrote this overview of his prosecution policy, 14 of the 41 local industries were subjected to a judicial investigation. Of course, as the investigations were ongoing, he was not able to give any information about which of these companies would eventually have to go to court. Six companies were also being subjected to a preliminary investigation. The military prosecution office, moreover, was looking into the possibility of sequestration for three local companies. Not all was going according to plan, however. The experts working on the bookkeeping of the companies took more time than planned because they themselves lacked the necessary qualified personnel, meaning 'connaissant parfaitement allemand, civique et compétent'.

In order to minimise the disruptive effects of the judicial investigations for the companies as much as possible, Trousse left the documents at the companies and allowed the confiscated documents and papers to be consulted by the personnel, under supervision. A small number of company leaders were arrested and put in jail. Trousse aimed for a serious cleansing of the region, with a minimum of damage for the companies concerned. This is why he preferred the civic purge measure to sequestration of companies. As in the rest of Belgium, leadership of the companies needed a new government document called 'a proof of civic loyalty' in order to obtain the right to import and export goods. Before delivering this important document to the leadership of the local companies, the mayors asked Trousse to get the necessary information about their wartime behaviour. He gladly helped the mayors out and even went so far as to describe to the companies the conditions to which they needed to adhere in order to get a positive evaluation. This allowed the company to purge itself and begin to produce in the post-war period without any concerns. Although it was out of the ordinary, Ganshof van der Meersch supported this special procedure.

A special case is the *Câblerie*. Trousse developed a special prosecution plan in order to be able punish certain leaders of this company on the grounds of breaking articles 118*bis* (political collaboration) and 121*bis* (delation to the enemy) of the

---

[17] CegeSoma. IG's. Z/238-9-7. File concerning the treatment of economic collaboration with the enemy in the area of Eupen.

Belgian penal code. When his superior military prosecutor expressed his doubts, Ganshof van der Meersch followed suit. They both deemed it logical for the judges to consider political collaboration crimes to be closely linked with economic collaboration, while a separate court case for delation to the enemy might be able to work.

A more important discussion specifically concerned which crime description should be used for economic collaboration crimes in the East Cantons. Trousse wanted to use the original article 115, not the more limited descriptions put into the penal code by the decree-law of 25 May 1945 (Luyten 1996). Trousse defended this quite surprising proposition because he considered the new fourth paragraph to refer solely to a territory occupied by the enemy, while the East Cantons were annexed to Germany. Again Ganshof van der Meersch took the opposite view. In line with his general policy choice to treat the inhabitants of the East Cantons on the same grounds as other Belgians, albeit with a clearly more lenient use of duress, Ganshof reminded Trousse that they had kept their quality as Belgian citizens. At the end of May 1946, Ganshof van der Meersch even urged his colleague Mahaux to stress in the following meeting concerning the East Cantons that duress must be used and accepted 'exceptionnellement généreuse'. This comes at the same time that for the whole of Belgium the general military prosecutor urged broadening the use of the simplified procedure as much as possible.

In January 1946, the general military prosecution Office also received an overview about the prosecutions in Sankt-Vith. German laws had been fully applicable there from May 1940. The military magistrates looked for proof of voluntary help for Nazi Germany and tried to determine how conscious perpetrators had been about the damage their behaviour could cause to Belgium and whether or not it helped achieve successful end of the war against the occupier. Lucre and special motivation for committing economic collaboration with the enemy in particular were taken into account as proof of these crimes. The political behaviour of the suspects concerned was usually used as a general context for explanations of their decisions (Van Haecke 2014, 351–352, 550–554).

This became very clear in the five actual court cases for economic collaboration with the enemy. The prosecuted companies all clearly had ties with the *Heimattreue Front* before the war or had developed close ties during the war with either national-socialistic or German State organisations. One of the more important reasons to punish the nephews Gerhard and Lothar Peters (linked to two different companies brought before the military court of Eupen), for example, was their membership of the HF and later the NSDAP (Quadflieg 2013, 125–128).

3 Some Concluding Remarks

The post-war repression of collaboration constituted a massive confrontation between the inhabitants of the East Cantons and the Belgian justice system. Several thousands of internments and opened instructions, more than 1500 sentences and the special decree concerning the loss of Belgian nationality led to a great number of persons in literally every locality facing the police or judicial authorities. The expectations of justice could not have been more different: on the one hand, the majority of the population in the region who invoked constraint as an exculpatory element, because of the region's annexation to the Third Reich; on the other hand, a spirit of revenge among some of the population in Belgium, especially in the neighbouring localities, visible in certain characteristics of the wild purge. In these chaotic circumstances, the Belgian authorities had to make up for a lack of knowledge with a surplus of emotions. The political aim, however, was clear: the territory had to '(re)become' Belgian. It was now impossible to only aspire to the 'passive loyalty' of the local populations as Belgian policy had accepted in the interwar years.

Post-war justice inevitably had a political function. It seemed unrealistic to only try a few leading members of the local collaboration movement, not only because many of them remained in Germany after the war but also because the judicial actors never considered a 'collective guilt' (in contrast to some resistance fighters or veteran's leagues). In the end, the basic method was a very pragmatic one: the military courts, based on the crimes listed in the Belgian penal code and on a more or less developed sense of comprehension towards the specific situation of the East Cantons, ultimately decided who was a collaborator and who was not. But this concerned only the 'regular' repression.

Nevertheless, add to that the more overtly political way in which the repression of economic collaboration was regarded, the 'civic purge' and the decree-law from June 1945—even if the draconian decisions of the beginning would later be reduced or even practically annihilated—and it becomes clear that the population of the East Cantons was considered to be a 'population at risk'.

From a historiographical point of view, two issues need a deeper and more thorough analysis, and more in-depth research. There is the question of studies based on trials (raising the 'classic' question about the accessibility of the penal files) and the establishment of a—at least comparative—link with repression in the rest of Belgium. The observation that in no other region was the proximity between local authorities and judicial actors so important marks a first important step in this direction. Another comparative link could be made with other European regions annexed by the Reich during the war. One could especially think of Alsace-Moselle, with which a resemblance exists with regard to the wild purges, although a great difference is constituted by the fact that French authorities gave a special juridical basis to the legal prosecution of collaboration. Interestingly, the historiography of the prosecution in this region is not very rich and mostly considers the two regions separately (e.g., Vonau 2005; Kohser-Spohn 2011). Nevertheless, such a comparison would stress the importance of a European perspective of the legal prosecution of collaboration in border spaces.

References

Aerts K (2014) 'Repressie zonder maat of einde?' De juridische reïntegratie van collaborateurs in de Belgische Staat na de Tweede Wereldoorlog. Academia Press, Ghent

Brüll C (2009) Belgien im Nachkriegsdeutschland. Besatzung, Annäherung, Ausgleich 1944–1958. Klartext, Essen

Brüll C (2011) Les enrôlés de force dans la Wehrmacht—un symbole du passé mouvementé des Belges au XXe siècle. Guerres mondiales et Conflits contemporains 241:163–174

Brüll C (2013) Das Gerichtswesen im deutschsprachigen Belgien seit 1920: politische Betrachtungen. In: Festschrift. 25 Jahre Gerichtsbezirk Eupen (French version: L'organisation judiciaire dans la Belgique de langue allemande depuis 1920: considérations d'histoire politique, 75–107). Kliemo, Eupen, pp 39–74

Collin F, Bekaert H (1949) De Belgische Wetboeken. Strafwetboek. Wetboek van Strafvordering. Bijvoegsel. Met aanteekeningen. Larcier, Brussels

Cremer F (2001) Von den 'inciviques' zu den 'Modellbelgiern'. Als man den aufrechten Gang wieder lernen musste. In: Cremer F, Fickers A, Lejeune C (eds) Spuren in die Zukunft. Anmerkungen zu einem bewegten Jahrhundert. Lexis, Büllingen, pp 99–116

Cremer F (2008) Eine Hypothese: Keine moralische Verpflichtung zur Selbsthinterfragung. In: Lejeune C, Klauser K-D (eds) Die Säuberung, vol. 3: Verdrängte Erinnerungen—340 Zeitzeugen berichten. Lexis, Büllingen, p 330

Cremer F (2012) Der 20. September 1920 in Geschichte und Erinnerung der deutschsprachigen Belgier. In: Brüll C (eds) ZOOM 1920–2010. Nachbarschaften neun Jahrzehnte nach Versailles. Grenz-Echo, Eupen, pp 73–102

Cremer F, Mießen W (1995) Spuren. Materialien zur Geschichte der Deutschsprachigen Gemeinschaft Belgiens. Einführung. Self Publishing, Eupen

De Vos L (2004) De Tweede Wereldoorlog. Davidsfonds, Leuven

Fickers A (2004) Gedächtnisopfer. Erinnern und Vergessen in der Vergangenheitspolitik der deutschsprachigen Belgier im 20. Jahrhundert. *Zeitenblicke* 3(1). http://www.zeitenblicke.de/2004/01/fickers/. Accessed 24 June 2016

Gilissen J (1951) Étude statistique de la répression de l'incivisme. Revue de Droit pénal et de Criminologie

Gilissen J, Cassiers P, Debroux F (1967) Crimes et délits contre la sûreté de l'Etat. *Les Novelles, Droit Pénal* 3:113–319

Hiegel C (1983) La répression de la collaboration et l'épuration en Moselle. Bilan statistique. Les Cahiers Lorrains 4:335–369

Huyse L, Dhondt S (1991) Onverwerkt Verleden. Collaboratie en repressie in België. 1942–1952. Kritak, Leuven

Kohser-Spohn C (2011) L'épuration de 1945 en Alsace, un vecteur de la réconciliation entre la France et l'Allemagne. In: Ludwig B, Linsenmann A (eds) Frontières et réconciliation. L'Allemagne et ses voisins depuis 1945. Peter Lang, Brussels, pp 179–198

Lejeune C (2005) Die Säuberung, vol. 1: Ernüchterung, Befreiung, Ungewissheit (1920–1944). Lexis, Büllingen

Lejeune C (2007) Die Säuberung, vol. 2: Hysterie, Wiedereingliederung, Assimilierung (1945–1952). Lexis, Büllingen

Lejeune C, Brüll C (eds) (2014) Grenzerfahrungen. Eine Geschichte der Deutschsprachigen Gemeinschaft Belgiens, vol. 5: Säuberung, Wiederaufbau, Autonomiediskussionen (1945–1973). Grenz-Echo, Eupen

Lepsius MR (1993) Soziologisch-historische Konstellationsanalysen. Ausgewählte Aufsätze. Vandenhoeck & Ruprecht, Göttingen

Luyten D (1996) Burgers boven elke verdenking? Vervolging van economische collaboratie in België na de Tweede Wereldoorlog. VUB Press, Brussels

Mennicken D (2016) Die Heimattreue Front 1936–1940. Geschichte der 'Heim-ins-Reich'-Bewegung in Eupen-Malmedy. AixPress, Aachen

Monballyu J (2011) Slechte Belgen! de repressie van het incivisme na de Eerste Wereldoorlog door het Hof van Assisen van Brabant (1919–1927). General State Archives, Brussels

Pabst K (1964) Eupen-Malmedy in der belgischen Regierungs-und Parteienpolitik 1914–1940. *Zeitschrift des Aachener Geschichtsvereins* 76(special print):205–515

Quadflieg PM (2008) 'Zwangssoldaten' und 'Ons Jongen'. Eupen-Malmedy und Luxemburg als Rekrutierungsgebiet der deutschen Wehrmacht im Zweiten Weltkrieg. Shaker-Verlag, Aachen

Quadflieg PM (2013) Ostbelgische Elitenkontinuität in der Industrie? Wirtschaftliche Anpassungsprozesse vor und nach der Befreiung 1944—Eine Bestandsaufnahme. In: Brüll C, Herrebout E, Quadflieg PM (eds) Eine ostbelgische Stunde Null? Eliten aus Eupen und Malmedy vor und nach 1944. General State Archives, Brussels, pp 115–133

Radermacher O (2015) Les réfractaires de la 'Wehrmacht' dans les 'dix communes' annexées au Reich pendant la Seconde Guerre mondiale. Unpublished Master's thesis. Université de Liège, Liège

Reip N (2014) Funkstille. Von Vergangenheitsverschwiegenheit und Geschichtsmanipulation. In: Lejeune C, Brüll C (eds) Grenzerfahrungen. Eine Geschichte der Deutschsprachigen Gemeinschaft Belgiens, vol. 5: Säuberung, Wiederaufbau, Autonomiediskussionen (1945–1973). Grenz-Echo, Eupen

Roberti-Lintermans M (2015) Le centre d'internement pour inciviques de Verviers (septembre 1944–novembre 1945). Contribution à la répression des collaborations dans les cantons de l'Est. Unpublished Master's thesis: Université Catholique de Louvain, Louvain

Rousseaux X, Van Ypersele L (2008) La Patrie crie vengeance! La répression des inciviques belges au sortir de la guerre 1914–1918. Le Cri/UCL, CHDJ, Brussels and Louvain-la-Neuve

Schandevyl E (2011) Walter Ganshof van der Meersch, een topmagistraat in zijn professionele en maatschappelijke context. Een kijk op het Belgische gerecht in de twintigste eeuw. Bijdragen tot de Eigentijdse Geschiedenis 24:97–133

Schärer MR (1978) Deutsche Annexionspolitik im Westen. Die Wiedereingliederung Eupen-Malmedys im zweiten Weltkrieg. Peter Lang, Bern and Frankfurt

Tiedau U (2006) Die Rechtslage der deutschsprachigen Bevölkerung in Belgien nach dem Zweiten Weltkrieg. In: Kittel M (ed) Deutsche Minderheiten 1945. Ein europäischer Vergleich. Oldenbourg, Munich, pp 435–522

Van Haecke L (2014). Repressie en epuratie. De bescherming van de uitwendige veiligheid van de Staat als politiek-juridisch probleem tijdens de Belgische regimecrisis (1932–1948). Unpublished Doctoral Thesis. Ghent University, Ghent

Vonau J-L (2005) L'épuration en Alsace. La face méconnue de la Libération 1944–1953. La nuée bleue, Strasbourg

Wynants J (2004) La situation des cantons de l'est 1940–1944. *Bulletin d'information du Centre Liégeois d'Histoire et d'Archéologie Militaires* IX(fasc. 1):15–26

After the Big Show: British Police Officers and Civil Affairs in Europe

Clive Emsley

Abstract There is a long-standing joke in England that after the splendour of the annual Lord Mayor's show through the streets of the City of London trudge the workers with shovels and buckets whose job it is to clean up after the horses. The workers, of course, are ignored in the accounts of the splendour. So it is with military history. It concentrates on strategy, tactics and battles and, sometimes, on the 'poor bloody infantry' who do the fighting. There is very little on the men (and now women) who have to clean up after the fighting and, often quite literally, get the streets tidy and useable. This dismissal of the need for such people in the recent conflicts has contributed to the disastrous aftermath, and is all the more surprising given the fact that in 1943 the Americans and the British had established a Civil Affairs organisation whose task it was to restore civil society to countries liberated from the Axis powers and to rebuild the Axis powers themselves. In both post-war Europe and Asia this restoration and liberation was to be based on ideas of liberal democracy. Police officers played a key role in Civil Affairs; focussing on the careers and experiences of two British policemen this essay will explore the role of such men in Europe during the mid-1940s.

There is a long-standing joke in England that after the splendour of the annual Lord Mayor's show through the streets of the City of London come the workers with shovels and buckets whose job it is to clean up after the horses. The workers, of course, are ignored in the accounts of the splendour. So it is with military history. It concentrates on strategy, tactics and battles and, sometimes, on the 'poor bloody infantry' who do the fighting. There is very little on the men (and now women) who have to clean up after the fighting and, often quite literally, get the streets tidy and useable. This role was largely ignored also by the architects of recent invasions of Iraq and Afghanistan and by those supporting the civil war that brought about the

Clive Emsley: Deceased.

C. Emsley (✉)
Open University, Milton Keynes, UK

M. Bost and A. Vrints (eds.), *Doing Justice In Wartime*,
Studies in the History of Law and Justice 19,
https://doi.org/10.1007/978-3-030-72050-6_11

destruction of Colonel Muammar Ghaddafi's regime in Libya. This dismissal of the need for such people in the recent conflicts has probably contributed to the disastrous aftermaths and is all the more surprising given the fact that in 1943, the Americans and the British had established a Civil Affairs organisation whose task it was to restore civil society to countries liberated from the Axis powers and to rebuild the Axis powers themselves. In both post-war Europe and Asia, this restoration and liberation was to be based on ideas of liberal democracy. Police officers played a key role in Civil Affairs; focusing on the careers and experiences of two British policemen, this essay will explore the role of such men in Europe during the mid-1940s (see Emsley 2017, Part Two).

The British had been aware of the need for some sort of Civil Affairs body as early as 1940, and the Americans established a training school at the University of Virginia, Charlottesville, early in 1942, but they did not begin serious joint planning until the end of that year. In October 1942 a senior British Army officer in the War Office contacted the Commissioner of the Metropolitan Police, various branches of local government, public utilities and various groups within the agricultural, commercial and trade sectors of the economy asking for volunteers for the new Civil Affairs body. Among the local government bodies approached were provincial police forces, those of both boroughs and counties. As far as the police were concerned, the War Office letter had broken the rules by bypassing the Home Office, but once the necessary apologies were made and the ruffled feathers were smoothed, the request for volunteers was launched. Policing was a reserved occupation, and, in consequence, it had not been possible for policemen to enlist in the armed forces easily. This had happened during the First World War and had led to a serious and worrying reduction in the size of police forces. There had been a loss of men at the end of 1939 when those who were reservists were called back to the colours, and, periodically, men were permitted to put their name forward when there were, for example, calls for men to join the Royal Air Force. The call for men to serve in Civil Affairs gave those who sought it the opportunity, in the contemporary parlance, 'to do their bit' for the war effort; but they still required the permission of their local police administrative authority to volunteer, since they could not be replaced by recruits—after all, other eligible and fit young men were required for the armed forces.

Leslie Tompkins, an inspector in the Bedfordshire County Police, and Albert Wilcox, an inspector in the Metropolitan Police, were among the first volunteers. Since the origin of bureaucratic police institutions in early nineteenth-century Britain, police officers had been drawn mainly from the unskilled working class. All ranks in the urban police forces, except those commanding in the largest cities, joined as the lowest form of constable; by luck, successful work and sometimes because they caught the eye and favour of the local civilian committees that supervised a local force, any man could reach the rank of head constable in a town. Chief constables in the counties were more commonly members of the county elite and were often recruited from men with military experience or who had commanded police forces somewhere in the empire. The Metropolitan Police in London, the only force directly responsible to the Home Secretary, also drew its most senior officers from the same kind of pool as the counties; the Commissioner in London was usually appointed from among generals or senior imperial police officers. Things began to change during the inter-war years, when the sons of the respectable middle class began to join the police, often because their family was in dire financial straits and there seemed few other openings for an ambitious young man with little money. Tompkins and Wilcox did not fit precisely into the usual categories of unskilled working class or educated young man from a financially impoverished family; they both came from less privileged sections of society but not the unskilled working class.

Leslie Arthur Tompkins was born in Dunstable, a small town in the south of Bedfordshire in 1904. When Tompkins was born, his father was a bootmaker and ran a general store, but then he and his brother branched out into running a garage. Young Tompkins left school aged 14 years and, probably partly because of his father's and uncle's business, became an apprentice at Vauxhall Motors, a major car factory in nearby Luton. Following the General Strike of 1926 and seeing rows of unsold cars outside the Vauxhall Works, Tompkins believed that there was no future in motor manufacture. He left the factory and applied to join the county police. Tompkins himself was a big man, over six feet tall with a burly physique, but in his two brief, unpublished memoirs Tompkins described being surrounded by equally big police officers, many of them former members of the Brigade of Guards sporting magnificent moustaches—'fully trained soldiers instead of the likes of me—an ex-engineer'.[1] Yet Tompkins's skills as an engineer were precisely what the police did need during the interwar period. He was rapidly appointed to run the motor transport section of the Bedfordshire Police; this, in turn, led to him advising on the kind of speedometers that should be attached to police motorcycles to enable accurate measurements of speed. He began writing articles on various aspects of policing motor transport for the *Home Office Journal*. All of this led to rapid promotion, and by the end of the 1930s he was an inspector. His fascination with engines and speed, however, led to a minor confrontation with the Chief Constable. In July 1938, concerned about the possibility of another war, the Secretary of State for Air announced the formation of the Civil Air Guard to assist the Royal Air Force in any emergency. Tompkins, keen to learn how to fly, enrolled. The Chief Constable, apparently concerned that he would lose Tompkins in the event of a war, ordered him into his office, accompanied by a superintendent. He asked to see Tompkins's personal membership card for the Air Guard, then tore it up and ordered the superintendent to march Tompkins out of the office.

Wilcox's background was very different from that of Tompkins.[2] His father, Albert Clements Wilcox, was what people like to call 'colourful'. He was the youngest of three brothers and had been born around 1849 in Bristol, where his father was a brush-maker and his mother a beer retailer. The 1871 census listed Albert Wilcox as an infantryman in the 50th Foot; ten years later he was following his father's trade

[1]Bedfordshire Police Archive, L. A. Tompkins, 'Friends, Romans, Countrymen' (unpublished memoir 1987); Imperial War Museum, Doc. 20713, Captain L. A. Tompkins, 'A Nomadic Policeman' (unpublished memoir 1988). The quotation is from the former, fol. 4. The account of Tompkins's life is based on these two memoirs.

[2]The evidence for Wilcox's father and early life is based on material from the ten-yearly British census and an unpublished memoir in the Hertfordshire Police Archive.

as a brush-maker in Lancashire. He married a local woman and moved to Yorkshire. Around the turn of the century his wife died, as did one of his brothers, leaving him a legacy. Albert promptly moved up the social ladder; he found a young second wife and on his marriage certificate described himself as a 'gentleman'. He also moved back to his native Bristol. His first marriage appears to have been childless, but his second marriage produced children, including the Albert Wilcox central to this chapter. Young Albert, born in 1910, was a bright boy who gained entry to a grammar school in Bristol. Unfortunately Albert senior rapidly ran through his brother's legacy; in the 1911 census he was no longer listed as a 'gentleman' but as a 'retired brush-maker'. Upon his death the family found itself in dire straits, and young Albert had to leave school and take a job in a boot and shoe warehouse. As soon as he was old enough he joined the City of Bristol Police, but here he became frustrated by the lack of opportunity; promotion in police forces, as noted previously, often depended little on ability, sometimes on favouritism and more often on length of service and the fact that an individual was the next in line. In 1934 Wilcox saw his opportunity.

Towards the end of the 1920s there was concern within the Home Office about the standard of leadership within the police. A plan was drawn up by a senior civil servant for a college that would train potential leaders of the police. It failed, partly because of the deteriorating economic situation but also because local government bodies that had responsibility for all police forces outside London were unsure about what the plan would cost them. Lord Trenchard, however, who had established the Royal Air Force at the close of the First World War and who, in 1931, became Commissioner of the Metropolitan Police, decided to press ahead with a college for potential police leaders. The college opened in 1934. Over the following four years 217 men took the 15-month course. The majority of places were taken by men already serving in the Metropolitan Police; there were a few students taken on from outside the police, and there were other young men accepted from the roughly 200 provincial police forces. Wilcox volunteered, passed the stiff entrance examination and was one of the first 32 students. On his graduation he found sufficient money to travel to the United States, where he spent several weeks studying police developments before returning to London as a junior station inspector. The report that he wrote on American police did not go down well at Scotland Yard, since Wilcox challenged the notion of police in Britain being superior in every department and having little to learn from elsewhere. Yet this did not hinder his steady promotion and the opportunity to serve in different geographical areas of London in different positions, from detective to manager of men in uniform. He also succeeded in being called to the bar as a barrister at Gray's Inn.

The departure of so many young police officers during the First World War, which left forces seriously under-staffed, with inexperienced men and others who were past their retirement date, led the government to restrict volunteering from the police into the armed forces. Tompkins had already shown his preparedness to fight by joining the Civil Air Guard. Wilcox had demonstrated his eagerness to take on challenges. When the request was made for volunteers to step forward as potential Civil Affairs officers, both men jumped at the opportunity, and Bedfordshire no longer had a chief constable ready to hold men back if it suited him. Tompkins and Wilcox had a brief period of training in London with men from other public services that were thought to be necessary for restoring essential services and civil society in liberated Europe; and since Civil Affairs was intended to have British and Americans interleaved with each other, there was a small group of American officers training alongside them.

Wilcox was among the first to go overseas. In August 1943 he had time for a short visit to see his two-week-old second daughter before taking ship for North Africa. On arrival in Algiers he was informed that, as part of the interleaving policy, he had been attached to the American Army's VI Corps. He had a brusque meeting with an American general, which concluded with the general saying that, above all else, Wilcox was to ensure 'that the dead were buried promptly'. He did not want 'mounds of rotting corpses spreading disease and infection among the troops'. Shortly afterwards, though all of his training had concentrated on Pas-de-Calais, he landed on the beachhead at Salerno, where he and the small group of Civil Affairs officers that was with him found themselves under fire with everyone else. Upon reporting to a harassed American colonel they were told: 'Get to hell out of here'. Determined to get on with their tasks, Wilcox and another Metropolitan Police officer, 'Steve' Stephens,[3] linked with the *carabinieri* lieutenant based in the district to the south of the fighting and then proceeded to 'liberate' the local villages.

At this point, liberation was not much of a problem. Wilcox and his colleague had an Italian-speaking driver; no-one had thought to teach them any Italian during their training. Driving into villages they were greeted with Fascist salutes—to which they responded with V for Victory signs. Children milled around them hoping for chocolates, while young girls asked for cigarettes. All that the Civil Affairs officers had were proclamations regarding the liberation, which they posted on key buildings, and red and black arm bands, which they issued to the mayors and other key individuals to show that they now worked for the Allied Military Government (AMGOT).[4] The Italian-speaking driver read out the main provisions of the proclamations: people were to hand over guns, binoculars and cameras; a movement pass was required for anyone moving after dark; and a curfew was imposed. Once these niceties were out of the way, the Civil Affairs officers were required to examine what was required among the population in terms of food, medical supplies and clothing and what was required in the way of repairs to roads, bridges, buildings and other vital parts of infrastructure.

Wilcox and Stephens saw a problem with all of this. They had simply reappointed, as mayors and their subordinates, men who had worked under the Fascist regime; and they had no power to replace members of the *carabinieri* or those local priests who had collaborated with Mussolini's regime. None of the locals appeared to object to the Civil Affairs officers' appointments, and elections seemed out of the question; moreover, in the south, when the allies first landed, if a *carabinieri* officer or a

[3]Dean Frederick William Stephens was rather more typical of police recruits. Born in 1897 in Kennington, London, he was more typically working class. He began life as a boiler-maker's plater in Sheerness Dockyard, joining the Metropolitan Police in 1919.

[4]AMGOT was the acronym for Allied Military Government for Occupied Territories.

priest advised removing an individual, any such removal usually appeared to meet with local approval. Prisoners were released from gaols because most of the records relating to them had been destroyed, if indeed they had ever been made; and there was no attempt to interfere with Italian soldiers making their way homewards.

When Naples fell to the advancing Americans at the beginning of October, however, things became more difficult for Civil Affairs. Wilcox was sent to Naples as one of a small body of police officers now referred to as Public Safety officers. The commander of the group was an American, Lieutenant Colonel Orlando Wilson, who as a civilian police chief had developed a reputation as an efficient and thoughtful organiser and who had been appointed to teach at the University of California, Berkeley, in the summer of 1939. The principal task of the group was to reorganise and re-establish the authority of the *carabinieri* and the other police institutions in the city and its hinterland. This was no easy task, given the shambles in which the allies found Naples. The local population had risen against the Germans, which meant that a large number of arms were in circulation and were invariably acquired by some of the more dangerous groups in the city. The docks became the principal entry point for goods bound for the allied armies and consequently attracted armed gangs who—if they did not pillage allied ships themselves for all kinds of clothing, foodstuffs, medicine, cigarettes and anything else that they could sell—knew the dockers who could. Goods in transit, in railway depots and in supply dumps equally attracted armed gangs of local criminals and allied deserters. It was estimated at the time that the equivalent of one cargo in three landed from allied ships at the Naples docks was stolen. A large black market flourished, and challenging racketeers could result in serious fighting, as another Metropolitan Police officer, Sergeant Roy Hobbs, discovered when he led a group of *carabinieri* against a Neapolitan gang. The Neapolitans were equipped with machine-guns; but Hobbs and his men won the day and made 56 arrests.[5] The situation of the population, however, made much of the black marketeering understandable. The city was in ruins; there was disease and little food. Any and everything became available, for a price, most notably in a market on the Via Forcella, not far from AMGOT headquarters. And, to some extent, everyone seemed to be involved. When the papal legate's car was stopped in a road check, by accident rather than design, it was found to have four new allied tyres. Small workshops sprang up taking new military uniforms to pieces and converting them into smart civilian clothing (Lewis 1983, 122–123). Similarly a careful eye had to be maintained on brothels, on young Italian men who assaulted young Italian women found to be, or suspected of, consorting with allied soldiers. And soldiers, on a few days leave, went in hot pursuit of both young Italian women and drink, leading to allegations of rape, problems of drunkenness and fights between different military units—often units of the different allied armies.

In March 1944, Wilcox was moved to a Public Safety post in the Headquarters of the Allied Control Commission. At this point, planning was underway for the capture and occupation of Rome. Tompkins had arrived in Naples and assumed command of a 'legion' of *carabinieri*, somewhere between 60 and 100 men. Tompkins had crossed

[5]T[he] N[ational] A[rchives], WO 220/492 fol. 37.

the path of Wilcox in February when the two had been involved with suppressing a mutiny by Italian troops objecting to a rest period being cut short. But while Wilcox planned for the occupation of Rome, Tompkins and his men were destined for the occupation itself. The sea trip northwards from Naples ended for Tompkins and his legion on the bridgehead at Anzio where, like all of the allied troops, they were forced to live in foxholes under constant bombardment. Like Wilcox at Salerno, however, Tompkins and the two other British policemen with him tried to get on with the Civil Affairs tasks for which they had been appointed.[6] According to the *Police Review*, which was essentially the trade newspaper of the British police, this was 'pioneer work, soothing and controlling the local population for the benefit of fighting forces'.[7]

Tompkins took responsibility for the handling of refugees, known as 'line-crossers', on the beachhead. His *carabinieri* had to screen them all to make sure, as far as they could, that there were no enemy agents among them. Tompkins also took over the church of Santa Theresa in Anzio and, by screening off the altar area, turned it into a maternity ward. Other sick and wounded were also put into the church, and another at nearby Nettuno, which was directed by one of his two comrades. Unfortunately there were no doctors and few nurses to help. Several of the refugees complained of *febbre*, and this led to an argument between Tompkins and a senior Army officer. The officer was concerned that the troops might start going down with a fever, particularly malaria, while Tompkins insisted that all 'fibre' (his spelling) meant was 'a runny nose'. Perhaps the officer was right, since the Germans cut drainage pumps in an attempt to flood the area, and the local marshland was notorious for malaria; fortunately there was no serious outbreak. Yet if Tompkins annoyed senior officers, and this was to occur again later in his career, he appears to have been popular with his *carabinieri*. To keep him safe they decorated his slit trench with pictures of the pope.[8]

When the allies finally extricated themselves from the Anzio bridgehead, they joined the rush to occupy Rome. Tompkins and his *carabinieri* were not among the first to enter Rome, but they were not far behind. Alf Saunders, a Metropolitan policeman leading a squadron of mounted *carabinieri*, was among the first, however, and he was given the job of ensuring that the pope had not been and would not be kidnapped by the retreating Germans. Saunders confronted some suspicious Swiss Guards who required him to leave his gun with them, and then proceeded to wake the pope and explain the developing situation to him; it was 2:00 in the morning.[9] Alf Saunders became the senior Civil Affairs officer in the Vatican, with Tompkins as his deputy. Rome was soon involved in the usual mayhem of an occupied city, and though not quite as chaotic as Naples, it experienced a flourishing black market involving

[6]Tompkins's police comrades at Anzio were Arthur George Mack, born in Bournemouth in 1906, who joined the Metropolitan Police in 1926 giving his trade as a 'grocer'; and A. E. Baker, who came from the Exeter City Police.

[7]*Police Review*, 19 May 1944: 236.

[8]Tompkins, 'A Nomadic Policeman', fols. 63–70.

[9]*Police Review*, 23 April 1982: 782–783.

ordinary people desperate for the necessaries of life as well as armed gangsters. An army jeep could be stripped of its wheels in a matter of moments. Women sold themselves to allied soldiers for money to survive or simply for food. Soldiers got drunk and fought each other, especially those wearing a different uniform and speaking a different language. One of the major concerns for AMGOT was the security of the Vatican's treasures; their safety and preservation became a major concern for Tompkins and his men. At the conclusion of his period in Rome, Tompkins received the personal thanks of the pope for the fact that nothing had been stolen or damaged. Tompkins claimed that he could not resist asking the pope whether he believed that the photographs that his men had put in his slit trench had really protected him at Anzio. 'As Christ's representative here on earth', came the reply, 'there may be some virtue in my photographs'.[10]

Tompkins did not remain long in Rome and was given the post of a spearhead officer. He and his men were to follow up immediately on an assault; in his words, they were to 'get in quickly to gather up the bad boys (Fascists) and create a new Mayor, restore water and food supplies and the thousand things never thought of'. In an article called 'Liberation—And then what' that he wrote for his local newspaper towards the end of the war he explained: '"Spear-heading" is a single-handed job. There is no-one above to appeal to for advice; there is no-one below you to appeal to for help; what you do, you do alone, of your own initiative'.[11]

The problem was that in the smoke and confusion of battle, a small Civil Affairs unit could easily become the tip of the spearhead; no-one in the infantry appears to have thought it necessary to notify the spearhead officer when a town had fallen or what the situation was. The first town in which Tompkins acted as a spearhead officer was Faenza, where he and his second in command, a *carabinieri* officer, almost walked into a German soldier whose unit was still in occupation. Tompkins and his subordinate decided to make 'a dignified retreat'. When a town finally fell, the spearhead officer, as Wilcox had been told by the American colonel, had to organise the burial of the dead. British and Imperial troops generally gathered up their own, but the German and civilian dead became the responsibility of the spearhead officer. Frank Rawlings, a station inspector of the Metropolitan Police, held the post with the Canadian troops that fought their way into Ortona in December 1944. He arranged for 'all able bodied civilians … to work in small groups under the supervision of one who appeared qualified' to clear the streets of the remaining dead and of debris. 'Unfortunately at the outset of this work one group, whilst clearing the debris, were blown up by a mine that had been placed there by the enemy, causing several deaths and serious injuries'. As he grew in experience, Tompkins and others learned to watch for booby traps, to keep away from possibly mined major buildings and not to light fires since these attracted German artillery. The spearhead officers had to impose law and order, and this could mean persuading nervous policemen to get back on the streets and to do their old job; but the policeman was told that the spearhead officer, for whom he was now working, would feed him. As Wilcox had

[10]Tompkins, 'A Nomadic Policeman', fol. 70.

[11]*Bedfordshire Times*, 5 January 1945: 6.

done south of Salerno, the spearhead officer would give the policeman an armband and proclamations promising respect for people's rights and requiring obedience to new laws. He had to find a worthy man to be mayor, and others to act as the town council. The spearhead officer presided over the first meeting of the council, to which the local priest, doctor, banker, police chief and leader of the partisans were also called. Gradually the spearhead officer became transformed into the local *governatore*, and as such he had to fix the price of food 'with due regard for it being within the reach of the poorest and to prevent underground sales (black market)'. There was also the problem of dealing with recalcitrant local leaders—Tompkins imprisoned a local doctor until he agreed to run a makeshift hospital—and criminal offenders. Prosecution for most offences initially came under the remit of a senior Civil Affairs officer. Tompkins and others appear commonly to have used their own initiative to decide how a particular individual should be treated. Again Tompkins got into trouble with senior Army officers for fining, rather than imprisoning, a 14-year-old boy who was carrying a pistol in a forward area. Tompkins believed that a subsequent run-in with a senior officer was responsible for blocking his promotion from captain to major, which had been promised when he left Rome. In this instance, when a senior officer demanded a return of wheat supplies around Ravenna, Tompkins replied: 'Please refer your request to General Kesselring. He is still there'.[12]

Some of the trickiest issues, however, for men like Tompkins as they followed the army up the Italian boot, were relations with the partisans and the fact that they were enmeshed not just in a war against the Germans but also in a civil war and an ideological conflict between communists and others. The partisan groups contained many communist units who saw the best future for Italy as governance by a communist regime. Both communists and non-communists were suspicious of the old police and even of those *carabinieri* units that had fought their way northwards under the command of men like Tompkins. For the anti-fascists, even anti-fascist *carabinieri* were compromised by their loyalty to the monarchy that had accepted Mussolini. Civil war and political hatreds abounded. One of Tompkins's grimmest tasks was supervision of the execution of a fascist by a *carabinieri* firing squad. The volley of shots did not kill the man immediately, and a *carabinieri* officer administered the *coup de grace* with his pistol. Immediately a lawyer also observing the execution stepped forward and insisted that the final shot was illegal; if the man was not dead then he should have been taken to hospital. The lawyer announced his intention to begin legal proceedings. The *carabinieri* officer waved his hand; he had no fingernails. They had been pulled out, he said, when he had been tortured by fascists. Angrily he promised that there would be no similar case in future when he was involved with a firing squad; he would use a submachine gun.[13]

The British government was immensely proud of its police. It believed its own rhetoric, and that of others, that Britain had 'the best police force in the world'. Indeed, it was suggested that if such policing could be exported, then the entire

---

[12]Tompkins, 'A Nomadic Policeman', fols. 71–78; Frank Rawlings, 'Forty Years On', fol. 16.

[13]Tompkins, 'A Nomadic Policeman', fol. 79.

world would be a better place and less likely to engage in war and other forms of conflict. In the autumn of 1943, for example, the *Police Review* declared:

> The British Police ideal has impressed all civilised nations by its remarkable success in the country of its origin. It is rightly regarded as a wonderful achievement that a body of 65,000 men should be able with so little friction and so high a degree of efficiency to maintain law and order among a population of some 45,000,000 people. If the secret of the success of the British Policeman could be communicated to others abroad in the liberated countries of Europe it would be a great and lasting contribution to the peace.[14]

A few weeks later the Home Secretary reiterated this sentiment by declaring that, at the end of the war, the whole world might benefit from an international police based on the unique nature of that in Britain.[15]

In the summer of 1945 it was suggested that an Allied Police Mission be sent to Italy to reorganise Italian policing. Wilcox was one of the two British police officers asked to make suggestions on the best way to conduct the reformation. Wilcox duly wrote his report, but the mission never got off the ground. Ministers in the Italian coalition government did not like to be told that their police institutions were badly managed and directed, while the communists believed that there must also be Soviet involvement in the mission.[16] Wilcox may have presented a report, but by now he was away from Italy, with Soviet troubles of his own.

Wilcox disliked the bureaucratic role that he had acquired in Italy and was keen to get back to acting with the troops. When the opportunity arose he volunteered to join that section of the Army about to move northwards into Austria. Early in May 1945, after an improvised journey that enabled him to visit some of the cultural treasures of Italy, especially Assisi and Venice, he was among the first Public Safety officers to cross the frontier into the Austrian province of Carinthia. Here he found two major problems: first, the countryside was flooded with refugees, many of whom were fleeing from the Red Army and Yugoslav partisans; second, there were armed Yugoslav partisans—known to the British as 'Jugs'—reluctant to yield territory that they had captured. Among the first tasks of the British was to round up the partisans, as best they could, and drive them back to their homeland in army vehicles. The problems of occupying enemy territory were also present, especially looking for ex-Nazis and following up reports of war crimes, but Wilcox appears to have found the early summer of 1945 generally pleasant—fishing, swimming, sampling the local wine. Wilcox was destined to become the chief Public Safety officer for the British occupation forces in Vienna, and he was ordered to move back to Italy while the four allied powers who were to occupy different zones of the country argued over the division of control in the city. When orders eventually came for Wilcox to move to Vienna, he was back in England being interviewed for senior posts in the civilian police. He arrived in Vienna in mid-summer, however, and found himself with the kinds of problems that had affected Civil Affairs from the first landings in Italy, but with the added complication of the developing Cold War.

---

[14] *Police Review*, 1 October 1943: 470.

[15] *Police Review*, 24 December 1943: 621.

[16] Hertfordshire Police Archive: unpublished Wilcox autobiography, Chapter 7, fol 3.

Table 1 Estimates of crime in Vienna compared with that in London

Classification	Vienna 20 weeks September–January 1945	Vienna annual average	Vienna adjustment by population[a]	London 1944	Proportion Vienna: London
Murder	86	224	1120	18	62:1
Crimes of violence	872	2267	11,335	240	47:1
Housebreaking	2786	7244	36,220	5249	7:1
Shopbreaking	1850	4810	24,050	7344	3:1
Theft of vehicles	606	1575	7875	539	15:1
Theft of bicycles	1076	3597	19,985	9305	2:1

[a]For the purpose of this comparison, it is estimated that the population of London is five times greater than that of Vienna. (Original table in Hertfordshire Police Archive: unpublished Wilcox autobiography.)

In the summer of 1945, the dead might have been buried, but Vienna still had a multitude of problems for Civil Affairs officers, problems similar to those that they had faced during the Italian campaign. There was the aftermath of bombardment and fighting; much debris remained to be cleared. There were refugees. There were deserters—possibly somewhere between 10,000 and 20,000 Red Army deserters. Worse still there were DPs (displaced persons), often former slave labourers, now sometimes armed and fully prepared to take whatever they wanted, including revenge on the civilian population. To compound the problems, everywhere the necessaries of life were in short supply—except among the British, American and French liberators. Many of the local police were old men who, but for the war, might by then have been in receipt of a pension. Some of the police, especially the commanders, were suspect. There were armed men—and arms remained plentiful—organised into gangs to run trafficking and the thriving black market. An additional problem with the black market was the involvement of large numbers of Soviet soldiers. The overall problem of crime in the city seemed far worse than in the Austrian countryside, and early in 1946 Wilcox attempted a comparison of the crimes reported to the Viennese police with those reported in London (see Table 1). Wilcox had a greater faith in crime statistics than most modern criminologists, but however sceptical modern academics might be over statistics, the numbers before him suggested a major crime problem. In his monthly report for November 1945, Wilcox noted that the Viennese police believed their figures to be 'reasonably honest' and that they could 'be taken as a true index'. Nevertheless 'the figures for "breaking and entering" offences are deceptive as many of the crimes were committed months ago but have only been discovered now that residents are returning to Vienna'. At the beginning of 1946, the method of collecting statistics was overhauled to require two separate report forms; the first for listing crimes reported to the police; the second giving full details when an arrest was made.[17]

[17]Hertfordshire Police Archive: unpublished Wilcox autobiography.

Table 2 Offences by allied troops reported by the Vienna Police, January to August 1946

	January	February	March	April	May	June	July	August
British	2	1	2	3	7	3	6	1
American	13	5	23	6	17	9	20	24
French	18	23	48	17	18	9	9	6
Soviet	210	133	119	70	102	78	60	45

The statistics available to Wilcox enabled him to declare, with a degree of pride, that the British soldiery was the best behaved of the allies (see Table 2). In his memoir he noted how, on his arrival, 'Russian soldiers with childlike glee were wearing two or three watches on their wrists'. During the time that Wilcox was present in the city, he received evidence of members of the Red Army shooting civilians and carrying out large-scale robberies as well as being heavily involved in the black market. If local people made a complaint to a Russian officer, they could find themselves arrested, held for several days and subjected to beatings. Such was the case of Franz Sverak, a railway employee who reported Russian soldiers for stealing salt from a railway goods wagon standing in Hauptzollampt Station. Paul Bottoli, a garage owner in the British Zone, and his wife were arrested by a Red Army squad on circumstantial evidence following the disappearance of a Russian major's car. The soldiers had entered the British Zone without authority, and while they released Mrs. Bottoli after a few hours, they held her husband for some time. The Russians would only let him go once he had agreed to provide a replacement car, and they refused to return it when the original vehicle was found in Hungary, with its driver, who was promptly arrested. British demands to give Bottoli his car back were ignored, as were initial British protests about the unauthorised Russian entry into their zone and Bottoli's arrest on very weak evidence.[18]

Sometimes the clashes between the allies were not confined to arguments among men responsible for restoring order and civil society in the ruins of Vienna. There were also conflicts between the ordinary soldiery, and sometimes the results were lethal. The war was over, men wanted to go home, they had money for women and drink, and they still had their guns. Fights between soldiers were matters to be resolved by military police, but the allies' military policemen also wanted to go home and, from the moment that the occupation was agreed among the four powers, it was also recognised that some form of Viennese Police needed to be re-established to deal with ordinary criminal offences and civil regulations. The French and the Russians were initially reluctant, arguing that such an institution could become the basis for a new army; eventually, however, they also accepted the idea of a city-wide police institution.

The thought that had gone into the training in London, together with the experience gained in Italy, had given the British and the Americans some ideas about re-establishing police institutions. The problem was that theirs were not the first

[18] Hertfordshire Police Archive, Wilcox Memoir, fols. 7 and 11–12.

armies in Vienna, and in the few months during which the Red Army had been in sole command and occupation of the city, the Soviets had ensured that all of the key posts in local government and the police were filled by communists or sympathisers. Few of these senior police officers had any experience of policing except, perhaps, for being on the wrong side of it—investigated, pursued and potentially beaten or imprisoned for trade union or political activity before the end of the war. The British zone was comprised of six districts (*Bezirke*), each one commanded by a British civilian police officer now a member of Civil Affairs and serving as a Public Safety officer (PSO). Wilcox and his PSOs had very few British military police to assist them. From the beginning they set about removing Soviet appointees to the senior police ranks, vetting the surviving Viennese police for Nazi links and sympathies and recruiting new young police officers.

Linked with the French and Russian concerns that the new police could form the basis of a future army, and with British Police ideas that a patrolman should be armed with nothing more than a wooden baton, there was uncertainty about whether or not the Viennese Police should be armed. But dangerous armed gangs continued to lurk in the bomb-damaged streets. In the early hours of 25 November 1945, for example, Josef Oberst a 20-year-old police recruit challenged a group in a street in the British Zone (*Bizerk 5*) near a fur shop that appeared to have been broken into. Oberst was shot dead. Eventually Viennese patrolmen were all armed and often acquitted themselves well against armed gangs. Six months after Oberst's death, the Viennese detective branch arrested a gang of 36 who were believed to be responsible for five murders, ten attempted murders, two robberies, 57 house and shop-breakings and 44 motor-car thefts. By this time the Viennese Police, trained at a new police school initially in the British Zone and subsequently in an old barracks in the American Zone, consisted of some 11,000 men, of which 7000 were uniformed patrolmen and another 844 were detectives. Wilcox remained concerned about the political police in the city (774 of them) and the potential for their use by politicians, but overall when he left the city in the late summer of 1946 he could feel some satisfaction with his input into the new force and with the reduction in the statistics of crime (which, if they were no precise measure of the problem, appeared to have an underlying reality). There was also some success in resolving disputes with his Red Army equivalents, generally through compromise. He and the British authorities had agreed, for example, to use the term offenders 'wearing Russian uniforms' rather than labelling them simply as 'Russian soldiers'; the Russian commanders had increasingly begun to clamp down on Red Army involvement in the black market.

Wilcox's role in Vienna was still largely a bureaucratic one, but in Vienna he was much closer to the day-to-day action of his police officers than he had been in the Headquarters in Italy. Tompkins, in contrast, remained at the heart of the action. At the end of the war he was transferred from running the police in the Italian province of Ravenna to the role of Public Safety Officer in the German *Land* of Westphalia. Here again he annoyed some of his military superiors. First he used the word 'please' in his instructions to his German subordinate police officers. Then, when acting as prosecuting officer in a German Police court with a bench of British Army Officers, he declined to offer any evidence. A group of German civilians was being prosecuted for having British food supplies, but Tompkins maintained in his memoir that 'enough was enough'. The Germans were starving and were exchanging what they had with troops to keep body and soul together; moreover, the prisons were full.[19]

After a relatively short period, Tompkins transferred from his old Civil Affairs role to a management position with the Police Training School at Munster. The allies were intent on de-Nazifying the police, and the aim, in the British Zone, was to recreate the British Bobby, which was regarded as a model for the world. Senior British police officers and politicians took very seriously the idea of the British Police as 'the best in the world'. A retired Prussian colonel became the senior German police officer in Tompkins's school; his wife, who clearly did not have the same confidence in British police officers, was initially wary of the 'savage English'. An exchange of English white for German black bread appears to have been a good first step towards smoothing matters. Tompkins was given an English-speaking German as his driver. The man claimed to have been a tank driver on the Eastern Front, but Tompkins suspected that he had been rather more than a tank driver.[20]

Like other Public Safety officers deputed to police training, one of Tompkins's jobs was to ensure that ex-Nazis, particularly SS men, were kept out of the police. The British and the Americans were pragmatic and in some instances a little lax in getting rid of former Nazis and Fascists in the police. In contrast, the Soviets were rigorous in their zones of Austria and Germany. The British and Americans rationalised that men had families to support and hoped for their pension eventually; if a police officer had wanted to keep his job in Fascist Italy or the Third Reich then he had to become a party member. This was probably much more the case in Austria and Germany than in Fascist Italy, but it also ignored the fact that Mussolini had been in power since the 1920s so that, by the mid-1930s, young men joining the Italian police had been schooled and socialised into the system. This was also the case with young recruits into the police of Austria and Germany after the war; they had been brought up and educated under the Nazi regime. Tompkins recounts how, after interview, recruits were required to remove their shirts and hold up their arms so that they might be checked for the tell-tale sign of an SS tattoo. He also describes putting a stop to recruits stiffening the front of their caps which, in his eyes, gave them a Nazi-style look. As an example, he removed the stiffening from his own cap and pulled the peak down 'Eighth Army style'.[21] The attempt to make good Bobbies out of good *Schutzmänner* was probably doomed from the outset; the systems of police administration and organisation, and the German understanding of British system and practice, were just too far apart. But having been joined by his wife for the end of his service in Germany, Tompkins saw a future for them both in a much wider world than that of the Bedfordshire Police.

---

[19]Tompkins, 'A Nomadic Policeman', fols. 83–84. Tompkins appears to have enjoyed such stories about him annoying army officers, and it is tempting to wonder how much of this is romanticised and how much actually happened as he described it. Nevertheless, it is the case that Civil Affairs officers were given advice on the 'German mind' that implied the only way to deal with Germans was to give them precise and sharp orders (Meehan 2001, 54–56).

[20]Tompkins, 'A Nomadic Policeman', fols. 84–86.

[21]Tompkins, 'A Nomadic Policeman', fols. 93–94.

It is always difficult to generalise about how similar events affect different people. Some of the Civil Affairs officers recruited from the police were content to return to the police when the war ended, while others saw new opportunities. Wilcox returned to policing and served as Chief Constable of Hertfordshire from 1947 to 1969. Tompkins, in contrast, seems to have had no desire to return to Bedfordshire. His wife sold the contents of their home and joined him while he was in Germany. When his contract for training the German Police expired, he applied for and got a post with the Foreign Office Administration of African Territories. He became a senior police officer in a series of imperial possessions—Somalia, Eritrea, Ethiopia, Nigeria—while the British Empire converted to the Commonwealth. He ended his career working as a security officer for UNRWA (the United Nations Relief and Works Agency) in the Middle East. Others followed similar routes, while still others found new careers not linked with policing but drawing on the experience and confidence learned in their wartime roles.

The impact of the various wartime duties is difficult to assess. In the short term they were reasonably successful in restoring a degree of civil society—supervising the burial of the dead and removing the rubble, re-establishing the necessities of life as far as they were able and reconstituting local government and police services by and large with the worst of the Fascist and Nazi party members removed from their posts. However, Germans, Austrians, Italians and others had their own traditions of police that had evolved from their legal and governmental systems long before the Fascist and Nazi takeovers. The perception of the British/English police as 'the best in the world' was not one that the peoples of continental Europe automatically acknowledged. Why would the Italians dispense with their *carabinieri*, especially when the Civil Affairs officers in Italy generally thought it the best police organisation in the country? Similarly, what was wrong with Italy having a distinct financial police, the *Guardia di Finanza*? Why should the Germans, like the English Police, forbid their police from joining trades unions? The British successfully abolished the German Administrative Police (*Verwaltungspolizei*) and the tradition of emphasising maintenance of public order and security (*Alfrechterhaltung der öffenlichten Sicherheit und Ordnung*), yet this re-emerged in the 1990s. Moreover, there was little that could be done to change completely the socialisation and education of the 1930s that had informed the formative years of those senior police officers who, in the 1960s, commanded the rank and file police who confronted student demonstrations and young people who asked for the truth about the war and the Nazis (see, *inter alia*, Reinke 2004; Weinhauer 2003).

References

Emsley C (2017) Exporting British policing during the Second World War: policing soldiers and civilians. Bloomsbury, London

Lewis N (1983) Naples '44: an intelligence officer in the Italian Labyrinth. Eland, London

Meehan P (2001) A strange enemy people: Germans under the British 1945–50. Peter Owen, London and Chester Springs, PA
Reinke H (2004) The reconstruction of the police in post-1945 Germany. In: Fijnaut C (ed) The impact of World War II on policing in North-West Europe. Leuven University Press, Leuven, pp 133–149
Weinhauer K (2003) Schutzpolizei in der Bundesrepublik Zwischen Bürgerkrieg und Innere Sicherheit: Die turbulenten sechziger Jahre. Ferdinand Schöningh, Paderborn

The manufacturer's authorised representative in the EU is Springer Nature Customer Service Centre GmbH, Europaplatz 3, 69115 Heidelberg, Germany. If you have any concerns regarding our products, please contact ProductSafety@springernature.com

Printed and bound by CPI Group (UK) Ltd, Croydon, CR0 4YY
28/09/2026
02224090-0002